futureagenda

Six Challenges for
the Next Decade

futureagenda
Six Challenges for the Next Decade

Caroline Dewing and **Tim Jones**

Third Millennium
Publishing

First published in Great Britain in 2016 by Third Millennium Publishing, an imprint of Profile Books Ltd.

3 Holford Yard
Bevin Way
London WC1X 9HD
United Kingdom
www.tmiltd.com

Copyright of text and figures © Future Agenda, 2016
Copyright of design and layout © Third Millennium Publishing, 2016

The rights of Caroline Dewing and Tim Jones to be identified as the authors of this work have been asserted in accordance with the Copyright, Designs and Patents Act of 1998.

All rights reserved. No part of this publication may be reproduced, stored or introduced into a retrieval system or transmitted in any form or by any means (electronic, mechanical, photocopying, recording or otherwise) without the prior written permission of both the copyright holder and the publisher.

A CIP catalogue record for this book is available from The British Library.

ISBN 978 1 908990 79 2
e-ISBN 978 1 908990 93 8

Editor: Michele Greenbank
Design: Sharpe Graphic Design
Production: Cambridge Publishing Management Ltd.

Printed and bound in Great Britain by Bell & Bain Ltd.

MIX
Paper from
responsible sources
FSC® C007785
FSC
www.fsc.org

Acknowledgements

The Future Agenda Programme is all about collaboration so it seems strange to have only our names on the front cover of this book. We have been highly dependent on the wisdom of others to shape this story – most importantly that of the core team. Nothing at all would have happened without their extraordinary efforts. Patrick Harris, James Alexander, Ali Draycott, Robin Pharoah, Marlene Han, Charlie Curson, Lisa McDowell, Alka Puri and Anupam Yog: we learned from and leaned on you all and are in your debt. Beyond the core team, there were many others who also gave generously of their time: Don Abraham, Chris Carbone, Nicky Chambers, David Coates, Shalaja Sharma, Cornelia Daheim, Roger Dennis, Rima Gupta, Katie Hodgson, Stephen Johnston, Dave McCormick, Bhupendra Sharma, Hamsini Shivakumar and Neal Stone – a huge, huge thank you.

Very little would have happened without the expertise and bravery of those who kindly wrote an initial perspective on each subject we covered. You set high standards for the subsequent conversations that took place in as many corners of the globe as we could muster. The workshops themselves were full of informed and knowledgeable people prepared to give freely of their time and experience. These enriched and enlivened our thoughts and brought colour to our ideas. And, of course, none of the above would have been possible without our hosts, too numerous to mention but whose support was fundamental to the whole programme. Thanks indeed.

We would also like to thank my agent Maggie Hanbury who provided sound advice and guidance with charm and efficiency and also Humphrey Price whose eagle eye spotted repetition and deviation when it occurred and helped us to smooth the rough edges of our text.

Finally any mistakes or misunderstandings that you spot are ours and we apologise for them completely.

Contents

Chapter 8:
Reflections on Common Views of the Future

Chapter 9:
Cross Topic Insights

Conclusion

Endnotes

Index

Introduction

- The Challenges We Face
- Looking Ahead – Why and How
- Uncertainty and Certainty
- Multiple Voices vs Single Opinion

Personalised medicine, autonomous cars, ISIS (Islamic State/Daesh), Snapchat, lower oil prices and data hacks: we live in a time when change seems to be happening faster than ever. Across health care, entertainment and transport – to highlight just three – technology seems to moving on apace. Equally, whether in politics, attitudes to social networks or who we trust, the way in which many of us behave is also in transition. Whether change is actually happening faster than ever may be a matter of perception, or it could be fact. We do know that we will see many new developments over the next decade and a host of issues will rise to the fore. If we are going to be better prepared, we need to see over the horizon. The problem is that no one can predict the future. Some think they have a clearer idea of what is coming than others. Most realise that it is about making intelligent bets. If we cannot predict the future, then to make such bets we need to anticipate what may happen next. If we can anticipate more effectively, then we can make better bets.

Taking the long view has never been easy. Rapid technological advances, shifting political movements, changing economic dynamics and accelerating societal change are seldom far from the news headlines and many of us struggle to understand their implications for day-to-day life. Indeed, such are the challenges that it seems clear that the major issues facing our planet are of such a magnitude that no single institution or organisation alone can truly understand their impact. As change accelerates in an increasingly connected world, more organisations are looking further ahead to better understand emerging opportunities and threats. We believe that sharing knowledge across disciplines and across continents can add real value to this process, particularly as much-needed innovation often occurs at the intersection of different disciplines, industries or challenges.

The Future Agenda is the world's largest global open foresight programme and is based on the idea that by engaging with others from different cultures, disciplines and industries, we can collectively create a more informed understanding of the world in which we live. This makes it easier to shape a strategy that will help to address what lies ahead. Our aim is to identify ways in which systems could function, consumers behave and governments regulate over the next decade, and give all organisations, large or small, access to insights which we hope will help them to develop their future strategy.

The first Future Agenda programme ran in 2010 and brought together views on the next decade from multiple organisations. Building on expert perspectives that addressed everything from the future of health to the future of money, more than 1,500 organisations debated the big issues and emerging challenges. Sponsored globally by the Vodafone Group, the programme connected CEOs (chief executive officers) and mayors with academics and students in 25 countries. Additional online interaction connected over 50,000 people from more than 145 countries who added their views to the mix. The results published both online and in print have been widely shared and used around the world by individuals and organisations seeking to be more informed. TV programmes, talks, workshops and additional discussions have followed as people have explored the potential implications and opportunities in their sector or market.

The success of the first Future Agenda programme led several organisations to request that it be repeated. As a result, the second programme, Future Agenda 2.0, ran throughout 2015, looking at key changes that the world could experience by 2025. Following a broadly similar approach, it added extra features, such as providing more workshops in more countries to gain an even wider input and enable regional differences to be explored in more depth. All in all, 25 topics were discussed in 120 workshops hosted by 50 different organisations across 45 locations (Figure 1). There was a specific focus on the next generation, including collaborating with schools, universities and other educational institutions. There was also a more refined use of social networks to share insights and earlier link-ups with global media organisations to ensure wider engagement on the pivotal topics. In addition, rather than having a single global sponsor, this time multiple hosts supported workshops on specific topics either globally or in their regions of interest. This book outlines the insights we gained from all these conversations.

Europe	Asia	Americas	Australasia	Middle East	Africa
Berlin	Bangalore	Lima	Brisbane	Abu Dhabi	Cape Town
Budapest	Beijing	Mendoza	Christchurch	Beirut	Johannesburg
Cologne	Hong Kong	New York	Sydney	Dubai	
Guernsey	Jakarta	Quito	Wellington	Istanbul	
London	Kuala Lumpur	San Francisco			
Munich	Manila	São Paulo			
Noordwijk	Mumbai	Stanford			
Rome	New Delhi	Toronto			
Vienna	Shanghai	Washington DC			
Zurich	Singapore				

Figure 1: Future Agenda Event locations 2015.

We have already witnessed a number of opportunities for positive change. These include ideas about how to tackle some of the issues in areas such as climate change, sustainable health and food supply, for example; ideas about how to use policy to best influence our right to a private life; and ideas for new products, services and business models that will ensure the legacy of the past does not become a burden for the future. We are delighted and humbled that so many people have given freely of their time and intellect to help ensure that these ideas become a reality. Run as a not-for-profit project, with the core team all donating their time for free, Future Agenda continues to be a major collaboration involving many leading, forward-thinking organisations around the world.

Our Approach

From the very beginning, our intention was not only to obtain new views for each topic on what the future would be, but also to understand perspectives on which direction we should take, why and with what consequences. To do this, we invited recognised experts in each topic from academic, commercial and government arenas to answer a number of common questions on the future. These were then edited into initial perspectives and placed in a standard format to ease navigation and to ensure a common structure. Each was grouped into four sections – global challenges, options and possibilities, the way forward, and impacts and implications.

We then initiated a nine-month programme of 120 face-to-face workshops around the world in order to build the debate. Some of these were held within single organisations but many brought together different expertise from multiple avenues. Some took place in corporate conference facilities, some in hotels and restaurants, others in universities – whatever worked best. In locations around the world, including London, New York, Singapore, Sydney, Shanghai, Munich, Beirut, Dubai, Mumbai, Lima and Mendoza, well-informed people from many cultures, of varied ages and with many different perspectives shared their views.

After all the workshops were complete, the Future Agenda team took the output that had been gathered and identified the major insights that were proposed to drive change. These are based on common subjects that were raised in several discussions – either across different countries or across different topics. As part of the overall synthesis, these insights have now been have been broadened into summaries and shared online. As with the insights gained from the first Future Agenda programme, organisations around the world are already using these new views variously to challenge assumptions, refine strategic directions, and identify emerging innovation and growth opportunities. Furthermore, all of the output from the Future Agenda project, including all the raw insights, has been made freely available for organisations around the world to use to help challenge, and build more informed views, of the next decade.

This book is the next step in the journey. What has already been shared online reflects what we heard from multiple expert discussions around the world. These are neutral, curated playbacks of the core issues that people think are important. The opinions expressed are therefore not necessarily ours, nor those of our hosts and partners. They are those of the independent experts whose views we respect, even if we don't always agree with them. This book, on the other hand, is what we think about what we have heard. Not only have we have added our additional thoughts and opinions, but in many cases we have moved away from a neutral position. We have done this partly to try to make sense of some of the contradictions we have found when talking about the future, and partly to try to knit what we heard into a coherent view.

We do not pretend to be experts in food, energy, cities or data, nor in any of the other topics addressed; however, during 2015 we talked to many thousands of informed people who are. Our contribution is to be able to stand back from the detail and identify the connections across topics and highlight some of the core connections. You may well not agree with some of the points being made, but perhaps you will see why others think the way they do. If we are going to build a better future, seeing the world and its underlying issues from the point of view of others is, we believe, pivotal to ensuring that we can really achieve something that will make a difference. We hope that this book helps.

Chapter 1

Twelve Common Views of the Future

- Twelve views of the future that we have heard repeatedly across different countries, different topics and different groups of people.
- Can we better understand which of these views actually hold water and which may well be less of an issue than we think?
- Can we separate myth from reality?

Many people around the world have different perspectives about the opportunities and challenges that lie ahead – and what these might be. Governments, large corporations and think tanks sometimes have an alternative view on issues to the self-employed or the layperson. Equally, people and organisations in different regions often also see things through a dissimilar lens – for example, East vs West and North vs South, or, on a more local level, urban vs rural.

In addition, where information comes from also shapes views: the state media, newspapers, TV, Twitter and other social media all take different angles, sourcing insights from multiple and varied groups, and so communicating perspectives in alternative ways. Likewise, depending on their faith, politics, wealth, education and health, individuals may hold closer some of their beliefs about the future. Of course, some see the world differently to others due to the experiences that they, or their friends and families, have had in the past.

Across all these multiple diverse ways of seeing things, however, there are several views that are shared. Some are nearly universal and heard across many groups; others are the majority perspectives, but all influence how we look ahead and the priorities we may therefore have. They are a useful stake in the ground, as they show received wisdom as well as some current assumptions and paradigms.

What follows is what we have termed 'twelve common views of the future', which we have heard repeatedly across different countries, different topics and different groups of people.

Several of them focus very much on negative issues and big concerns:

1. Too Many People

With more than seven billion of us now living on the planet, our ability to cope with another two, three or four billion by the end of the century is widely questioned: will we have enough land, food or water to cope with a 50 per cent growth in global population? Where will everyone live? How will we preserve our nations, our societies and cultures, our ways and standards of living and quality of life?

2. Running out of Resources

With all these extra people, many of the key resources that we depend upon will come under stress and may even run out: if we are already using 1.6 times the resources that the Earth can naturally replenish, how can we accommodate further growth? Will there be enough for everyone? Equally, is there enough energy and rare metals to enable us to continue living the lives we lead?

3. Pollution is out of Control

Most of us now accept that we are in an era where the world is becoming increasingly polluted due to human activity: many see that we need to live green lives. If we have already overshot the safe planetary thresholds for biodiversity and nitrogen, is there any way we can repair the damage? Will the quality of our cities, oceans and air continue to decline? What has been the effect of artificial fertilisers on food production? And what about the increasing impacts of climate change? Is there a magic technology solution around the corner or not?

4. Migration is Bad

While some in countries such as Canada and the Philippines see migration as a positive lever to use to rebalance population and resource supply, others see it as a negative. In many regions people ask: how can we cope with ever more refugees and migrants putting strain on our systems and resources? How can we stop millions of people moving our way, taking our jobs and changing our culture? What can we do to help people stay where they are, live better lives at home and not want to move to other countries or into cities?

5. There will not be Enough Jobs

With more of us on the planet, more students being educated and more technology in the workplace, will there be enough paid work to go around? Will artificial intelligence and robots replace many of our low- and middle-income jobs? More migrants coming into our societies will be prepared – or desperate enough – to work for less, and so drive down all our wages. The increasing social burden of more people living longer will mean that fewer old people will stop working and release their jobs for the young. What will the people who do not have any work do, and will those in work have to support them?

But on the plus side, a good number of people see positive changes taking place:

6. Female Education can Address Many Issues

Many believe that providing better and wider access to education to girls in particular will have a positive knock-on impact for society as a whole. If girls stay in school beyond primary level, they can become more economically active and make a bigger contribution to progress. They are also likely to have smaller families and so help to reduce fertility ratios and bring population growth under control. And, in some countries, the view is that having more women in areas of political and commercial influence will help to rebalance male-dominated societies and institutions, and better manage our world.

7. Technology will Solve the Big Problems

We have faced many challenges in the past and yet have always overcome them, largely through advances in technology. This will happen again: the 'Internet of Things' (IoT) connecting everything will provide more data and information and so enable us to significantly improve efficiency. For instance, scientists will be able to enhance food yields, and engineer plants that are drought tolerant and able to grow in salt water; electric cars will provide clean transport, reduce carbon emissions and help to clean up our cities; and innovations in data-sharing and communications technology will help take better care of the sick and reduce the risk of global epidemics.

8. Solar is the Answer

Specifically, a growing number of governments and companies are backing advances in solar energy to have a major impact on the world's energy supply and beyond. More solar energy is available to us than we could ever use and it is 100 per cent renewable – the sun rises every day. If we improve the efficiency of solar cells and batteries, then we can provide low-cost energy at scale anywhere in the world. Moreover, if we have (nearly) free energy, then we can use that to provide (nearly) free clean water and so the availability of increasingly cheap or free food.

And some issues that people highlight have varying positive or negative impacts – depending where you come from:

9. We Need to Rethink Retirement

Because of improvements in health care and consequent increases in life expectancy, most of us will live longer, but in many countries this may place a burden on the work-pension balance. Most state pensions are designed to last ten years and therefore we need to keep on working until 'death minus ten' years. If we are all healthier for longer, then we can remain economically active well into our 70s, especially if we move to part-time rather than full-time working. Experienced older workers can be highly effective within organisations, but we need to redesign systems to better support them within the workplace. Equally, loneliness is a growing concern for elderly, so should we rethink how older people are integrated into our communities?

10. Health-care Spending will Only Go Up

As more of us live for longer and we develop new medicines, the cost of health care to all societies will continue to increase, and this may break some systems. Some countries are already spending well over ten per cent of their GDP (gross domestic product) on health care – both public and private. Chronic diseases such as diabetes, cancer and Alzheimer's are on the increase, and collectively they could double the overall health-care burden in many societies. But there may be better alternative approaches, being developed in Asia and Africa, which could provide more effective health care for all of us. Can prevention play a more significant role – not just in the control of chronic diseases, but also in pandemics such as Ebola?

11. This is the Asian Century

If the 20th century was the American century, then maybe the 21st is the Asian century, with China and India leading on economic growth, becoming more externally active and deploying their economic and military power to exert more global influence. China and India have been principal economies for the majority of the last 2,000 years and are steadily regaining a global leadership position. In recent years China has achieved amazing growth, brought millions out of poverty and is now using its huge population and financial resources to help others. But China is also in a rush to get rich before its population gets old – as the long-term impacts of its one child policy become evident, its economic growth will decline and so, as with all great powers, will its influence. And what of India? It has a much better population demographic. Will it become as important as China economically, militarily and diplomatically?

12. GDP Growth is the Best Way to Measure Progress

As some nations see stagnating growth, many are questioning whether our obsession with using GDP as the primary measure of success should end. A focus mostly (or fully) on GDP growth prioritises money above other things that may well be more important to us as a society – such as well-being, education and happiness. This GDP growth obsession forces many companies to prioritise growing shareholder value above all other outcomes, and drives short-term thinking in the financial markets that in turn impacts on society's norms and values. And 20th century capitalism may not be the best system for the 21st – more consumption is unsustainable, and a growing number of people see that we need to find a better model – whatever that may be.

Six Key Challenges

While few people share *all* of these views, most agree on a good number of them. They could be seen to be the underlying assumptions held by many individuals, groups and societal actions. Given this, if we are to help citizens, companies and governments make better decisions for the future, can we better understand which of these views actually hold water, and which may well be less of an issue than we think? Can we separate myth from reality? What are the real global challenges that lie ahead? And, ultimately, what are our best options for the future?

The following chapters explore these and other issues, and share what informed people around the world think about the major challenges and opportunities for the next decade. Split into six core sections on Future People, Place, Power, Belief, Behaviour and Business, they not only help us to address these 12 common views, but also include additional perspectives on many other issues for the future.

Chapter 2

CHALLENGE 1:
Future People

With an increasingly unequal and ageing population in many countries, how will we generate the wealth to rebalance society fairly and afford better care provision?

- Imbalanced population growth
- Shrinking middle
- Agelessness
- Working longer
- Rising youth unemployment
- Care in the community

- Affordable health care
- Enhanced performance
- Mass engagement
- Skills concentrations
- Female choice dilemma
- Currencies of meaning

Around the world, the macro shifts for population are clearly evident – we are living in an older, and less equal, culture. Although these are not evenly distributed changes, at the global level they are the two that cause greatest concern for governments in terms of both funding and maintaining societal balance.

That we are all living longer is due in part to great improvements made in health care in recent years, but in many regions the cost of care for the elderly is stressing the system. As global life expectancy increases by an average of six months each year, so the share of GDP spent on disease prevention, sick care and general care for the ageing is also rising. In countries where this share is now ten per cent or higher, serious questions are being asked about how to sustain this spend.

At the same time, economists and politicians are all lining up to highlight the rise of inequality and are discussing the issue with increasing concern. While the United States of America (USA) is always the reference point for income inequality, there are many other countries with a greater problem – not just much of Latin America but also South Africa, India and China. Moreover, beyond raw income inequality, many other countries are seeing greater gaps in other areas such as education, transport, health care and connectivity.

After half a century of evident progress – fewer wars, less disease, improving access to education and health care – it is clear that the two issues of ageing and inequality link to many other related transformations on the horizon. This chapter explores *Future People*, how societies are changing and what may be some of the core implications in the years ahead.

Imbalanced Population Growth

A growing population adds another billion people but it is also rapidly ageing: a child born next year will live six months longer than one born today. While migration helps to rebalance some societies, increasing dependency ratios challenge many.

While there are a number of different views on what the total population will be in 50 years, no one disagrees that this growth is going to be imbalanced. Be it ageing, fertility or geography, increasingly we are going to have more people living in the places and demographic zones where we are least comfortable. Dependency ratios in some countries are fast reaching unsustainable levels and, thanks to wars and global warming, we are going to see significantly increased migration as the system across many societies seeks to rebalance itself. This in turn will lead to economic, political and social stresses around the world, bringing greater pressure on the overall system in the next decade.

The global population hit the 7 billion mark in 2012; the latest projections see this rising to 8.5 billion by 2030, and maybe up to 10.5 billion by 2050 (Figure 2).[1] With

Population (in billions)

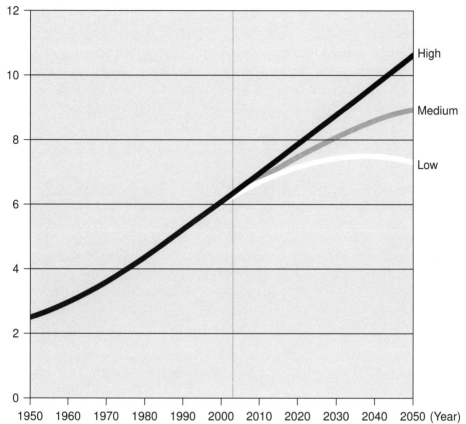

Figure 2: World population projections to 2050.
(Source: UN)

better use of food and land, this is thought to be possible; however, regionally, the numbers and speed of increase vary considerably. In Europe, the natural population is actually set to decline: having peaked at 740 million in 2010 today it is down slightly to 738 million. By 2030, without mass migration from elsewhere, it is expected to be 734 million and by 2050 it will have dropped further to 707 million. Other countries with naturally declining populations include Japan, South Korea, Taiwan and Singapore. In all, the populations of 48 countries or areas in the world are expected to decrease between 2015 and 2050. Those countries face significant structural issues; if they are to maintain sustained economic growth, one of the biggest challenges they face is how to achieve this with an increasingly imbalanced domestic population.

Overall, though, the world will be adding an average of 60 million people a year to the planet between now and 2050. Africa, the fastest growing region, is growing steadily and is expected to move from a population of 1.1 billion today to 1.7 billion in 2030, and 2.5 billion by 2050. Elsewhere, the trend is somewhere in-between: in North America, the population is expected to grow by two million a year, rising from

358 million today to 433 million by 2050; in South America, the increase is from 634 million today to 784 million by 2050.

In Asia, currently the population of China is approximately 1.4 billion compared with 1.3 billion in India; within seven years, the population of India is expected to surpass that of China. With China's population growth plateauing, by 2022, both countries are expected to be home to approximately 1.4 billion people. Thereafter, India's population is projected to continue growing for several decades, to 1.5 billion in 2030 and 1.7 billion in 2050.

There are three core drivers of population growth: ageing, fertility and migration. It is the first of these that is clearly visible in most societies today. One of the great successes of the last 50 years has come from better health care: all over the world we have improved public health, created new drugs that cure ailments, eradicated many diseases, improved water supply and sanitation for many and helped to reduce, but not yet erase, hunger. As a result we are living longer: 900 million people – around 12 per cent of the world's population – are now aged over 60; this figure is projected to rise to 1.4 billion by 2030. While most of the overall increase will come from health improvements that have, for example, brought the average age in Africa to beyond 50, it will be in Asia, America and Europe where the elderly will be most visible. Currently, 24 per cent of Europe's population is aged 60 or over; this is projected to rise to 33 per cent by 2050. In North America over the same period, the numbers are expect to rise from 20 per cent to 27 per cent, and in both Asia and Latin America we will see a doubling of the over-60 population share from 12 per cent to 25 per cent.

Today life expectancy at birth is around 70, ranging from 46 years in low-income countries to 79 years in high-income countries.[2] This is still increasing. If the success of the last 50 years continues, a child born next year will live six months longer than one born today.

At the same time, in pretty much every country in the world, the number of babies being born per family is on the decrease. This is widely seen to be a good thing, as it reflects both better health care and puts a brake on runaway long-term population growth. Infant mortality is decreasing, so families no longer see the need to have so many children to ensure that at least some of them will make it through to adulthood. However, the single biggest factor in reducing fertility is widely seen to be female education. This has become a major focus for many governments worldwide over the past 50 years; it was a priority United Nations (UN) MDG (Millennium Development Goal) and is now part of the fifth SDG (Sustainable Development Goal). Women empowered through education tend to have fewer children and have them later in life.

Countries where women average six children each are those that are generally low income. But not all low-income countries have high fertility rates. This is shown in Bangladesh, where GNI (gross national income) growth per head has been one of the lowest in South Asia and the number of children per women has dropped from 6 to 2.5 since 1970. Equally, religion has little to do with it: the same downward trends are true for Christian and Muslim majority nations alike. The single biggest factor in reducing fertility is widely seen to be female education; here Iran and Mauritius are often held up as leading examples but the same is true for Bangladesh. Globally we are nearing the average level for natural replenishment of 2.2 children per woman.

In many regions, however, low fertility rates are a problem. Fertility in all European countries is now below the level required for full replacement of the population in the long run. In the majority of cases, fertility has been below the replacement level for several decades.

China's one child policy was introduced in 1978 to manage population growth. Although it has many detractors, many believe that it has worked – maybe too well. During this time, population growth has been brought under control but there have been consequences. Since most young Chinese adults have no siblings, the so-called 4-2-1 problem – a single child caring for two parents and four grandparents – is intensifying.[3] As a result, official policy now allows couples to have two children. China has too many men, too many old people and too few young people, and hence a crushing demographic crisis. If people don't start having more children, China is going to have a vastly diminished workforce to support a huge ageing population.

Bringing all this together, within and across countries, demographers look at the balance of society by calculating dependency ratios.[4] This is a measure showing the number of dependents (those aged 0–14 and those over the age of 65) proportionate to the total population (those aged 15–64); in other words, the number of people being supported by the system in proportion to the population available to work and so pay taxes into the system.

There are ongoing debates about whether this measurement should be changed, to include or exclude the unemployed or public sector workers, for example, but in principle it reflects how a society can afford to support its young and old. It can be deconstructed into two parts – the youth dependency ratio and the elderly dependency ratio – but, overall, economists seek to look at the overall total figure. A high total dependency ratio indicates that the working-age population and the overall economy face a greater burden to support and provide social services for the youth and elderly persons, who are often economically dependent. Concerns are raised when the total ratio increases beyond 60 per cent, and the elderly ratio is more than half of that. This shows not only a high level of social burden, but one skewed by an ageing population. Overall the world has a total dependency ratio of 52.3 per cent but an elderly dependency ratio of only 12.6 per cent. As the elderly dependency ratio globally is set to double by 2050, a good number of countries have cause to be worried, including Japan (total dependency ratio of 64.5 per cent), Sweden (59.3 per cent), Italy (56.5 per cent) and Germany (51.8 per cent).

Similarly, the PSR (potential support ratio) calculates the number of working-age people per single elderly person. As a population ages, the PSR tends to fall, meaning there are fewer workers to support the elderly. Currently, African countries, on average, have 12.9 people aged 20–64 for every person aged 65 or above, while Asian countries have PSRs of 8.0, Latin America and the Caribbean 7.6, Oceania 4.8 and Europe and Northern America at or under 4. Japan, at 2.1, has the lowest PSR in the world, although seven European countries also have PSRs below 3.[5] By 2050, many countries are expected to have PSRs below 2, underscoring the fiscal and political pressures that the health care systems, as well as the old-age and social protection systems, of many countries are likely to face in the not-too-distant future (Figure 3).

Shorter term options for rebalancing populations are few – perhaps the most visible is migration. Around one in seven people today is a migrant, and net migration is projected to account for 82 per cent of population growth in high-income countries. Migration is an increasingly political concern the world over, but, while the current conflict-driven movement of people out of Syria is ever present on our TV screens, globally the great majority of displaced people have been uprooted by weather-related disasters. Since 1990, the number of international migrants has increased by 65 per cent in the northern and by 34 per cent in the southern hemispheres. Although still seen as a negative issue in many countries, in others such as Canada, New Zealand and the Philippines (actively involved as either migration magnets or providers), it is already considered part of a positive economic and social mix.

From 2000 to 2015, average annual net migration to Europe, Northern America and Oceania averaged 2.8 million people per year. With climate change now seen to be having a sustained impact, 2°C – let alone the more likely 3°C or 4°C of global

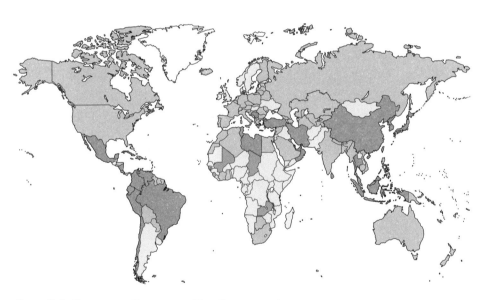

Growth in the proportion of 65+ population from 1985 to 2030

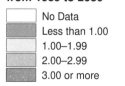

No Data
Less than 1.00
1.00–1.99
2.00–2.99
3.00 or more

Top five countries:
1. South Korea
2. Singapore
3. Thailand
4. United Arab Emirates
5. Bosnia & Herzegovina

Figure 3: Growth in the proportion of population aged 65+, to 2030. (Source: UNDP)

warming over the rest of the century – is likely to continue to be the biggest driver of migration.[6] While gap filling of populations by a million or so a year is attractive to several governments, dealing with tens, and maybe hundreds, of millions of people moving North and inland is going to overload the system.

As the rate of growth drops globally, thanks to longer lifespans, and we continue to move towards a steady state of around 2 billion babies on the planet, what remains uncertain is how societies will seek to cope with high dependency ratios and low potential support ratios, and what role increased migration will play as the 21st century's primary population-balancing mechanism. Self-evidently a rising political challenge, many are calling for those in the driving seat to take the hard decisions on this proactively.

Shrinking Middle

As the global middle class grows, in the West increasing inequality for some drives a relative decline in middle-income populations. Coupled with the erosion of secure jobs, the USA in particular sees a steadily shrinking middle.

When taking a global view, one of the major demographic shifts underway is the development of the middle class. Middle-income workers first emerged in force in Europe during the Industrial Revolution and then in the USA after the Second World War. Growth now is taking place elsewhere. Today, other parts of the world – Asia, Africa and Latin America – are collectively set to add 3 billion more to the middle class by 2030. However, across the USA and Western Europe, some detect a shrinking middle class: 'the middle-class is no longer America's economic majority'.[7] Or perhaps it is about a broader shrinking middle that encompasses not just the idea of the middle class but of middle-income jobs and roles?

In 2011, 13 per cent of the world population were middle income, defined as living on between $10 and $20 a day.[8] Most middle-class growth is expected to come from more of the 56 per cent low-income people crossing the $10 threshold; the Asia-Pacific's share of the global middle class will have increased from 28 per cent in 2009 to 54 per cent in 2020 and 66 per cent by 2030.[9] By contrast, the middle class in the West is not declining steeply, but rather stagnating – a bit like its economic growth (Figure 4).

In the USA there has already been a significant drop in the middle-income population. In 1970, 65 per cent of Americans lived in middle-income neighbourhoods; by 2010 this had fallen to just over 40 per cent.[10] Meanwhile, the proportion of families living in affluent neighbourhoods doubled to 15 per cent and conversely those living in poor neighbourhoods grew from 8 per cent to 18 per cent, hence the term the 'squeezed' (or shrinking) middle. As the numbers of rich and poor have both increased, the middle has shrunk. Research by the Brookings Institution[11] shows that larger US cities have more unequal income distributions than small ones.

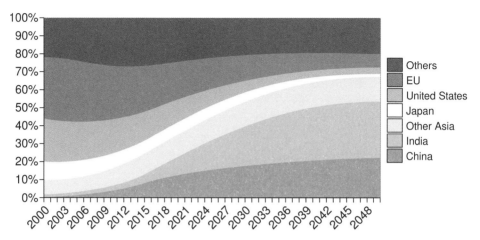

Figure 4: Shares of global middle-class consumption to 2050, by region/country. (Source: Quartz)

There are a number of reasons for this. Most importantly middle-class jobs are on the decline – again, a concern mainly in the West rather than the rest. Intriguingly, when you talk to the IT and automation firms keen on using new technology to improve or replace human roles, their core focus is no longer in the manual arena of factory and agricultural workers. Even replacing a $15,000 hairdresser with a robot with the required dexterity is simply not practical; however, there is a wealth of prime middle-class jobs in their sights. For instance, the vast majority of back-office legal and accounting roles are repetitive but require good levels of knowledge and memory, which makes them ideal for replacement by AI (artificial intelligence). As a result, a growing number of $50,000 roles across the West are, potentially, at risk – a cause for concern for many.

More hidden from some is the fast growth of the on-demand or 'gig' economy.[12] Whether it is Axiom, Eden McCallum, Freelancer.com or Upwork, a host of specialist service intermediaries are matching skills-to-project – from lawyers to consultants, designers, copy-editors and marketers – and cutting out the middlemen. Upwork (formerly Elance) alone connects 9.3m workers to 3.7m companies. As half of the 160 million-strong US working population is expected to be freelance or independent contractors by 2030, the scale of the opportunity for replacing this shrinking middleman of service organisations and employment agencies is huge. This is not restricted to the USA; India is another prime example, with 25 per cent of its workforce already freelancing,[13] and similar shifts are also occurring in the Philippines, Kenya, Indonesia and Brazil. As the global supply of talent and the growth of the service economy align, location and national boundaries cease to restrict workers. Some predict that this will bring a levelling of the international marketplace, driving more effective matching of people to projects and, over the long term, a normalisation of global freelance rates to between $40 and $50 per hour.

Others are not so sure.[14] In some arenas, middlemen are more important than ever: while many people already buy insurance direct from the insurer and subscribe to digital news direct from the publisher, estate agents for one are still around and, in some cities, flourishing. Confused by the overwhelming choice the Internet brings, people need trustworthy guides and other sorts of intermediary. Curation and coaching seem to be a growing need.

Several Western governments are clearly concerned about the implications of this global market on taxation. Not only may personal income tax incomes drop as individuals move from being employees to self-employed, but there could also be a big hole in corporation tax revenues as whole rafts of established organisations disappear and are replaced by networks nominally hosted in suitable low-tax regions. With less money to play with, this may in turn, it is argued, reduce the level of state and government expenditure on areas such as education, health care and social benefits which in turn would further increase the rich/poor gap and shrink the middle.

What is clear is that this is a lumpy shift – not like the relatively smooth growth in global population. The overlay of local economic shifts, regional population trends and a global, connected marketplace is, in some countries, likely to have a significant impact. At the moment, the signs point to the US middle class bearing the brunt of this. But the same drivers of change are having an impact elsewhere so it may not be long before other countries start to feel that squeeze.

Agelessness

A person's physical age becomes less important as society adapts to the new demographic landscape. New opportunities arise for creators and consumers of all ages, though benefits are often only for the wealthy.

'Chronological age is completely irrelevant,' says Sarah Harper, professor of gerontology and director of the Oxford Institute of Population Ageing. While exaggerated for effect, the comment speaks to how society is increasingly adapting to an older population and reducing age-based limitations. The demographic transition the world is going through is as unprecedented as it is profound. In historical terms, change has come very quickly: in 1990 we reached 500 million people over 60; there will be a billon by 2020 and 2 billion by 2050 (Figure 5). By then, one-third of people will be over 50 (up from 18 per cent in 2000).[15] The pace of change is accelerating, and these dramatic shifts are taking place in countries all over the world.

In January 2016 the first of the baby boomers (1946–1964) will start turning 70, and they are changing the experience of ageing, just as they have led cultural and societal changes over the past half-century. The cohort has been the largest and wealthiest the world has ever known, and continues to adapt society to meet its needs. Baby boomers control 80 per cent of personal financial assets; over the next ten years, they will change the nature of the workforce, the consumer market and shift societal attitudes around ageing – as well as dictating insurance and health-care financing.

Older people are increasingly healthy – the average 65-year-old today is as healthy as a 58-year-old was 40 years ago – and more active, and are not necessarily ready

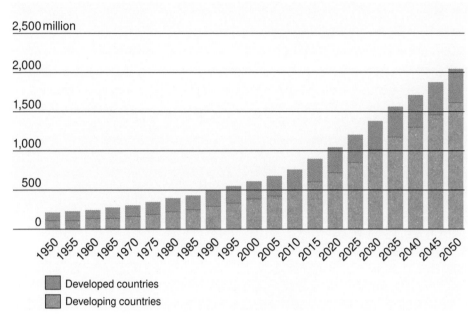

Figure 5: The number of people globally aged 60 and over, by 2050.
(Source: UNDESA)

to retire. With better health, older people are looking for ways to continue to be engaged, productive and connected. Companies are beginning to recognise that older people are an economic powerhouse and source of growth. By 2020, the 60+ market will account for around $15 trillion total globally – approaching half the GDP value in many Western countries. As marketers will be keen to capitalise on those who can afford to pay, expect a shift away from the youth sector (created by Madison Avenue in the 1950s) to a broader audience. Growth will come from the overlap of health and lifestyle: senior living, new opportunities for lifetime planning, ageing in place, pharmaceuticals, travel and leisure, beauty and cosmetics, fashion and retail.

However, the picture is *not* universal. Life expectancy, while growing on average, is not growing for all. Income, health and life expectancy are highly correlated. In the United Kingdom (UK) and the USA, the difference in life expectancy between the poorest and the richest sectors of society is around ten years, and across Northern Europe, around seven.[16] In certain demographic groups, for example, middle and lower income American women, life expectancy has actually fallen over the past decades; white males with a high-school level education have been dying early at an unprecedented rate, often due to early onset heart disease and suicide. As the divide between the haves and the have-nots increases, so will this trend. Addressing these health and longevity disparities present some of the greatest opportunities for innovation and for new models of collaboration between government, community-based organisations and the private sector.

While many compare and contrast demographic data between countries and regions, few look for differences within cities. One graph that came to light focused on variations in life expectancy within London. A view of life expectancy along the

Travelling east from Westminster, each tube stop represents nearly one year of life expectancy lost

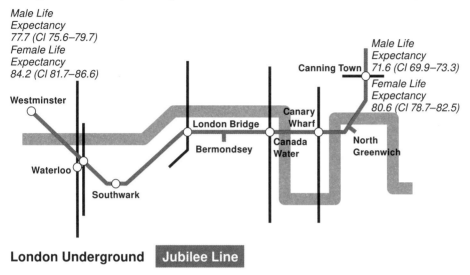

London Underground   Jubilee Line

Figure 6: Life expectancy in London along the Jubilee Line. (Source: London Health Observatory)

Jubilee line of the Tube network by the London Health Observatory reveals a notable shift.[17] Starting in Westminster and heading east to Canning Town, average male life expectancy drops from 77.7 years to 71.6, over six years in seven tube stops – not far off one year per stop (Figure 6). As we move ahead and grapple with an increasingly ageing and also increasingly unequal society in many urban areas, how this evolves and how similar contrasts can be made in other cities may well be an interesting indicator of progress or failure.

As we look forward to 2025, the extent to which we achieve an ageless society will be determined largely by how readily we embrace a new model of long life. How older workers are kept on or taken back into the workforce, what skills these 'wisdom workers' can pass on, what products and services they will need and wish for, and how society will adapt to embrace a positive view of older people – these are the challenges ahead.

Working Longer

People are having to work for longer to support longer retirements. Flexible working practices and policies are emerging, but some employers continue to remain ambivalent about older workers.

People are staying in the workforce longer. In Europe, 50 per cent of 55–64-year-olds continue to work, compared to just 37 per cent a decade earlier. In the US, the number of people who say they retired after the age of 65 rose from 8 per cent in 1991 to 14 per cent in 2015.

Financial concerns will mean that for many the dream of a long retirement will remain just that. Many older people simply can't afford to retire. The National Institute for Retirement Savings estimates that the balance in median retirement accounts across all American households in 2015 was just $2,500, while just one in three working Americans aged 55–64 has accumulated a year or more of salary in savings. Coupled with the lack of a meaningful social safety net, poor access to universal health care and far-flung families, these numbers mean that retirement is increasingly challenging for many in the USA. In Europe, where social safety nets have been lauded, current policy changes and budget cuts are threatening commonly held expectations of comfortable retirement. Women everywhere have lower lifetime earnings, take more time off for family caregiving and have longer life expectancy; older women in particular need to get back to the workforce to make ends meet.

In developed economies 2015 was the year in which the working-age population (15–64-year-olds) peaked. From now on it is in decline: by 2050 it will have shrunk by five per cent. Corporations in need of talent will have increasing incentives to make their workplaces suitable for all ages and capture the value of 'wisdom workers', rich in experience and judgement. For individuals with good health, a longer life will allow them to extend their careers, remain creative and involved and potentially develop new ventures.

As populations age, businesses will be developed to support them. The work of organisations such as Encore.org focuses on having a productive and engaging 'third age', retraining older professionals as teachers without having to join a class of 20-year-olds. Workforce productivity is another area of innovation – BMW made changes on its production line in Germany to accommodate the needs of older workers, and found that the productivity of all workers went up.

More employers are recognising the benefits of employing older workers.[18] Although memory and processing speed become impaired with age, other capacities, such as judgement, pattern recognition and decision-making, improve. These improved skills are well suited to the advanced knowledge work that makes up many economies as we move away from manual work. More experience can make older workers more effective as entrepreneurs too. The Kauffman Foundation found that business creation by older adults increased by 60 per cent between 1996 and 2012, and entrepreneurs older than 45 were the most successful demographic at creating sustainable businesses.

The flexible work experience sought by older workers is becoming increasingly possible with the advent of new technology platforms and the 'sharing economy'. One-quarter of Uber drivers in 2015 were over 50, higher than those aged under 30. Ten per cent of Airbnb's hosts are over 60, driven by the desire to generate additional revenue (which can serve as an alternative to a reverse mortgage) and to stay connected, social and active.

There is also an enormous economic benefit to supporting an older workforce. A June 2014 report by the UK's Department for Work and Pensions found that if there were as many older people in the workforce (defined as those between the age of 50 and the state pension age) as those in their 40s, British GDP would have risen by one per cent in 2013, a not insignificant number given trends of shrinking working-age populations. By 2050, working-age populations will have shrunk by a quarter in the advanced economies of South Korea, Japan, Germany and Italy, and the workforce will contract by 21 per cent in less affluent Russia and China. To put this in stark relief, by 2020 China will have 212 million fewer workers available, approximately equivalent to the entire population of Brazil. The USA fares somewhat better – its working age population is set to expand by ten per cent due to more favourable demographics and more migrant workers. Globally, this reduction in the labour force over the next 50 years could reduce GDP growth by up to 40 per cent.

As such, a number of countries, particularly in Europe, are developing innovative public policies. In Sweden, employers can qualify for a subsidy of up to 75 per cent for employing older workers; Germany is opening up sabbaticals for its older workforce and the Dutch government has introduced age-discrimination legislation and policies to promote flexible working. Japan, one of the first 'super aged' societies, provides part-time options for older workers and encourages them to be mentors. Groups such as Trading Times in the UK match employers with 50+ workers, while in the USA, the Columbia Center on Aging and the Center on Aging and Work at Boston College have been developing innovative initiatives to provide data and best practices to support productive later-life employment.

Holding back older workers are subconscious biases in hiring practices, such as a desire for very specific qualifications and a favouritism towards youth. This can be changed with improved coaching for line managers, investing in training for people of all ages, retraining for older workers, providing resources for maintaining good employee health, creating more flexible working schedules and providing support for workers who are caring for elderly relatives. The rapid arrival of robots and automation into the workplace will have positive and negative effects: while robots (or smart exoskeletons) could complement an older person's physical failings, others will reduce the employment prospects of anyone – at all. Similarly, migration by younger workers, from countries affected by environmental disasters, political conflict and continued economic disparities, and willing to do the jobs that locals do not want to, will alter the market.

Finally, will pension policies evolve? Although someone of typical retirement age is now healthier, it doesn't mean that the pension age should necessarily increase, since manual workers and those with lower income and skill levels – precisely those who need pensions the most – have not benefited to the same extent.

Germany's EU Commissioner Günther Oettinger has suggested, 'We have to talk about 70 as the new retirement age.'[19] He is not alone. Faced with the need to take the long view and balance their budget, the Swedish government has shifted responsibility and asked a non-partisan commission to propose long-term reforms.[20]

As a result the Swedes have gone some way to rescuing their pension system from collapse. An independent commission suggested pragmatic reforms, including greater use of private pensions and linking the retirement age to life expectancy. Maybe a model for others?

Rising Youth Unemployment

With unemployment rates at more than 50 per cent in some nations, access to work is a rising barrier. Especially across North Africa, the Middle East and southern Europe, a lost generation of 100 million young people fails to gain from global growth.

On the flip side to older people working longer, in some regions we can see a mirrored trend – that of youth unemployment. It is also high on many an agenda. Each one of the world's 1.2 billion young people aged 15–24 has the potential to lead productive, independent lives and contribute positively to society. Yet far too many lack the skills and opportunities to stay in school, obtain and keep a decent job, and become constructively engaged in their community. Across the globe, today's young people simply don't have the resources or support they need to succeed in an increasingly competitive, complex and often-threatening world.

The world is plagued by youth unemployment. The numbers are stark: there are currently about 75 million young people looking for a job around the world (Figure 7).[21] In some countries in the Arab world, up to 90 per cent of 16–24-year-olds are unemployed. In the USA the youth unemployment rate is 23 per cent. In Spain and Greece it is nearly 50 per cent; in the UK, 22 per cent. The International Labour Organization (ILO) predicts that by 2019 more than 212 million people will be unemployed, up from 201 million today. Irrespective of location, young people, especially young women, will be disproportionately affected: unemployment is expected to be around three times higher for them than for their older counterparts. In some regions, the proportion of young people without work is already five times as high as the adult rate.[22] Globally, young people account for nearly one in four of the working poor, stuck in low-quality jobs with no hope of progression. For many, the transition from education to a full-time job does not run smoothly: they lack the necessary skills, there are no available jobs in their area and they find it too expensive to move house to find work.

It is not just the under-qualified who are affected. In some places it is quite the reverse: higher education does not necessarily guarantee a decent job. In Tunisia, 40 per cent of university graduates are unemployed against 24 per cent of non-graduates.[23] In the Middle East and North Africa, highly educated young women are particularly disadvantaged: in Turkey, the unemployment rate among university-educated women is more than three times higher than that of university-educated men; in Iran and the United Arab Emirates, the figure is the same; and in Saudi Arabia, a university-educated woman is eight times more likely to be unemployed.

Aside from being unable to contribute to the economy, widespread youth unemployment can rob a whole generation of the capacity to enjoy mental and physical well-being. At its worst it can lead to social and political instability, constrained productivity and poor economic growth. Its effects can last for years, and those affected can lose all expectation of a full and productive life.

While economic downturns are one reason for youth unemployment, others include the growth in automation and lack of relevant skills. New technologies are changing the nature of work across every sector, from agriculture to industry to services, while new skills are needed for even the most traditional of roles. A generation ago manufacturing jobs required manual ability, and perhaps basic literacy, but now they require technical capabilities. Worse, increased automation and AI mean that both unskilled and skilled jobs are decreasing – just as the number of people seeking work is increasing. In many areas there are simply not enough jobs to go around. Such is the extent of the problem that, to make up for jobs lost during the economic crisis and to provide productive opportunities for those in or entering the labour market, including young people, the ILO estimates that 600 million jobs will have to be created over the next decade.

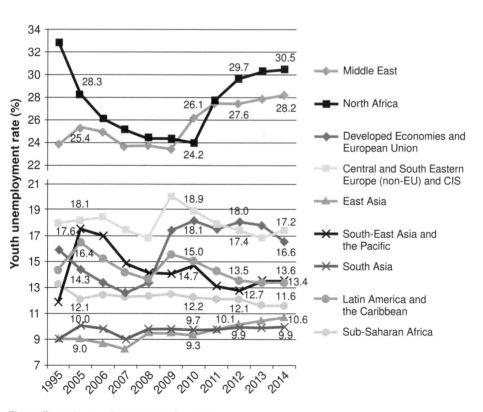

Figure 7: Youth unemployment rates by region.
(Source: ILO)

Location has a big impact on employment prospects; the inability to move to where the jobs are can limit opportunity. In the West in part this may be due to attachment to home, but rules around social housing and poor transport links also play their part. In Europe, only 2.8 per cent of young people move for work, compared to the USA where almost 30 per cent of Americans now live in a different state to their birthplace. Language barriers, cultural differences and non-transferable qualifications make it much harder for Europeans to move, but public policy also shapes behaviour. Most euro-area countries support their unemployed for more than a year. In most US states the incentive to go where the jobs are is significant as jobless workers qualify for only 26 weeks of unemployment benefits.

Europe's young have borne the brunt of recent economic woes: across the EU unemployment for those under 25, although dropping, still stands at more than 20 per cent. Experiencing unemployment at levels not seen in half a century, Greece has been particularly hard hit. Despite having good qualifications, many of its young are accepting low-paid jobs abroad. More than 100,000 educated youngsters have left over the past four years, mainly for Britain and Germany. As Greece's travails continue, expect more of its young people to seek their fortunes away from the land of their birth. Following six years of austerity, most of the Greek middle class have become significantly poorer, are unable to support their children's education as they did in the past and the young people who have moved elsewhere in the EU to study or work see little reason to go home any time soon.

In developing economies, a relatively high share of young people are likely to be involved in unpaid family work, starting their working life supporting (informal) family businesses or farms. The World Bank estimates that this affects 99 per cent of working teenagers in Zambia, for example. In the rich world, it estimates that a third of under-24s are on temporary contracts. Although it is better than not working at all, informal sector jobs are generally unregulated, don't pay much and often involve poor working conditions with no benefits or protection. Young people in the Middle East and Africa are particularly susceptible to this and there is enormous dissatisfaction in the region over the quality of jobs available. Among youth surveyed by the ILO, 58 per cent reported disillusionment with the availability of good jobs.

However, not everyone is looking for a job. Some people choose not to or are unable to work. Many South Asian women, for example, do not work for cultural reasons. In the Middle East only 15 per cent of women are in formal employment and in North Africa it is 16 per cent. To avoid increases in unemployment rates, the ILO estimates that 15 million new jobs will have to be created in the region each year for the next decade.

Managing the balance of their society, not just financially but also in terms of economic activity, is clearly one of the core priorities for many governments. With stagnating global growth, more automation and more competition for the jobs that are available, it is no wonder that concern about rising youth unemployment is increasingly in the spotlight.

Affordable Health Care

The escalating cost of health care is further exacerbated by the need to support the old and the chronically ill. Spending 20 per cent of GDP on health care is seen as unsustainable so hard decisions are taken around budgets and priorities.

Given the preceding issues, it is little surprise that many countries are facing stresses on key parts of their systems, none more so than health care. As nations develop and their economies grow, so does spending on health care. Improved health is a priority issue and the challenge for governments is how to provide an efficient, cost-effective system. This is no easy task and many are buckling under the pressure of rising costs, ageing populations and increased public expectations; across the world the whole health care system seems to be imploding. Fear of failure has not quite reached a point that will instigate change; although many agree that something has to be done, fewer know quite what this should be.

Of the global population just 30 per cent has access to decent health care. It comes at a cost: most developed countries use upwards of 9 per cent of their GDP on it – in the USA, it's more than 17 per cent. Emerging economies are also seeing a rise. In Indonesia spending on health care is now more than 3 per cent, in India it is more than 4 per cent and in China it is approaching 6 per cent.[24] In part this is because of the increasing health care solutions available. In the USA, the system is geared towards inflated prices so pharmaceutical companies are able to charge more for the same product, but, because of the size and scale of the industry, what is paid for drugs in the USA generally sets the benchmark in other markets. Much has been written about the varied attempts to address this but there seems little control over the pharmaceutical companies and costs continue to rise. For example, Gleevec, a drug sold by Novartis to treat blood-based cancer, was considered expensive when it was first sold in 2001 at around $30,000 for a year's supply, yet the price has still tripled in the past decade.[25] In most developed countries funding for this is picked up either by the state or the insurance system so the patient rarely has to come to terms with the real cost of health care. But the money has to come from somewhere.

From the very beginning of life, health care is expensive. Many countries are lowering the threshold at which they are able to support premature births from 26 weeks to 22, but this costs: around £250,000 for a birth at 23 weeks, 30 times the cost for a full-term baby.[26] Meanwhile, global life expectancy is increasing on average by six months every year, largely due to better health-care provision. Although each of us needs more overall medical attention as a result, our main requirements are associated with the last two years of life when more frequent admittance to hospital will account for around 80 per cent of our lifetime health-care costs. Better end-of-life provision is therefore a big issue – and one where the balance between hospital and palliative care is key.

The downside to longevity is that more of us are now living past the point at which we become susceptible to diseases such as cancer, dementia and Alzheimer's. These are expensive to treat and require long-term care. As we age, we are likely to have more disorders and so require more complex support. The average 80-year-old today has more than four separate disorders, all of which require treatment, often with conflicting side effects. The elderly, however, are not to blame for all the escalating cost of care. Our sedentary lifestyles and appetite for alcohol and cigarettes has led to a huge rise in chronic conditions such as diabetes, heart conditions, emphysema and cirrhosis – all expensive to treat. Most seem to agree that we need an alternative solution, one that focuses on preventive health-care measures rather than treatment of preventable conditions. We also need technology that delivers improvements at scale and at low cost. Controversially, some believe we need to start reducing the level of health-care cover to a good proportion of some populations – smokers and the obese.

More positively, India has become a standard bearer for redesigning processes that deliver high quality health care at a fraction of the usual cost. For example, Aravind provides $50 per patient cataract surgery, or $2,000 cardiac surgery from Naranaya, innovation that drives the delivery of world-class surgery at 1/50th of the cost of the same care in the USA. Naranaya Healthcare has now opened facilities in the Cayman Islands to better serve the fast-growing medical tourism industry.

High-tech, personalised treatments tailored to an individual's genetic make-up rather than generic profiles are another fast-developing area. Significant investments have already been made by the biotech industry and will have an impact soon, particularly in the provision of bespoke drugs that can dramatically increase efficacy. The cost of such treatment is prohibitively high because it requires the development of specific drugs for small populations and, in all probability, the additional provision of customised support systems. While some are sceptical of this having large-scale impact by 2025 because of the expense, all agree that personalised health care is a great opportunity for those who can afford to pay.

In the world of health care, there is also much debate on how automation and robotics will either enhance or replace jobs. While high-knowledge, high-cost, repetitive roles such as pharmacists are seen as being highly likely to replaced by a combination of artificial intelligence and robotics in the near future, the idea of a robot conducting surgery solo in probably a good decade or so away.[27] The nearest we have to date is the da Vinci system which, with quite a bit of set up, can already perform key operations and has fast become a selling point for some hospitals in China as well as in the USA. The key question, however, is whether this, and subsequent improvements, will replace the role of the surgeon or enhance it. While jobs such as truck drivers, accountants and even paralegals are all seen as replaceable jobs by leaders in IT and AI, in the world of the operating room the fully robotic surgeon is still seen as a long way off. While the technology to undertake routine surgery automatically is clearly either here or in development, the general view is that the surgeon will still need to be present to oversee the operation and be there in case something goes wrong. A close parallel is to be found on the flight deck of pretty much every commercial aircraft. Planes can now take off, fly and land all by themselves, but we still have a couple of fully trained pilots on board every flight – increasingly there just in case they are needed. The future surgeon will probably certainly do less, as automation and more highly trained support-staff do more, but as team leader or captain on deck, their physical presence will remain a mainstay for some time to come.

Perhaps it all comes down to the business model. For the pharmaceutical industry, the system is based on the expectation of a $1 billion revenue windfall from an occasional blockbuster, but as R&D (research and development) budgets can only to be justified on the promise of a major drug discovery, this takes time and is extremely expensive to deliver, which explains the high average costs of patented drugs. There is a general acceptance of high failure rates in product development, and the reality is that very few of the drugs currently coming out of the system deliver reasonable returns, from either a financial or a health-care perspective. For example, the 70 most recently approved anti-cancer drugs provide a median extra life for patients of just two months.

Some believe that sequencing technologies will help to improve the efficiency of drug development, while others hope that big data will reduce or even eliminate costly clinical trails. As long as share prices are based on high drug prices, few believe that any of the big pharmaceutical players will seriously consider a different approach. Most 'big pharma' companies prefer to focus on developing drugs to treat problems rather than vaccines to prevent them. Financially this makes sense: the benefits of a $250,000 a year drug for cancer is more attractive to some than a $500 vaccine to prevent the same disease. Many consider that so long as the current system in several countries is tilted towards rewarding sick care rather than prevention, high development costs and high health-care costs naturally follow.

Nevertheless, the principle of preventive health care is lauded, especially when tied into improving overall public health, but the system is not set up to align with this and there are few economies that are prepared to fund it at the scale required. More time is needed before the cash flows towards prevention rather than cure and this explains why some see predictions by the likes of McKinsey, which suggest that the opportunity for mobile health in preventive health care will be worth $50 billion by 2020, are optimistic.

Improved public education is an integral part of the process. Little things matter; in India 4 to 16 per cent of pregnant women are anaemic, and better education around diet could have a dramatic impact on child survival rates at birth. However, such is the scale of change required that few see a dramatic shift in public awareness any time soon, particularly as the cost-saving benefit does not come for 20 to 50 years down the line.

Paying for health care is a balance between state intervention and personal responsibility. Shifting from a national system towards private health-care insurance is supported and rejected in equal measure. Some support the notion of each citizen having a personal health-care budget, where there is a limit of spending beyond which the state either stops providing support or reclaims it via tax or benefits. Generally speaking, there are increasing expectations of 'co-pay' whereby sick patients will pay, directly or indirectly, for an element of their treatment, whether drug or hospital costs.

In emerging economies, where private health care is already in place for the better off, the big challenge is to develop appropriate systems for everyone else. While most support the concept of the UK's National Health Service (NHS), many believe that it is simply not sustainable in the long term. Potential alternatives being explored in India and South America are focused around micro health insurance, where people pay a small amount a month extra on their mobile phone bill, which is used to fund a workable health-care insurance system for the majority. Outstanding questions remain: What level of support can be provided, and how much additional government financing is also required? India is never going to spend as much on health care as the USA, but will a combination of more innovation, effective use of data, new pricing systems for drugs, micro-insurance initiatives, more public-private partnerships and a slight rise in government funding provide an equivalent service?

Certainly scalable, sustainable health-care solutions are needed. Most likely we will see few global answers, but more probably there will be a host of regional and local shifts, all aimed at a more cost-efficient, more effective and more equitable health-care system for a growing, ageing but still, on average, healthier population. As one US health economist put it, ideally 'we want to die quickly as late as possible'. Achieving that for all in the next decade really would be a success.

Care in the Community

> *The desire to 'age-in-place' meets a health-care reform agenda that promotes decentralisation. A new care model is customer-centric, caregiver-focused and enhances coordination across care settings.*

The issue of 'right to die' is powerfully addressed in Atul Gawande's recent book, *Being Mortal*, which vividly illustrates the crushing financial and emotional costs a dysfunctional end-of-life care paradigm can inflict on patients and their families. Many see that our whole approach to care for the elderly needs to change, and change fast. The economic and social implications of this issue are clear and the consequences of not getting this right are becoming increasingly visible.

Ahead of the end of life itself is one of the fastest growing markets, and also one of the biggest costs to society: providing care for the elderly. Understandably, most people, when given the choice, would elect to stay in their homes and in their communities rather than move into residential senior care – a recent survey by AARP (formerly the American Association of Retired Persons) in the USA put the numbers of people wanting to 'age-in-place' at more than 90 per cent.[28]

However, until recently the services, enabling technologies and business models didn't support this, especially as people start to get sick. And people do get sick: according to the World Health Organization (WHO), 70 per cent of people aged over 65 need some form of support, and two-thirds of Europeans will have two or more chronic conditions by the time they are 65. Already dementia costs society more than all cancers (yet receives much more limited research funding). By 2030, chronic conditions in total are estimated to cause a global GDP loss of $47 trillion.[29]

The trouble is that our health systems were designed for acute, not chronic, care. The challenge ahead is managing decline and improving quality of life, rather than curing disease. Europe, for instance, devotes around 75 per cent of its health-care spend to managing and treating chronic disease, but only 3 per cent[30] on prevention.[31]

Public and private payers are increasingly coming to terms with the challenges of the current system and its unsustainability in light of the demographic changes underway, and a new model is emerging in which the metric of success shifts from *preserving* life to enhancing the *quality* of life. This new care model can be characterised in three ways: customer-centric, caregiver support and care coordination.

The home is increasingly becoming the focal point of care, and technologies such as the IoT, smart home solutions, wearables and robots will all play a role in delivering remote care that allows patients to stay at home for longer. Smart gadgets, consumer-friendly mobile apps, 'tele-health' and other sensors allow for tracking and data creation, which can be used to make predictions about a patient's future needs, develop the most effective care plan and triage high-risk patients. Shareable electronic medical records are already commonly used and allow both doctors and patients more visibility and control. If they are able, patients, especially those with multiple chronic conditions, can effectively become their own care managers – tracking drugs, interventions, stakeholders and finances on a daily basis. This is challenging for anyone, particularly older people and those with impaired sight, mobility or cognition, which is why caregivers are such an important part of the equation.

Caregivers generally fall into two camps – family (unpaid) and professional (non-medical) caregivers. Family caregivers, who provide the informal care necessary to keep frail elders independent, often perform the highly stressful and underappreciated role, with limited support. In the USA the ratio of people in the 'family caregiver' segment to people in the 'care-receiver' segment is fast declining. A report by the AARP suggests that by 2030 the proportion will decline from eight caregivers per person over 80 to just three. To support a more stretched caregiver generation, new services for family members are being developed in some countries.

In the USA, the lifetime cost of being a family caregiver (in terms of missed earnings) is more than $300,000 per person, according to a 2011 MetLife study.[32] As there are 44m unpaid caregivers in the USA, this translates into billions of dollars if they were to be compensated at the market rate. However, family caregivers are generally not rewarded financially, and often suffer professionally and personally. A family caregiver can expect a 19 per cent reduction in their professional productivity, incur significant stress and face accelerated decline into their own chronic disease or depression. In recognition of this, new caregiver platform services such as CareLinx, Honor and Hometeam, supported by more than $100m in venture funding in 2015, are aiming to help them. At the same time, online portals (Unforgettable.org), social robots (Jibo) and on-site education services (Care at Hand) will also change the picture by aiding care coordination and delivery.

The need for care coordination matters most for those with chronic conditions as patients can often feel overwhelmed if left alone to manage their treatment programme. To address this, hospitals in the USA are actively penalised if a patient is readmitted for a recently treated condition, thus providing the motivation for the health-care provider to check in regularly with their patients and deliver care in the community setting where possible.

Treatment at home is not everything, however. As new technologies and new models of care are introduced, maintaining human contact and overcoming loneliness and isolation will be an ongoing issue.

Female Choice Dilemma

> *Women in richer economies have greater choice, and with it increased control and influence over their lives. This continues to drive change and decision-making but, globally, the battle for female equality has a long road to travel.*

Debates about equal rights for women have been on the agenda for over a century. Despite the best efforts of the UN's MDGs, more girls than boys still don't go to school, and in Africa and South Asia boys remain 1.55 times more likely to complete secondary education than girls. Even in rich countries life isn't particularly equal – the average wage gap between men and women is 20 per cent.

And yet, when girls do go to school, almost universally, they do better than boys and these days their educational dominance persists into university. In countries making up the Organisation for Economic Co-operation and Development (OECD) women now account for 56 per cent of students enrolled, up from 46 per cent in 1985; by 2025 that may well rise to 58 per cent (Figure 8). Women who go to university are also more likely than their male peers to graduate, and typically get better grades. In the next ten years this, surely, will have an impact on equality.

Most governments are keen to encourage more women into work as it makes good economic sense. Some estimates suggest that global GDP would rise by between 5–20 per cent if women's participation in the workforce increased. The McKinsey Global Institute's report suggests if the gender gaps in participation, hours worked and productivity were all bridged, the world economy would be $28.4 trillion (or 26 per cent) richer by 2025.[33] The potential gains are proportionately greater in places where fewer women are already in paid employment. India, for instance,

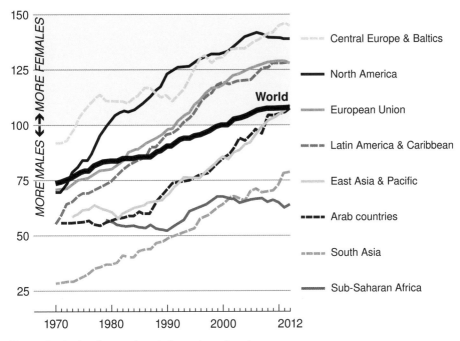

Figure 8: The female-to-male ratio for tertiary education.
(Source: *Economist*, World Bank and UNESCO)

could be 60 per cent richer. To date, however, gender parity in business is a long way off pretty much everywhere. Across the EU only one-third of managers are women.[34] In some countries, such as Luxembourg, it can be half that. Only one in 20 bosses of a Fortune 500 company is female.

Sometimes gender equality is the result of poverty rather than opportunity. The smallest gaps in participation rates are in some poor African countries, where men and women are almost equally likely to work at home, probably growing food. India, despite its impressive economic record, remains one of the world's most unequal societies: women make up less than a quarter of the paid workforce and account for just 17 per cent of GDP, a measure of output that excludes unwaged work. The United Nations Development Programme (UNDP) recently ranked it the worst-performing Asian country, excluding Afghanistan, for gender inequality, ranking it 132nd out of 137 countries. In other parts of South Asia, women carry out up to 90 per cent of unpaid care work, including cooking, cleaning and looking after children and the elderly. They are far less visible than men in work outside the home. By contrast, women contribute 41 per cent of GDP in China.

In richer countries, opportunities for many women are on the up. Better access to education, effective contraception and, arguably, rising divorce rates, all mean that more women choose to build a career and delay having children until later in life. As increasing numbers of women work, they became less accepting of discrimination. Women whose level of education is on a par with men are more likely to find well-paid jobs, but there remains an overall imbalance in pay. They earn about three-quarters as much as men. Since 2006, the number of women in the global workforce has risen from 1.5 billion to 1.75 billion, but the average annual pay for women today is the same that men were earning in 2005.[35]

Inequality judged purely on finance, however, is not the whole picture. Sometimes the reasons why women earn less than men is due to the type of career path they choose and the choices they make about lifestyle. Although men and women may start work on relatively similar salaries, family responsibilities often take priority for women and therefore decrease their earnings relative to those of men as they get older. In some countries the cost of childcare makes going back to work financially challenging, so the primary carer, generally female, either cancels or postpones their return. Anyone who chooses to put their career on hold to have a family and do the bulk of the baby-minding will find it hard to catch up.

Increased flexibility would help, but a flexible schedule often comes at a high price simply because for many corporations hours of work are worth more when staff are available at particular moments and when hours are continuous. Some argue that the gender gap in pay would be considerably reduced if firms could consider a different approach to working and did not, for example, have an incentive to disproportionately reward individuals who work long and particular hours. There will, of course, always be jobs where flexibility is not an option – CEOs, trial lawyers and surgeons, for example – but for many others pay does not need to depend on being available during a standard nine to five working day.

Often women get fed up waiting to be accommodated by their employers and decide to go it alone. This in part explains why nearly 30 per cent of all US businesses are majority female-owned[36] and why in the UK women have account for more than half the increase in the self-employed since the 2008 recession.[37] In emerging economies, innovations such as mobile phones, microcredit and even the humble scooter (over 60 per cent of which are bought by women in India), have freed up female entrepreneurs. There are further promising ideas to reduce the drudgery of women's lives: foot-pedalled water pumps, the 'micro-franchising' of heating and lighting provision in rural areas not served by the electric grid, and the 'crowdsourcing' of work to local communities.[38]

Many agree that for women to be truly equal in the workplace men will need to be equal in the home, and this change is gradually happening. To encourage this, women who in the past focused on redefining femininity might themselves have to change their perceptions on the nature of masculinity. Rather than embrace the image of male success as being a high-flying, high-earning superhero, perhaps they should celebrate men who can care for children and be content to earn less than their partner.

Conclusion: Nordic Answers

Although many see some of the issues discussed above as independent of one another, they are evidently interlinked. More people living in increasingly imbalanced societies is one of the few certainties for the years ahead. Managing this imbalance is therefore one of our greatest challenges. With an increasingly unequal and ageing population in many countries, how will we fairly generate the wealth to rebalance society and afford better care provision? Given all the variations within regions, never mind across the world, this will be far from straightforward, however. Those looking for answers are increasingly exploring the interconnections and hence some of the potential causal effects. Although it is not just about the money, this is an important core issue.

Most of us want to see a more equal society where poverty is reduced. Some at the top, however, are not so keen on relinquishing their influence. Many believe that this needs to change. In many countries income inequality has only risen in the past 20 years and has certainly not been embedded in society for a century. Many trace the recent growth of inequality in Europe and the USA back to around 1985. If we are going to address the burgeoning health- and sick-care crisis born out of an ageing population and better expectations of health for all, then there has to be a shift. While 20 per cent of GDP spending on health care may be possible in the USA for a time, it is not credible for many other nations. Whether via taxation or greater philanthropy, and the societal expectation of both, a redistribution of wealth will clearly play a part. So, we patently need to not only manage our population growth and its mix, but also to administer the finances that provide for affordable health care as well as support for the elderly and the unemployed. Many understandably ask: where can we find the right role models?

A number of the more equal societies are found in small Northern European nations. Many of the approaches taken in Scandinavia and the Netherlands clearly work and therefore probably merit further exploration as to how scalable they are. In a discussion in Bangalore on education, one government representative said that Finland's world-leading school system was not a credible model for a country with a population of over 1.3 billion; others in the room disagreed. They felt that even though the Nordic approaches are focused on smaller populations, many of the successes that have been achieved there warrant further attention. Although many point to the high levels of recent taxation, others looking deeper see many of the positives as being more cultural, not only in terms of education, but also health care, wealth distribution, openness and a very strong sense of community. Indeed, several now highlight that 'the desirable aspects of Scandinavian societies, such as low income inequality, low levels of poverty and high economic growth predated the development of a generous welfare state and the explosion of taxation over the 30 years from 1960'.[39] Scandinavia was also not alone in developing comprehensive social welfare systems in the 20th century. Across Western Europe, the kernel of a social compromise around the building of universal welfare institutions emerged in the early 20th century. The Nordic countries' institutional blueprints were produced by a strong labour movement in alliance with other popular forces. Some therefore see that 'the only way to get Scandinavian levels of redistribution and social protection is to start building powerful popular movements capable of advancing this agenda'.[40]

Although not yet operating at all the extremes, many of the Nordic nations are indeed getting older, have high dependency ratios, youth unemployment around 20 per cent and high social costs. And yet they have been among the nations more

	Human Development Index (HDI)		Inequality-adjusted HDI (IHDI)	
	Value	Value	Overall loss (%)	Difference from HDI rank
HDI rank	2015	2014	2014	2014
Very High Human Development				
1 Norway	0.944	0.893	5.4	0
2 Australia	0.935	0.858	8.2	–2
3 Switzerland	0.930	0.861	7.4	0
4 Denmark	0.923	0.856	7.3	–1
5 Netherlands	0.922	0.861	6.6	3
6 Germany	0.916	0.853	6.9	0
6 Ireland	0.916	0.836	8.6	–3
8 United States	0.915	0.760	17.0	–20
9 Canada	0.913	0.832	8.8	–2
9 New Zealand	0.913	...	...	...
11 Singapore	0.912	...	...	...
12 Hong Kong, China (SAR)	0.910	...	...	...
13 Liechtenstein	0.908	...	...	...
14 Sweden	0.907	0.846	6.7	3
14 United Kingdom	0.907	0.829	8.6	–2
16 Iceland	0.899	0.846	5.9	4
17 Korea (Republic of)	0.898	0.751	16.4	–19
18 Israel	0.894	0.775	13.4	–9
19 Luxembourg	0.892	0.822	7.9	0
20 Japan	0.891	0.780	12.4	–5
21 Belgium	0.890	0.820	7.9	1
22 France	0.888	0.811	8.7	0
23 Austria	0.885	0.816	7.8	2
24 Finland	0.883	0.834	5.5	10
25 Slovenia	0.880	0.829	5.9	8

Figure 9: Inequality-adjusted Human Development Index, 2014.
(Source: UNDP)

open to immigration, score well on both gender balance and education, are moving statutory retirement ages back and have some of the best care systems in the world. What is more, Scandinavian countries stubbornly continue to prosper. One relevant view of note, published by the UNDP, is the HDI (Human Development Index), a composite statistic of life expectancy, education and income per head indicators that are used to rank countries into four tiers of human development.[41] It has the explicit purpose 'to shift the focus of development economics from national income accounting to people-centred policies'. The inequality-adjusted HDI is a 'measure of the average level of human development of people in a society once inequality is taken into account'. For the past decade, the likes of Norway, Denmark, Sweden and the Netherlands have never been outside the top ten (Figure 9). Perhaps as we look for solutions to this, the first of our six key challenges, there is more to learn from the Nordics and their neighbours.

Chapter 3

CHALLENGE 2:
Future Place

As the shift to urban living puts pressure on the infrastructure, how do we create lasting cities that deliver better quality of life and also support rural communities?

- Citizen-centric cities
- Accelerated displacement
- Access to transport
- Air quality
- Intra-city collaboration
- Infrastructure deficit

- Basic sanitation
- Flooded cities
- Plastic oceans
- Off-grid
- Eco-China

May 2007 was the date when, for the first time, more than 50 per cent of the world's peoples were living in cities; by 2030, there will be 5 billion city dwellers; by 2050, more than 70 per cent of us will be urban (Figure 10).[42] According to the London School of Economics (LSE) Urban Age project,[43] in 2015 every hour more than 40 people moved into the likes of Mumbai, Karachi, Lagos and Dhaka – all one-way traffic. With greater internal migration occurring across Africa and Asia, the global picture is one of yet more people coming into cities. And yet there is rarely the infrastructure in place to accommodate them. The UN estimates that around a third of the urban population currently live in unplanned areas – townships, slums, ghettos and favelas – and this too is set to rise.

Despite having few tall buildings, the peak population density in Mumbai can be found in Kamathipura, where there are over 120,000 people per square kilometre. This is eight times the peak density found in London. How we use our urban space more effectively is a core area of focus; housing everyone is a major headache for many a city planner. Mass migration and localised population explosions will drive up the cost of both access to housing and home ownership. In many cities, this will need to lead to the development of new living spaces and ownership models that try to accommodate more of us. Moreover, beyond housing, others are struggling to upgrade the transport infrastructure needed to move us around in an efficient yet environmentally sensitive manner.

While apartment blocks and mass transit systems are therefore priority areas for many cities, some are also concerned about potentially even greater issues, such as air pollution and the increasing risk from flooding, both of which are already killing and displacing millions, and threatening more of the same in years to come. In many rural areas, it is no easier; providing access to transport, health care and education is coupled with ensuring that basic levels of sanitation are put in place.

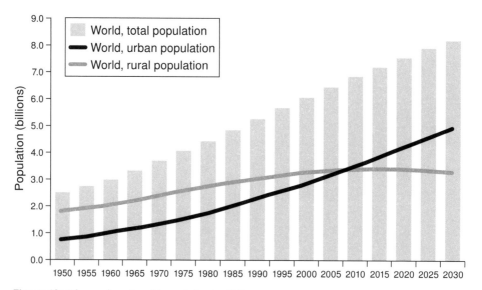

Figure 10: Urban and rural world population to 2030.
(Source: UNFPA)

Solutions, however, are in the mix. From more citizen-centric design and inter-city collaboration, to whole-scale reinvention of how the Chinese live are all at various stages of development. Bringing these visions to reality is the priority for many. *Future Place* looks both at the issues and the potential answers for how we can all live a better life – whether urban or rural.

Accelerated Displacement

> *Climate change, conflict, resource shortages, inequality and political elites unable or unwilling to bring about necessary change all trigger unprecedented migration to the North. Over the next 50 years, as many as 1 billion people could be on the move.*

In 2015, more than four million Syrians attempted to escape the conflicts in their home country. More than one million made their way to Europe, sparking political crises across the continent as politicians and communities struggled to get to grips with both the physical needs of those at their borders and the political and social implications of mass immigration.[44] The media was awash with images of an increasingly desperate caravan of people marching, from country to country and border to border, hoping to find their way to a new life. They are still moving; the Syrian exodus is the single largest conflict-driven mass migration event in living memory.

But this European tale, for all its impact on attitudes towards migration in the West, masked a far bigger migration story that has been taking place right across the world and one in which the Syrian movement to Europe plays only a minor role.

For sheer scale, the number of people migrating from rural areas to urban areas around the world dwarfs Syrian out-migration. Best estimates put this figure at more than three million people *every week*; in China and India, it was in the tens of millions in 2015 alone.[45] And this kind of internal movement can happen suddenly, even if some of its impacts are only temporary. Typhoon Haiyan, for example, was estimated to have displaced four million residents in the Philippines in as little as a few hours. Many have returned to their original homes, but others have permanently relocated. Cross-border migration too is not a phenomenon unique to the West: Indonesia and Malaysia, for example, have been coping with periods of similar daily arrival rates from Bangladesh and Myanmar.

Historical and economic connections between countries also play a part in regional migration-flows often ignored by the international media, such as those from the former Soviet states to Russia. The scale of this migration is sometimes hidden because the receiving countries also have a high rate of out-migration, resulting in negligible *net* migration figures.

Furthermore, while citizens in Western countries often see themselves uniquely as victims of a mass migration that distort their populations, they would do well to understand that other parts of the world are already defined by such imbalance. Tiny Lebanon, for example, with a native population of just four million, is home to a far higher proportion of people born elsewhere than the vast majority of Western countries – currently over 1.5 million Syrian and one million Palestinian refugees. We cannot yet predict how many of those will stay, but most are thinking decades.

The causes or triggers of this scale are complex. War and conflict show no signs of abating, while climate change, or rather its localised effects, are beginning to have the displacement impacts predicted over the last two decades. The United Nations High Commission for Refugees (UNHCR) suggests that 2015 saw global records in terms of the number of people who have been forcibly displaced, claiming: 'one in every 122 humans is now either a refugee, internally displaced, or seeking asylum'.[46] Meanwhile the factors that lie behind movements to find better economic opportunities, escape from persecution or to gain better access to natural and societal resources, are all being exacerbated by regional population growth and widening wealth and access inequalities.

Often, attempts are made to categorise different kinds of migration and migrant according to the reasons for push and pull. Commentators talk of 'climate migrants', 'refugees', 'asylum seekers', 'political migrants' and 'economic migrants'. But it's often difficult to distinguish one from another – someone migrating from a warzone may have had their home destroyed, or be suffering from the deleterious economic impact that war is having in their region.

The impacts of mass migration are manifold. The most visible are changes in social attitudes reflected in popular and social media comment, as those in receiving countries or cities vocalise perceived threats posed by immigrants to their culture, livelihoods and security. These changes in social attitudes often lead to macro-level policy shifts. Recent trends in Western migration policy, from all sides of the political spectrum, seem to point towards a coming slew of draconian laws and policies designed to discourage immigration. Weakening of immigrant rights and benefits, tougher asylum rules and tighter border controls are a given, but formal criminalisation and harsh penalties for certain types of migrant, and even military intervention in borderlands, are not impossible in the future. Some of these measures will challenge the very fundamentals of the constitutions that produce them, causing anguished national soul-searching, a phenomenon we are already witnessing in relation to the plight of the Syrians.

In many emerging countries policies have been designed to slow or halt rural-urban migration, such as the implementation of China's infamous *hukou* system of residency rights or rural tax, and investment incentive schemes in places like Mozambique. At a more local level, cities are planning their infrastructure and services to cope with fast-rising and sometimes statistically invisible populations, to avoid pitfalls such as squalid slums and shantytowns. In these responses we may also see the seeds of a more balanced approach to weighing the pros and cons of migration in specific regions.

So what of the next ten years? The displacement of people due to the effects of climate change looks set to become a feature of the 21st century as coastal areas become more prone to severe flooding, extreme weather events become the norm, and arable land and fresh water become ever more scarce. Rising economic inequalities will also push even more people to move in search of better jobs. People trafficking of both voluntary and involuntary migrants is likely to become too profitable a business to prevent. And local population growths will increase pressure on localised resources, leading more governments to encourage emigration in the hopes of easing local pressures and benefiting from the remittances of overseas diasporas.

Despite the bluster emanating from certain politicians, the scale of migration and predicting its impacts are actually extremely difficult to measure, with statistical vacuums leading to ill-informed and reactionary policy-making. However, over the next decade, as many as a billion people could be on the move, often heading away from danger and distress towards to the metropolis. We will have no choice but to find sustainable ways of responding to this unprecedented human march.

Infrastructure Deficit

Infrastructure again becomes a source of competitive advantage. Emerging economies invest in new railroads and highways for more effective movement of people and goods, while developed nations suffer from poor legacy.

All these new urbanites are adding greater pressure to cities in several ways. Infrastructure – ports, pipelines, hospitals, highways, water, sewage and phone systems – matters, providing the bedrock of prosperity and well-being. Facilitating transport, promoting communication, providing energy and water, boosting the health and education of the workforce, the infrastructure enables the whole economy to flourish. The costs of building infrastructure are vast, but the human costs of failing to make such investments are incalculable.[47]

For a country or a city to be competitive, it needs roads and airports to provide access to markets, power sources to fuel homes and businesses, and reliable water to generate productivity. Improved infrastructure produces abundant benefits for the economy, environment and social progress, unlocking growth and generating economic and social benefits and progress. As INSEAD academic and co-author of the World Bank's global innovation index Bruno Lanvin says: 'Infrastructure spending will be increasingly important for future economic growth, especially for the development of high-tech and knowledge-based industries ... Major infrastructure projects help to diversify the economy by indirectly encouraging new industries. There are things you can do in countries with good infrastructure that you just cannot do anywhere else.'[48] According to the World Bank, 'Research shows that every ten per cent increase in infrastructure provision increases output by approximately 1 per cent in the long term.'[49] These findings are consistent with a substantial EU study that demonstrated causality of electricity and transport infrastructure investment driving GDP growth in the long run.[50]

Despite the compelling case for investing in infrastructure, there is still an enormous infrastructure deficit. The World Bank believes that there is a US$1 trillion per annum gap (or 1.4 per cent of global GDP) between what is required and what is currently being spent.[51] The development of environmentally clean infrastructure would raise this estimate by an additional $200–300 million yearly. According to the McKinsey Global Institute, 'the world needs to increase its investment by 60 per cent'[52] until 2030 just to maintain current levels. Critically, this figure does not include the cost of maintenance, renewal and backlog – or the cost of climate change adaptation – and will not raise the standard of infrastructure in emerging economies beyond their present level.

In the developed world, a particular concern is that so much legacy infrastructure needs too much maintenance and rehabilitation, owing to the ageing of assets, stricter environmental regulations and the globalisation of supply chains. At the same time, 'the supply of new infrastructure cannot keep pace with demand because of various impediments; notably, the public sector's budget constraints following the global financial crisis, and the reluctance of private financiers to commit capital to long-term and risky projects'.[53]

Looking forward, there are a number of actions that can be taken to narrow or close the gap. Governments can theoretically pull three levers: reduce infrastructure demand, build new assets, or optimise existing assets through efficient operation and maintenance. The solution could take all three actions, but many believe it is the last lever that may offer the most potential,[54] with big-data and digital networks helping us to use current infrastructure more efficiently, or even bypass it entirely. It is also likely that policy-makers will increasingly bet on longer-term options with built-in adaptability for changing technologies and infrastructure use. One emerging challenge will be around who will take, and be trusted to take, overall responsibility for its development.

Adjacent to this will likely be a continued evolution in the sources and mix of funding. According to PricewaterhouseCoopers (PWC), 'the trend for governments to seek private-sector involvement in projects rather than go it alone will likely grow, as will participation by funds dedicated to specific kinds of infrastructure – water, for example. And high-growth economies such as China, India, Russia, Brazil, South Korea and Indonesia may consume an increasing share of world investment capital.'[55] To collectively address major urban challenges, as best shown by cities such as Medellín in Colombia,[56] governments will need to increasingly collaborate openly with business to improve not only the institutional fabric of cities but also core infrastructure.

Building the right infrastructure in the right place at the right time clearly requires a lot of future planning. As ever more people enter the cities in increasingly unpredictable waves, some see that more proactive approaches are called for. Not only does this mean that we need to be better at building the required facilities, but also that these facilities need to be progressively flexible.

Built-in Flexibility

The path to a connected, accessible and distributed infrastructure is fraught with complex, costly and risky issues. Upgrading and repurposing systems to make them more open plus ongoing maintenance need significant resources.

Much of the world around us today is shaped by historical infrastructure, such as canals, railways and roads. Infrastructure through the years has naturally morphed as new opportunities are realised (the introduction of the steam engine to sailing fleets, and digital communications displacing analogue). Often, this world of large, mainly state-owned, suppliers distributing products to consumers in one direction, was developed to operate in isolation. Why would electricity providers *want* to talk to water distributors? Indeed, regulatory bodies have a remit to prevent overzealous collaboration within a sector.

Today, however, the infrastructure around us is changing. It is becoming more flexible, more open to multiple parties and more capable of separating its various flows. The effects of this shift will be profound. By 2025, the infrastructure will not only be smarter but also inherently adaptable. Energy flows will become more bi-directional and distributed as more 'prosumers' – individuals who both consume and produce energy – come online. Systems are also becoming more intelligent. As one example, water supply will be more readily captured, treated (or not) and separated to make best use of individual water types such as grey water, storm water and tap water for more specific usage. Transport will become smarter, with vehicles that know (or can be told) of errors and repairs, which can communicate with their manufacturer, owner and service provider, as well as with the environment and road around them.

Buildings and communication systems today are already demonstrating smarter operations. The Global Change Institute's Living Building in Brisbane, where we ran three workshops, is a good example. It generates more energy than it consumes, is naturally ventilated, captures its own power through solar panels and stores up to 60,000 litres of rainwater.[57]

One driver for the rise in built-in flexibility is the need for increased efficiency, particularly where key resources are involved. Infrastructure providers and their regulators will continue to aim to do more with less, reuse products, produce less waste and avoid misdirected supplies. Doing so not only saves costs and (often precious) resources in the short term, but also feeds a hunger for the same organisations to develop longer-term plans. The creation of what have been termed 'virtual plants' by aggregating swarms of smaller decentralised plants (that is, wind and solar farms) into what the grid recognises as one is already under way. Grids in countries like Denmark, currently converting its energy/heating system to a 100 per cent renewable energy system by 2050, are managed so well that they can accommodate more than a 40 per cent share of renewable electricity. When using ICT for modernising distribution grids, the share can even be higher.[58]

How much will change by 2025 depends, like the numbers of prosumers of energy we may see, on how many people will be sharing key assets like cars and how many will reuse and repurpose vital resources like water. The incentives will come from heavily weighted subsidies, feed-in tariffs, tax breaks, market penetration and more. The proliferation of smart metering will help greatly with forecasting; global water metering is expected to grow to 1.8 billion meters in 2025 – from $2.8 billion per year in investment in 2015 to $6.6 billion in 2025.[59] But until this time, if the outputs of the 2015 UN Conference on Climate Change in Paris (COP21) are in any way adhered to, look for the pace of change in adaptability and openness of infrastructure to quicken.

In developed economies, the transition from the 'old state' to new thinking will predominantly come from innovations in and repurposing of existing systems instead of a new build. For regions where infrastructure is absent, or obsolete, wholesale change is possible, as best illustrated in the 1990s with the arrival of mobile phone networks that 'leapfrogged' the need for further fixed telephony networks. But there could well be limits to leapfrogging; for most situations, hard assets are still required – plumbing, roads, wires and buildings.

Fuelling all of this is access to more data. Whether big data, personalised, or anodised, access to data and the ability to use it intelligently is key – and of course, collaboration, because truly flexible infrastructure systems will require much coordination with other systems.

Integrating systems such as water, resources, food and energy is also pivotal. Rather than independent conversations that pit one resource or industry against the other, the increased ability of systems to communicate and change their flow/supply/ direction will transform previously independent systems. One simple example of such a nexus is in using solar energy to operate water pumps to irrigate crops to feed local populations: energy, water, food, people.

That said, there is a price to pay, well beyond the pain and costs that this transition brings: increasingly open and connected systems will, by their very nature, be more vulnerable to cyberterrorism. Infrastructure is an enticing target for any group hoping to gain a little attention, cause disruption or worse. Infrastructure providers will need to be diligent in their cyber-security measures, while at the same time opening up their systems to all and sundry: a balancing act, if ever there was one.

Benefits that we can expect to see are increased specificity of supply for particular uses, more adaptable supply-demand relationships, improved efficiencies and the much-welcome by-product of helping infrastructure providers to incorporate a longer-term view. Built-in flexibility is not an either/or concept to fret over; rather it is a wave of change coming our way. Only the rate of adoption is still in question.

Access to Transport

The widespread need for individuals to travel short distances becomes a key feature of urban design and regeneration. Planners use transport infrastructure to influence social change and lower-carbon living.

Most visible within many cities are their transport infrastructures. The impact that transport has had on society is all around us. The past century's near-universal love affair with the automobile shows that transport can shape landscapes, stimulate economies and feed desires. The US Federal Highway Administration says that every $1 billion invested in highways supports 27,823 jobs.[60] Globally, many road-building strategies rest on that premise, and the CIA Factbook estimates that in 2013 there were more than 64 million kilometres of (paved and unpaved) roads in the world.[61] Led by the USA, India, China, Brazil and Russia make up the top five countries by road network (Figure 11). Car-based systems have brought much accessibility, connectivity and convenience but at the cost of introducing noise, pollution, high land-use needs, urban sprawl, urban decay and, in some high-use areas, increased social isolation. Nations like the USA are very car-dependent – compounded by underinvestment in maintenance

Rank	Country	(km)
1	United States	6,586,610
2	India	4,689,842
3	China	4,106,387
4	Brazil	1,580,964
5	Russia	1,283,387
6	Japan	1,210,251
7	Canada	1,042,300
8	France	1,028,446
9	Australia	823,217
10	South Africa	747,014
11	Spain	683,175
12	Germany	645,000
13	Sweden	579,564
14	Indonesia	496,607
15	Italy	487,700
16	Poland	412,035
17	United Kingdom	394,428
18	Turkey	385,748
19	Mexico	377,660
20	Pakistan	262,256

Figure 11: Top 20 countries by road network, 2013.
(Source: CIA Factbook)

of other forms of transport. But not all countries are equally dependent on the car. According to the World Economic Forum Global Competitive Index, the United Arab Emirates (UAE) and Singapore top the rankings for (all) transport infrastructure, and in the EU the Netherlands is the highest-ranking country (fourth overall).[62]

Transport is much more than the journey – it can positively influence how we move, and even why we might *want* to move. It can be a transformative tool in shaping the societies that we hope for, addressing significant challenges such as inclusivity, mobility, urban design and adjustment to lower carbon living. For instance, inclusive transport solutions will challenge inequality, while flexible and integrated solutions develop mobility. Design and environment-led transport solutions can improve urban living (better serving our growing urban populations) while low-carbon lifestyles help address climate change.

Part of the thinking required is to focus less on providing transport and more on providing access. In its Future Demand Scenarios, looking forward to 2042, the New Zealand Ministry of Transport states: 'We should recognise we are trying to improve access not just mobility. There are three different ways we can achieve this: with good transport systems; with good spatial planning; or by improving digital access.'[63]

Fuelling these wider conversations is the increase in urbanisation, where inhabitants require other forms of transport and a variety of services. Other drivers of this change include new ownership and usage models, such as Uber and its like. But, as many experts of the phenomenon of 'peak cars' have pointed out,[64] a fundamental shift certainly needs to take place. With transport today contributing around a third of all greenhouse gases, it is an obvious place to seek improvement.

What can we expect of integrated, inclusive transport? Greater choice, better connections (and thus efficiency as well as ease for the traveller) and more green and sustainable options. Many are discussing the need for and success of integrated transport hubs. However, the ingredients for each hub vary considerably, given their locality. In Singapore, the addition of shops and air conditioning while waiting for buses and trains is critical, while Shenzhen aims for a hub with five underground railway stations, a border control point and numerous commercial areas.[65] Hammarby Sjöstad is an eco-friendly urban development in Stockholm, and its sustainable transport mix features a tramline, bicycle and pedestrian networks, carpooling and a ferry. Infrastructure here was planned as 'closed loop' systems for water, waste and energy – all feeding each other.[66]

Transport solutions that address key societal needs, benefiting the urban poor, are a key focus. The less well-off typically suffer from a lack of mobility options and are often exposed to greater pollution and unsafe conditions.[67] To counteract this, avoiding the spatial marginalisation of areas inhabited by low-income populations, improving (heavily relied upon) informal transport options, facilitating bicycle ownership for poor and low-income groups, and providing an adequate infrastructure for pedestrians (safe walkways, seating, toilet facilities, etc.)[68] are all vital. Transport poverty, though, isn't just a developing world issue – the charity Sustrans says that it's a daily reality for millions of people across the UK as well.[69]

Much can be learned from 'social transport' solutions such as those highlighted in *Pro-poor Mobility*.[70] Consider the ways in which poorer travellers move – for example, bicycle taxis (*bodabodas*) in East Africa and eco-friendly dial-a-rickshaw services in India are both low-cost, low-carbon options.

Of course, integrated solutions won't happen overnight. Doing 'new' is hard. But technology and visibility can play a huge part in the transition that is taking place. These areas can instil a greater expectation on providers and showcase solutions for all to see. But governments cannot do this alone; such a shift requires partnerships that include new players, tech-enabled, and new business models.

Autonomous Vehicles

> *The shift to fully autonomous transport is an evolution via truck platoons on highways and small urban delivery pods. Connected cars create the networks and test the technologies for the eventual revolutionary driverless experience.*

In nearly every discussion we had on the future of transport, the role that driverless or autonomous vehicles may play, came up. Talked about for years, the reality of cars, trucks and buses that navigate and drive themselves is getting increasingly closer and, over the next decade, many expect to see some pivotal advances introduced at scale in some parts of the world, although at different speeds in different sectors and regions.

Over the past 30 years there have been numerous proof-of-concept tests that have set the direction, proved the principles, and raised many questions about driverless vehicles (such as data access, ownership and sharing, as well as network reliability). Some car manufacturers have since become confident enough to put major stakes in the ground – Volvo, seeing the ability of a car to take over when an accident seemed likely, declared that by 2020 no one would be killed in a Volvo. Recent work by the likes of Google, Apple and Amazon has shown how innovation from outside the automotive sector can speed up development. By 2025, will we see fully autonomous vehicles at scale – or more assisted driving, rather than the complete autonomous experience? The key question, it seems, is whether the next decade will be an evolution or revolution.

The connected car, a forerunner to a world of autonomous vehicles, is a priority for many. In 2013, Nissan, with a dedicated proving ground in Japan, announced its plans to launch several driverless cars by 2020; BMW and Mercedes have connected vehicles now motoring along German autobahns. Here autonomous driving is working as an evolution of adaptive cruise control and assisted driving, with automated lane keeping, parking, acceleration, braking, accident avoidance and driver fatigue detection. In 2014 Tesla introduced its AutoPilot systems in its Model S electric cars, and in 2015 a car designed by Delphi Automotive completed a coast-to-coast trip across the USA, 99 per cent of which was done using automated driving.

The recent acknowledgement by Apple that its autonomous car project 'Titan' is a 'committed' project has brought much speculation about what else is also underway in Cupertino.[71] Google, though, is probably furthest ahead, with more than 100 vehicles already having clocked up over one million miles. It started working on driverless cars as far back as 2005, when it won the DARPA grand challenge. In the past few years the company has successfully lobbied for regulatory approval for autonomous cars, started road testing in 2012, and set a launch date of 2020 for its car. The fundamental issue here is whether or not it can pull off vehicles that work in cities, can deal with roundabouts, avoid unpredictable actions by pedestrians – and do not crash.

Much attention is also focused on moving goods, within and between cities. Already in off-road applications such as mining and farming, many of the ingredients of autonomous and driverless vehicles get large-scale traction in this area. The advent of truck platoons or trains, lines of long distance trucks electronically coupled to each other running along the highway, is upon us – Daimler's Freightliner highway pilot has been given approval to operate in Nevada, while rivals such as Volvo and Scania are undertaking similar trials in Sweden.[72] However, the real revolution in this space is for small, urban delivery vehicles – slow-moving, driverless electric pods delivering packages to homes, offices, drop-off points and even the boot of your car. It is no surprise that many are looking to Amazon to take the lead here; the opportunity to simplify the last mile of delivery in terms of both reducing human cost and optimising drop-off schedules is a hugely attractive business proposition.

What remains to be determined are the all-important issues that sit around the core platforms. Mobile operators are already sharing data, but who owns the shared data required to make the whole system work, and how is it accessed? This is matter of trust, value and liability and, depending on where you are in the world, the balance between government, tech companies and vehicle manufacturers shifts significantly. These are issues that need to be addressed, as most business models require visibility of 100 per cent of the vehicles on the road – 99 per cent is not good enough.

And there is the tricky issue of risk. From an insurance perspective, the advent of autonomous vehicles should mean that cars do not crash and we do not need motor insurance. But insurance companies see the risk as simply shifting from the owner to others – the vehicle manufacturer, the road network or the whole system. With the costs of system failure likely to be significant, this is a big issue yet to be resolved.

As things stand, the technology is being proven, the money is being invested and the potential for safer, less congested roads is a big social benefit. Governments are starting to discuss regulatory issues in both the USA and EU, and some of the ingredients (such as automated connections like eCall) will become mandatory in major markets in the next few years. By 2025, we will certainly see more assisted driving and autonomy on highways for both cars and trucks, where everyone is going in the same direction with controlled entry and exit, and maybe there will be full autonomy in cities for goods delivery pods. At the moment, though, it looks like full autonomy in cities for passenger vehicles is a few years away.

Air Quality

> *Rising air pollution in many cities is killing people and becomes a visible catalyst for changing mindsets and policies across health, energy, transportation and urban design.*

Delhi, Patna, Gwalior and Raipur are the four most polluted cities in the world and all of them are in India – in fact 13 of the top 20 most polluted cities in the world are in India (Figure 12). Beijing has a worse reputation, with its visible smog formed mostly from 10-micron particulates, but many Indian cities have more of the more dangerous, smaller sub-2.5 micron ones that kill as they go deeper into the lungs. Delhi's air is 15 times more polluted than the WHO safe maximum.[73]

Whether from vehicle emissions, industrial smokestacks or paraffin stoves in the slums, this pollution is manifested across many Indian cities in escalating asthma rates, higher incidence of cancer and more heart attacks and strokes. About 620,000 people

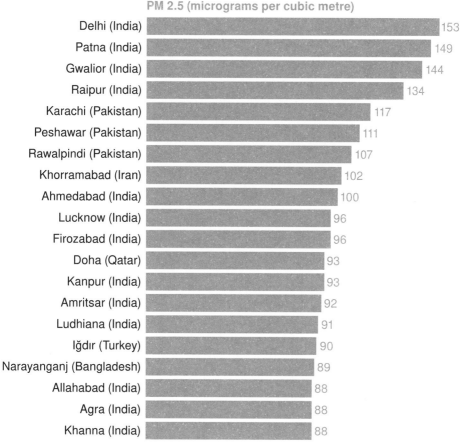

PM 2.5 (micrograms per cubic metre)

Delhi (India)	153
Patna (India)	149
Gwalior (India)	144
Raipur (India)	134
Karachi (Pakistan)	117
Peshawar (Pakistan)	111
Rawalpindi (Pakistan)	107
Khorramabad (Iran)	102
Ahmedabad (India)	100
Lucknow (India)	96
Firozabad (India)	96
Doha (Qatar)	93
Kanpur (India)	93
Amritsar (India)	92
Ludhiana (India)	91
Iğdır (Turkey)	90
Narayanganj (Bangladesh)	89
Allahabad (India)	88
Agra (India)	88
Khanna (India)	88

Figure 12: World's most air polluted cities, 2014.
(Source: WHO)

die in India every year from pollution-related diseases, but they're not alone. Air pollution in China kills about 4,000 people every day – accounting for around 17 per cent of all deaths – and in many Chinese cities lives are more than five years shorter than the national average because of air pollution. Eighty per cent of the population are exposed to below-safe levels, and the air in Beijing is so polluted that breathing it does as much damage to the lungs as smoking 40 cigarettes a day.[74] The omnipresent paper masks of recent years are being replaced by heavy-duty facemasks, and some are even delaying having children because of poor air quality. Having said that, according to the World Bank, when measured across whole nations, the most toxic air today is found not in India or China but in the UAE.[75]

Globally, in 2012, seven million people died because of the impacts of poor air quality. With increased industrialisation, wider car ownership and climate change adding to the problem, things are going to get a lot, lot worse. The OECD believes that pollution will soon become biggest cause of premature death.[76]

A pivotal issue about poor air quality is that it has multiple causal factors and impacts on multiple areas. From industrial strategy and energy policy, to vehicle emissions to city design and transportation choices, the forces driving increased pollution intertwine. Equally the health consequences of rising asthma, heart attacks, chronic obstructive pulmonary disease and cancer combine with poor visibility and grey skies to make many of the world's cities increasingly unattractive and unhealthy places to live.

In some Western cities, progress in improving air quality has been made over recent years. The Mayor of London, for example, has launched public awareness campaigns aimed at helping Londoners to reduce their exposure to pollution and help improve air quality.[77] Alongside tightening standards with the city's Low Emission Zone, retiring old taxis, cleaning up the bus fleet and retrofitting 400,000 buildings with clean air facilities, a primary activity to meet 2020 targets is to rethink traffic management. Meanwhile, the EU is taking legal action against 17 states with a consistent record of poor air quality. Bulgaria, Latvia and Slovenia are being asked to urgently address an ongoing issue that kills more citizens than road traffic accidents every year. In the USA, outdoor air quality has improved since the 1990s, but, according to the Center for Disease Control and Prevention (CDC), many challenges remain. Based on current projections, pollution in the USA is set to increase not decrease by 2025.[78]

With public attention rising and concerns over poor health influencing political agendas, India and China are ramping up their response. The Chinese government has set up a nationwide network of sensors, and regularly publishes data online. A comparative index has recently been launched in India to monitor air quality, while three industrialised states – Gujarat, Maharashtra and Tamil Nadu – are about to launch the world's first market for trading permits in emissions of particulate matter. In the town of Surat, in Gujarat, 300 textile plants, which typically burn coal to produce steam, are likely to be the first to trade such permits.[79] Monitoring equipment has already gathered emissions data from these and other plants.[80]

Beyond monitoring and permits, others are trying more radical measures. In the western Chinese city of Lanzhou, officially deemed by the WHO to have the worst air in China, officials have proposed digging gullies into the surrounding mountains in the hope of trapping polluted air in a gigantic landscape gutter. But Lanzhou's poor air quality is caused less by burning coal or car fumes and more by the local penchant for blowing up mountains. More than 700 peaks have been levelled to provide swathes of flat land for development – blowing out a huge gulley only adds to the problem.

New approaches to city design are being called for that will encourage healthier urban dwellers, thereby increasing productivity and life expectancy, improving community resilience, with fewer demands on health services. Reducing our dependence on cars is top of the list. Given that most people in India, even in the cities, still commute by foot, bus or bicycle – and that only five per cent of households own cars – the country still has time to set up systems for mass public transport before the car becomes king. Already 14 cities have, or are building, metros.

Most of the world's population will be subject to degraded air quality in 2050 if current trends in human-made emissions continue. The OECD believes that air pollution will become a bigger global killer than dirty water and, as such, is encouraging faster change.[81] The challenge in many countries is in balancing the public health impact with the desire for sustained economic growth – primarily still powered by fossil fuels. In regions where energy access is a higher priority than clean energy, many are increasingly seeing that it may well be air pollution, and not carbon emission targets, that captures the public imagination and acts as a catalyst for change.

More children with asthma, permanently grey city skies and increased breathing difficulties for all are seen by some as the triggers for widespread change – both bottom up and top down – and consequently, air quality is fast becoming a core part of the climate change vocabulary. Seeking to improve where and how we live will not only force us to face the myriad issues at play, but may also change the way we think about our cities and how we use them. However, for some, air pollution is not the only concern.

Flooded Cities

The vast majority of our cities are not prepared for flooding. Many districts and households can no longer get flood insurance and are in jeopardy. It's going to get worse before it gets better.

The year 2015 was the warmest year on record and, arguably, one of the worst for natural disasters: the Nepal earthquake, the worst flooding for 100 years in Chennai, one of longest heatwaves in years in India, huge monsoon rains in Myanmar, Bangladesh and India, massive flooding in Mozambique and Malawi, another drought in Ethiopia. Alongside flooding in Europe there was a strong El Nino that warmed the Pacific and led to heavy rainfall, flooding in the USA as well as more storms, poorer harvests and more flooding in South America.

In all, 23,000 people were killed as a result of natural disasters in 2015, many in the Nepal earthquake in April, and more than the total 7,700 deaths the previous year, but well below the ten-year average of 68,000. Insurers say that although the overall cost of natural catastrophes dropped to its lowest level since 2009, and claims fell to $27 billion, looking ahead, demand for cover will double in high-growth markets and rise by around 50 per cent in mature markets by 2020. Are things getting better or worse?

The consensus today is that climate change is here and we need to do something about it. As some have suggested, since 2000 we have been in the Anthropocene – the epoch that begins when human activities started to have a significant global impact on the Earth's ecosystems. Our past actions are having a potentially irreversible long-term effect on the planet. While ocean acidification, the nitrogen cycle and biodiversity loss are often highlighted as the most significant of these, there is little doubt that it is in the area of climate change that is the focus of greatest political attention.

With the recent agreements in Paris at COP21 now being worked through, some hope that actions to be taken will mean that overall global warming can be kept down to 1.5°C or 2°C. Others are less confident and think that our actions to date have already contributed to at least this and that, within this century, we are more likely to see 3°C or even 4°C of global warming.

To address this, there has to be significant change not only in the energy system but also in our behaviours. In the UK, the energy consumed in driving cars each day is greater than can be conceivably be supplied domestically from all three renewable options of wind, solar and wave. Add in heating, air travel, manufacturing and electricity for all our devices, and we are using way more than can be provided from existing green technologies. With current consumer behaviours, few countries can deliver a carbon neutral energy supply; without growth in nuclear or solar energy, coupled with hyper-efficient batteries, preventing the 2, 3 or 4°C rise in average temperatures is a big ask.

No one really knows exactly what this means, but the UK Met Office has created one map of likely consequences based on the Intergovernmental Panel on Climate Change (IPCC) Assessment Report.[82] Alongside further melting of the Arctic and Antarctic ice sheets, this shows desertification in the Amazon, the southwestern USA, southern China and large parts of Africa. However, although drought and hurricanes are going to increase in frequency and strength, and seasons will shift, the biggest issue that we need to prepare for seems to be flooding. Resulting either directly from rising sea levels and more heavy rainfalls, or as a by-product of more unstable weather patterns, dealing with more water than our systems were designed for is the top issue in many regions.

A lot of the problems of increased water flow stem from deforestation and more intensive farming on hillsides, meaning less absorption into soil and faster run-off, causing big problems downstream in urban areas where there is little option for run-off or containment.

As most of us live in cities and most of the largest of these are on the coast, the numbers likely to be affected are huge.[83] New York, Miami and Boston, alongside Guangzhou, Mumbai, Nagoya, Shenzhen and Osaka, are among the most vulnerable (Figure 13). The ten most 'at risk cities' globally already have combined populations of more than 150 million and are projected to have grown by a further 50 per cent by 2025, adding another 75 million people.[84] Twenty-two of the 50 wealthiest cities are prone to serious flooding that will also impact on housing, poverty, cost of energy and social breakdown. By 2070, the total asset exposure could rise more than tenfold from today, reaching $35 trillion, more than nine per cent of projected annual global economic output. In the longer term, experts estimate that, globally, up to one billion people will have to migrate inland or North as a consequence of climate change.

Climate change affects more than just humankind. Longer, more intense droughts threaten crops, wildlife and freshwater supplies. On the upside, we are seeing success in the development of saltwater-tolerant and more drought-resistant crops, and Canada and Siberia will both be warmer and able to accommodate more people.

For the majority, though, dealing with the impact of climate change will become their biggest priority. Over the past decades, many of us have consistently built where we should not have and in many regions flood plains have not been respected. Moreover, other than in the Netherlands, few buildings have been designed to accommodate regular flooding. In other countries few tangible schemes have been proposed.

There is an opportunity to rethink infrastructure in terms of resilience, and not just rebuild it. In a few cities more effort is being put into building new infrastructure similar to the Thames barrier in London. Designed in the 1960s and operational since 1982, this helps to defend London from high tides. Originally planned to be used only once or twice a year, in 2014 it was closed 48 times – without it, Trafalgar Square would have been underwater 17 times that year. Sustainable flood-risk management schemes are now being discussed and planned for areas like the Pearl River Delta in China where currently the practice is to deliberately flood rural areas in order to protect the cities.

1	Guangzhou
2	Miami
3	New York
4	New Orleans
5	Mumbai
6	Nagoya
7	Tampa
8	Boston
9	Shenzhen
10	Osaka

Figure 13: The ten most 'at risk cities' globally from flooding, 2015. (Source: OECD)

Nobody is expecting people to stop living in cities or for cities to voluntarily relocate any time soon, but with insurance being withdrawn from some, such as New York, and more regular flooding occurring in many, the need for action will be ever more visible over the next decade. If global warming plays out as many expect, attitudes to flooding will shift considerably; a more prevalent view around better preparing for resilience will take hold.

Basic Sanitation

Poor sanitation continues to impact on public health and restrict social progress, particularly for women. Governments and donor organisations prioritise measurement of sanitation, education and innovation in a bid to drive change.

While flooding and the availability of clean water are big, headline-grabbing issues, another less publicised but related water concern – sanitation, which should have been sorted years ago – is still affecting many millions of people in both urban and rural areas.

Although investments in sanitation can reduce disease, increase family incomes, keep girls in school, help preserve the environment and enhance human dignity, the world has missed the MDG target by almost 700 million people. Goal 6 of the newly adopted SDGs is to ensure the availability and sustainable management of water and sanitation for all by 2030. It is a tough challenge as, according to WHO, lack of access affects approximately 2.5 billion people, or more than 30 per cent of the global population, the majority of whom are living in extreme poverty across parts of rural Asia and Africa.

Some 130 million households still do not have access to a toilet. This means that more than a billion people defecate in the open, behind bushes, in fields or by roadsides. One gram of faeces carries up to one million bacteria and ten million viruses, meaning diseases can easily spread. As a result it is hard for health workers to control outbreaks caused by contaminated water and unhygienic food preparation.

This particularly affects women and young children. For a girl, lack of access to a clean, safe toilet, especially during menstruation, can lead to absence from school and increases the risk of harassment as many have to leave home in the cover of night to relieve themselves. This has long-term impacts on their health, education, livelihoods and safety, ultimately limiting the productivity of half of the potential workforce and therefore impacting on the economy.

India faces a particular challenge due to the widespread belief in the countryside that it is unclean to defecate inside and that only low-caste Dalits should deal with excrement. This has subjected generations to poverty and also prevents others from cleaning up their own mess, particularly within the Hindu community.[85] Indian Prime Minister Modi acknowledged this by taking up a brush himself and sweeping up rubbish in a Delhi street as part of a campaign to eliminate defecation in the open, but it will take many years for attitudes to change. The most recent national government survey in 2005 found that 67 per cent of all Hindu households, rural and urban, practised open defecation, compared with 42 per cent of Muslim ones.

Primary health-care facilities, critical in responding to outbreaks of diseases, such as cholera or Ebola, frequently lack good sanitation even though they are the first point of care, especially in rural areas. Lack of basic water, sanitation and hygiene facilities compromises the ability of health-care workers to carry out proper infection prevention and control measures, and demonstrate safe practices to communities, both of which are especially important in controlling and stopping outbreaks.

MDG and SDG status has done much to change the political cachet of sanitation policy. However, accountability for its provision is complex and crosses a number of different government departments – ministries for health, water and local government, of the environment, for example, and those with central, regional, district and city responsibilities. All are becoming increasingly aware of the pollution problems which on-site sanitation can cause to groundwater, coastal waters and surface water, and the net result is often a tangled web of overlapping, uncoordinated, unworkable policies, low-budget allocations and low prioritisation.

As better understanding emerges of the health impacts that improved WASH (water, sanitation and hygiene) can have on populations, expect new collective government bodies to make more strategic investments in projects. The World Bank Group is currently taking a lead in this area and is integrating WASH, nutrition and health in at least 13 projects across India, Pakistan, Lao PDR, Cambodia, Vietnam, Ethiopia, Mozambique, Uganda, Zambia and Haiti at a cost of around US$440 million.

Alongside this is the need to strengthen the mechanisms for tracking investments, better measurement and research is vital. Although the number of public toilet available is relatively easy to monitor, personal sanitation habits are not. Often developing countries are ill-equipped to monitor the many sector indicators simultaneously, especially if these indicators themselves are not easily measurable to begin with. The WHO and UNICEF (United Nations Children's Emergency Fund) are now committed to addressing this,[86] and are working with a number of countries to identify and use simple, measurable indicators essential to providing planners and decision-makers with relevant information. Campaigns that address the issue of personal habits may benefit from turning the spotlight on the personal advantages of sanitation, such as convenience, status and safety, rather than the more distant, albeit important, impact of sanitation on public health. Such campaigns not only mean government-built latrines have a better chance of being used, they may also encourage households to build them for themselves.

Aside from education and investment in facilities, innovation – both in the processes around building new facilities and in funding – will have a significant role to play going ahead. In emerging markets one of the main obstacles is often complexity: people have to cobble together all of the components and tradesmen from different places and then find the materials for the toilet separately. This can take time and energy so innovative processes to change this will make a huge difference, as will improved efforts around the mechanical waste removal and treatment.

Recently, the Gates Foundation challenged designers to reinvent the toilet, to make it suitable for developing world markets. The winning product, by Michael Hoffman of CalTech, uses solar panels to power an electrochemical system producing hydrogen and a compound that oxidises the salts in urine to generate chlorine, creating a mildly disinfecting solution to flush the toilet. The hydrogen is suitable for cooking or for powering a fuel cell to produce electricity. The solid residue from the process can be utilised as fertiliser. Prototypes will soon be tested in the field, and may well be deployed in as little as two years. The Foundation now intends to spend up to $80m a year on sanitation, an investment that WHO estimates will produce a return of 900 per cent in the form of social and economic benefits coming from increased productivity and reduced health-care costs.

At a time when some cities are focused on the opportunities provided by a more digital infrastructure, it is amazing to some that sanitation remains a major world problem at all. Without addressing the basics of clean air and water provision, they ask if there is really benefit in creating more travel apps. Some say no. Others see that this is all part of the global–local jigsaw of challenges to be addressed to enable better quality living.

Eco-civilisation

> *Over the past 40 years China has grown apace, mostly without concern for long-term environmental impacts. However, now faced with major challenges, a bright light of sustainable development is emerging.*

Faced with these considerable challenges, many see that the future as pretty stark. While some may be addressing water, air and infrastructure challenges, many believe that time is running out in core emerging nations. There is, however, change afoot – and it is coming from an unexpected direction. If you ask the man in the street which countries have some of the most ambitious targets for protection of natural resources and improving their environments, few, if any, would name China. If you look at rankings such as Yale's Environmental Performance Index for 2016 (Figure 14) then you will find China way down at 109 out of 178 – and even lower when you consider specifics around issues such as air quality and agriculture.[87]

But in Shantou, Shenzhen, Tianjin or Chengdu, or any of the other fast-growing Chinese mega cities, some people have a different perspective. They will talk about how China wants its local officials to stop ignoring the environment in favour of the economy, about an 'ecological civilisation', how the Chinese Communist Party is driving a huge shift in direction and, in order to do this, is making major changes to the whole government system. More than most, China is taking the sustainability imperative to heart and literally rewriting the rulebook. Whereas other countries debate, publish reports, develop frameworks and guidelines, and lobby for potential changes 20, 30 or 50 years out, China has set in process real changes that will take place by 2020. It has to.

At the Paris COP 21, many commentators were inspired by China's recent change of tone and tack on climate change, and its pledge, at a preceding UN Summit in September 2015, to be a carbon neutral state by 2030. Experts such as Dr Jackson

Rank	Country	Score	Peer Comp
1	Finland	90.68	↑
2	Iceland	90.51	↑
3	Sweden	90.43	↑
4	Denmark	89.21	↑
5	Slovenia	88.98	↑
6	Spain	88.91	↑
7	Portugal	88.63	↑
8	Estonia	88.59	↑
9	Malta	88.48	↑
10	France	88.20	↑
11	New Zealand	88.00	↑
12	United Kingdom	87.38	↑
13	Australia	87.22	↑
14	Singapore	87.04	↑
15	Croatia	86.98	↑
16	Switzerland	86.93	↑
17	Norway	86.90	↑
18	Austria	86.64	↑
19	Ireland	86.60	↑
20	Luxembourg	86.58	↑
21	Greece	85.81	↓
22	Latvia	85.71	↓
23	Lithuania	85.49	↓
24	Slovakia	85.42	↓
25	Canada	85.06	↑
26	United States of America	84.72	↓
27	Czech Republic	84.67	↓
28	Hungary	84.60	↓
29	Italy	84.48	↓
30	Germany	84.26	↓
109	China	65.10	↓

Figure 14: Yale's Environmental Performance Index, 2016.
(Source: Yale University)

Ewing, of the Asia Society commented, 'China's position has seen the greatest evolution on environmental and climate policy in the past years.' However, if you look at what is under way this should come as no surprise. Not only does China face some of the greatest environmental challenges, but given its scale and industrial capacity, it also has the wherewithal to do something about them.

To address these and other challenges going forward, the Central Committee of the Communist Party of China (CCCPC) is driving the concept of the ecological civilisation. The Central Committee, the highest authority in the system, is where significant change starts. At the third plenum of the 11th Party Congress in 1978, the historic 'Reform and Opening-Up' policy launched China's recent economic growth. Since then its GDP has increased from US$59bn to over US$10trn, with more than 470 million people lifted out of poverty between 1990 and 2005.

With economic growth now slowing, attention has shifted to a more sustainable view of future direction, linking growth with the environment. At the third plenum of the 18th Party Congress in November 2014, the ecological civilisation blueprint was officially launched. Former leader, Hu Jintao, stated that 'the essence of the construction of the ecological civilization is building a resource-saving and environment-friendly society based on the environmental carrying capacity of resources, the laws of nature and sustainable development'.[88] Eco-civilisation, the Chinese interpretation of the notion of sustainable development, is also fast becoming a new path for China's focus on innovation. In 2015 the UN commented: 'China's commitment to ecological civilization as a national strategy and the new post-2015 development framework are of huge significance to the world.'

Specific actions now on the table and coming into play include establishing property rights for the first time; using regulatory systems to manage natural resources; establishing a system for paid use of resources that better reflects the true costs rather than the previously heavily subsidised price; establishing a system for developing and protecting China's geography, including more zoning of key areas and monitoring of natural resource depletion; drawing ecological red-lines around sensitive terrestrial and maritime resources; and implementing eco-compensation mechanisms in accordance with the 'polluter pays' philosophy now gaining ground internationally. Eco-civilisation as discussed in China is very much a China-focused strategy, but in its use the term is also seen as a critique of Western-style industrialisation.

Among a host of targets and edicts, perhaps one of the most significant top-down shifts is the rebuilding of the government's performance indicator system. Whereas GDP has been the primary focus for China for the past few decades, the Central Committee has proposed a performance-evaluation system that moves away from this. New indicators will include resource consumption, environmental change and eco-efficiency – all underpinned by international COP21 commitments.

Although few report it, the change is underway. China has doubled its solar production to 20GW in 2015 and is targeting 1000GW; by 2030 China will cut its CO_2 emissions per unit of GDP by 60–65 per cent from 2005 levels. The country sees the battle against climate change as a major opportunity to accelerate its economic restructuring and so achieve more sustainable future development.

Whether or not China will be able to balance a possible economic slowdown with the move to the next stage in the chain of human civilisation is clearly up for debate. But against a background of global imperatives around climate change, the national dependency on coal-powered energy having significant detrimental impacts on public health, and the opportunity to take a world-leading position on green technologies in the mix, few would bet against China's eco-civilisation having an impact in the long term.

Intra-city Collaboration and Competition

Increasing competition between cities overrides national boundaries and drives change. They compete to attract the brightest and the best but also collaborate to avoid the downside of success – overcrowding, under-resourcing and pollution.

Global trade and power is generally defined between governments at a national level. Nations act collectively to negotiate deals to their mutual benefit, on occasion with the support of organisations such as the World Trade Organization (WTO). For city administrations, this time-consuming process can be particularly frustrating; they are disproportionately responsible for most of the world's output – 600 urban centres generate 80 per cent of GDP.[89] Some cities have become more actively involved in generating trade and business opportunities, their influence increasing depending on the amount of revenue they generate. Such is their success that some argue that the focus in the future will be between cities rather than between nations. The concept of the city-state, last seen in the 18th century, is about to enjoy a renaissance.

Cities offer opportunities for prosperity that cannot be found elsewhere; sheer population density allows businesses to make connections, attract funding and find customers. While economic size and growth are important and necessary, several other factors determine a city's overall competitiveness, including its business and regulatory environment, the quality of human capital and, indeed, the quality of life they offer.

To truly prosper, cities need more than office buildings and research parks. Cafes, concerts, art shows and open spaces are all necessary to allow citizens to meet and interact. Huge investments are being made to create liveable, healthy cities, encouraging more walking or cycling, improving public transport and adding green spaces – New York's High Line, London's Olympic Park and Seoul's rediscovered Cheonggyecheon River are all good examples.[90]

Urban developers are keen to focus on culture. Abu Dhabi, for instance, is developing the new Saadiyat Island cultural district, an area a quarter the size of Paris with three new museums (the Louvre, the Guggenheim and the Zayed) at its centre. It aims to position the city as a leading showcase for art in the Middle East and is at the heart of a plan to reshape Abu Dhabi's oil-dependent economy by 2030.

For cities, 'brand' is also important. Projecting the right image to attract the right kind of people works. New York, for example, is proud of its 'never sleeps' byline while Austin, Texas, promotes a different image using the slogan 'Keep Austin Weird', highlighting the city's commitment to creativity. Branding such as this acts as a reminder that urban growth should not drive out the culture that shapes a city's identity and appeal.

A group of elite cities are now playing an increasingly significant role in innovation. Mayors of mega cities such as Istanbul, Paris, London or New York are directly accountable to their constituents for their decisions, are more nimble than state and national elected officials, and take decisive action, often with immediate and impactful results – from trade to migration to education, their influence is key. Congestion zones in London, 'fat taxes' in New York, bicycle rentals in Paris (and elsewhere) and multiple mass transit systems improving urban transport are all examples of standards set by cities. Consider also Melbourne's 1,200 Buildings programme, which encourages energy efficiency upgrades to commercial buildings, and the environmentally sensitive building codes deployed in Hong Kong, New York, Singapore and Sydney. Oslo has announced that it will ban all private cars from the city centre by 2019. Although not yet independent, many predict that it will be city councils, and not state governments, that will drive significant urban change in the future.

The downside is that as city influence extends beyond the confines of national governments, government interest in the rural hinterland will diminish. City dwellers can become increasingly disengaged from those who live in rural areas, which leads to growing social problems – an estimated 60 million Chinese children remain in the provinces while their parents find work in the cities.[91] They are much more likely to be undernourished and underperform at school than their urban peers. Other countries with large-scale urban migration, such as Sri Lanka or the Philippines, are experiencing similar problems.

Continued growth makes cities vulnerable to the by-products of their success. Cities now consume 75 per cent of the world's natural resources and produce more than 60 per cent of the greenhouse gas emissions. Rapid urbanisation makes many of them unpleasant to live in, sometimes even for the rich. Cracks are forming in multiple locations. In South Africa the lack of public transport obliges slum-dwellers to take expensive minibus-taxis to work; many cities, from Lahore and Manila to Dar es Salaam and Delhi, are plagued by brownouts and poor sanitation (forcing citizens to resort to drinking costly bottled water). In London the city centre has become a ghetto of the super rich and has become simply too expensive for key workers to live in, leading to a shortage of nurses, teachers and policemen. Unless cities provide effective transport, power, sanitation and security, they will fail to attract the right workers to ensure they fulfil their economic potential. Many are solving these problems through collaboration. The C40 Cities Climate Leadership Group, for example, connects policy-makers from major cities around the world in order to address climate change, by learning from each other about issues such as waste management, building efficiency and transportation (Figure 15).[92]

We often heard that the C40, as a conduit for sharing best practice between cities, is an increasingly powerful organisation – maybe more so for tackling future challenges than the G20. After a workshop in Quito, Ecuador, at the IDE business school, I sat next to Quito's deputy mayor at dinner. Recently elected, she was keen to talk about how other cities were making progress. We had already talked about the transformation of Medellín in Colombia from a crime capital to a progressive, modern city with a string of public private partnerships now in place. She highlighted how she

Figure 15: C40 cities
(Source: C40)

saw the C40 as potentially the best source of support, so as to quickly identify, adopt and adapt the approaches, that could make a difference in Quito.

Cities, of course, do not always grow. In some places they are in decline. This is the case in the USA, where almost one city in ten is shrinking, as are more than a third of German cities. Chinese cities may well suffer the same fate as its population reaches its peak by 2050 – some of its older industrial boomtowns are already in decline. In order to survive, planners will have to work hard to identify policies that will be successful, with only a few brave enough to follow the example of Dessau-Rosslau in Germany and Pittsburgh in the USA, where derelict buildings were simply knocked down and the land allowed to return to nature.

Off-grid

People living off-grid, by inequality or choice, can exacerbate societal division or improve privacy, health and well-being. Either way, doing so provides fertile ground for innovation.

While the general trend is for people to move to urban areas and seek a more connected life, we should also recognise that for others the opposite may be true. People living off-grid, due to inequality or by choice, can either exacerbate societal division or improve their privacy, health and well-being, even with the world and humanity unquestionably more connected than ever before. According to Internet.org[93] 90 per cent of the world's population lives within range of a mobile signal and three billion people were connected to the Internet in 2015.

In Mendoza, Argentina, we met a good number of travellers who have successfully used this connectivity to merge work and holiday – the so-called 'bleisure' trend of mixing business and leisure. Whereas in the past long holidays for some in their 20s and 30s might involve three to six months spent backpacking, today's equivalent are doing it in style and for longer. Most of those we met were on year one or two of a multi-year journey around South America or beyond, while still working for their employer back home part time, or else freelancing. As long as they could find good Wi-Fi connectivity for two days a week, then they could continue to work and earn while travelling. As such, they were not having to keep control of tight budgets by staying in youth hostels and catching long-distance buses, but could stay in good apartments via Airbnb and share car rides. Most significantly, their employers, be that in the public sector or a number of IT and marketing organisations, were fine for them to work in this way. Maybe as freelancing grows and more of us become project- rather than job-focused, will we see, in certain sectors, more Wi-Fi nomads.

That said, this only applies to the lucky few and it is worth noting that 60 per cent of the world's population has yet to be connected to the Internet. A number of people are living off-grid for different reasons: this has the potential to improve well-being, or to further increase societal division and strain.

There are several drivers behind this. The first and most obvious is inequality of access. The barriers to access are principally quality of infrastructure, affordability and relevance. Inequality of access applies not only to the Internet, but also to education and health care. A key consequence of inequality of access can be increased social inequality, as the divide between the haves and the have-nots grows. The UN's SDG 10 is aimed squarely at reducing inequality within and among countries. More than one billion of us are, for instance, living without access to electricity – that's around two million villages globally still operating without something that has been taken for granted in many cities for more than 100 years. Many of the one billion off-grid population are not only failing to gain the basic benefits of electricity – from light at night to food preservation – but are also suffering from air pollution and associated public health impacts of using wood, candles, kerosene or paraffin.

After years of relative inactivity, there are, however, signs of significant movement in addressing this challenge. In Africa, India and Latin America a host of start-ups, government initiatives and CSR (corporate social responsibility) projects are starting to gain traction. M-Kopa and Off Grid Electricity in Kenya and Tanzania are just two of the prize-winning leaders in a field that is helping remote communities jump straight to a 100 per cent renewable solution.[94] Just as much of Africa skipped landlines and went straight to mobiles, so we are seeing a similar leapfrogging in power supply. Decreasing costs of solar panels, improving battery storage and low energy LED lighting are being coupled with innovative business models to provide accessible and affordable energy for all. Whether at a village or household level, pay-as-you-go electricity is starting to transform lives. Children can read at night and so improve their education, parents can work beyond sunset and food can be chilled enough to last a week instead of a day. Basic shifts that many of us have taken for granted for a century are fast coming to many of those previously left behind.

The other side of off-grid living is the positive choice some individuals make to be digitally disconnected. Driven by economic, political, social, cultural and privacy concerns, increasing numbers of people are opting or buying out. Many, as data becomes more ubiquitous, are actively choosing to avoid the digital ecosystem, or in some cases to hide from it; for others, this is about self-sufficiency and resilience. Being off-grid can be a permanent or temporary choice. Many individuals, families and communities now elect to be temporarily off-grid by, for example, choosing a digital detox to cut down screen and web time, to improve social, health, well-being and educational outcomes.

Digital off-grid living potentially provides both benefits and challenges. Key benefits include reducing stress, increasing happiness, reducing environmental footprint, (ironically) increased connectedness (with the planet, those around you) and reduced cost. Regularly cited challenges include increased inequality: digital inequality of access creates division, with many studies showing that that the digital divide exacerbates economic, social and democratic inequality, whether real or perceived, which can lead to tension between the haves and the have-nots, and instability.

Looking forward, the intent, enshrined in many of the UN's SDGs to ensure that 'no-one is left behind', provides an incredible innovation opportunity for many. This could be around improving access through increased infrastructure investment or subsidy, or finding ways to ensure that those left behind are shielded from social and political instability, worker strikes or the potential for increased mental health issues as hopelessness and unhappiness increases.

Conclusion: Smart Cities vs Smarter Citizens

No two cities are the same; each has its unique characteristics, so there is no global blueprint for the best place for us all to live. For example, in terms of personal mobility, in Mumbai over 55 per cent of people walk to work, in London it is 20 per cent and in New York it is 10 per cent (Figure 16). Equally in New York, 58 per cent of people use public transport every day, in London it is 41 per cent and in Mumbai it is 39 per cent.[95] From a pollution perspective, CO_2 emissions per head in Shanghai are 45 per cent greater than in New York and twice the average found in Mexico City, London, Berlin and Johannesburg. The answers are in evidence, but not in one location. Led by Bogotá, Latin American cities are seen as the most efficient for bus transportation but Latin America is also home to many of the world's most violent cities in terms of homicides per head.[96]

Much is now being made of the potential of so-called smart cities. In India a recently launched $15 billion initiative has the vision of developing 100 smart cities as satellite towns of larger cities, by modernising existing mid-sized cities. The aim is to improve basic infrastructure of these cities by providing good water and power supplies as well as improved waste management and public transport, but also to significantly enhance IT connectivity – and thereby provide 'smart' solutions to the urban challenges.

Elsewhere, others have already gone further with the IT-enabled smart city dream. Many see the perfect smart city as one where renewable energy systems, effective transport networks and digital infrastructures all align to create a super-efficient sustainable environment for everyone. While Dubai et al all have plans in place for realising this, several notable examples have started the move forward via city-corporate partnerships. IBM's Smarter Cities/Smarter Planet initiative has been embraced by mayors in many key cities such as Rio de Janeiro where massive sensor networks, Cloud-based storage and predictive analytics have all been integrated. Intel's collaboration with the city of San Jose, as a demonstrator of the capability of the IoT, focused on improving air quality, noise pollution and traffic flows via a more connected infrastructure. Although behind schedule, Masdar in the UAE is still aiming to be one of the most sustainable, environmental and smart cities on the planet, and Songdo in South Korea has embraced Cisco's 'Smart+Connected' view of the city. Here ubiquitous data sharing, automated buildings, high-speed networks and pervasive interaction are all part of the connected ideal.

However, while many of these initiatives are seeking to make cities smarter, a big question concerns how far cities can be intelligent in themselves vs enabling citizens to be more informed, take better decisions and so participate more in the development and execution of key strategies. With ever more people in our cities, it will take smarter citizens who are better engaged and keen to participate to make them more liveable, as well as underlying smart city technology. Changing how we use cities and the spaces within them is just as much about how citizens relate to these spaces as it is about the technology overlay.

For instance, with its population doubling, Singapore sees mass transit as a core driver for a more effective city – by 2030, 80 per cent of households will be within a ten-minute walk of a train station and 75 per cent of journeys will be on public systems. Nudging more people towards even greater public transport use is clearly a win-win. London has more open public data sets than any other European city and is fast becoming a leading centre for more intelligent use of shared information to enable greater collaboration and better decision-making. Implicit within this is collaboration within cities between different groups and, especially, government departments. For example, in Dubai, despite all the impressive hardware progress in recent years, innovation has largely taken place in pockets – either by district or government department. There is little cooperation between different parts of the public sector. If big issues such as poor air quality and rising urban obesity rates are going to be addressed, then they require deep collaboration across government departments – health, transport, planning, economy and tourism to name just a few. Designing our cities with citizens at the fore is a common call.

We clearly face many challenges in how we live in both urban and rural locations. Hopefully, if we can enact joined-up policies and implement those approaches most conducive to a better quality of life, we can take a major step forward. As is often the case when looking forward at how to address emerging challenges, it is often also worth taking a look in the rear view mirror. Are there lessons and pertinent insights from the past that are relevant? Maybe. More than half a century ago, in 1961, Jane Jacobs, in her seminal book *The Death and Life of Great American Cities*, highlighted that 'cities have the capability of providing something for everybody, only because, and only when, they are created by everybody'. Sounds pertinent today?

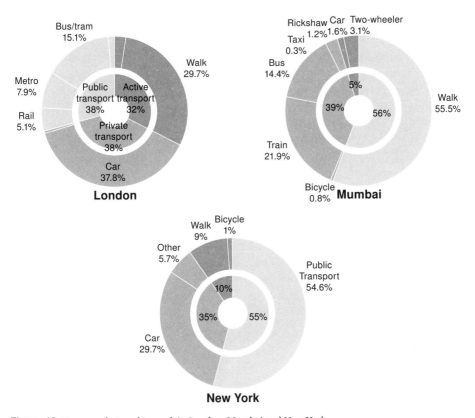

Figure 16: How people travel to work in London, Mumbai and New York.
(Source: LSE Cities)

Chapter 4

CHALLENGE 3:
Future Power

With Western governments ceding influence to cities and networks at the same time as Asia and Africa assert greater authority, how will global leadership be defined?

- Shifting power and influence
- Rise of the Cult of China
- Africa growth
- Declining government influence
- Everything connected

- Open supply webs
- Privacy regulation
- Built-in flexibility
- Energy storage
- Standards Driving Trade

Globally, significant moves are taking place which affect who, where and how power is being created and used. At a geopolitical level, many questions are being asked not only about the growing influence and re-emergence of China and India but also on the future role of Africa – economically as well as politically. As the West reluctantly cedes control of more areas of influence to the 'Rest', people around the world are speculating whether, faced with greater competition, Europe and the USA in particular will be able to continue to exert the influence they had in the 20th century. Will the 21st century turn out to be the next China era? Will a wider pan-Asian collaboration take the lead, or will the USA retain its influential position? Will security, technology or trade define future leadership?

Simultaneously, cutting across numerous regions, many are seeing shifts that will impact on the role and power of government. While in some areas government-led change is still in the ascent, in others the private sector is gaining greater sway, either directly or, more often, in partnerships – especially with cities as opposed to nation states. In some cities, mayors have already become more important than national governments.

As the IoT becomes a reality and technological dependence continues to grow, concerns around data security and ownership are being raised: data recognises neither national boundaries nor corporate firewalls. As we increasingly live in an always-connected world where everything can be part of the network, issues such as regulation around privacy are therefore in the ascent for some. For others, there is more interest in the underpinning changes around power supply, the shift away from fossil fuels to renewables and the fundamental issue of energy storage.

Across these and other core issues, what is clear is that it is the *nature of power* – as much as how it is exerted – that is in transition. We are moving into a world that is both more fragmented and yet more connected. This chapter explores *Future Power*: how, through different lenses, it is emerging and what, in different areas, may be some of the most significant shifts from the status quo.

Shifting Power and Influence

The centre of gravity of economic power continues shifting eastwards, back to where it was 200 years ago. Recent superpowers seek to moderate the pace of change but the realities of population and resource locations are immovable.

Significant for any view of future influence is to encapsulate what is being said about the macro view of geopolitics, globalisation and the role of the great powers. Are we, for instance, witnessing the end of an era in globalisation and international trade? The structures set up in the wake of the Second World War seem to be out of date and may, in 2015/16, no longer be fit for purpose. Adjustment is omnipresent: Western markets are weakening, the USA's appetite to act as overall arbiter and keeper of the peace is diminishing, and Europe faces its own constitutional challenges. Asian countries, which have in the main benefited from a youthful workforce and rising middle class, are beginning not only to influence world trade but also to play a greater role on the diplomatic stage. Africa and South America have yet to make a significant impact, but with a wealth of natural resources at their disposal, the next ten years should begin to change this.

Whether or not this is the Asian century, as some forecast, the next decade or so will witness the post-war trade routes gradually being eclipsed by the power of the Indian Ocean region. South–South trade doubled in the decade 2000–10, and is likely to account for more than a third of global trade by 2025 (Figure 17).

After centuries of growth, Europe's days in the economic sunshine are, many think, in relative decline. Some argue that the euro experiment has had its day and that Europeans will have to spend the next decade dealing with the repercussions of this failure. Some believe that the region will continue to muddle through as is, while others predict three possible options: that the euro will be split in two, probably along a North–South divide; second, a couple of major former currencies such as the Deutschmark and Lira will be reintroduced; or, third, there will be a complete refragmentation of the eurozone into individual national currencies and hence economic interests.

We heard rumours, during discussions in Asia, that the Germans had already printed Deutschmarks ready for the day they were needed. A couple of months later, I found myself in Berlin, speaking about some of our views on the future of payments. I shared

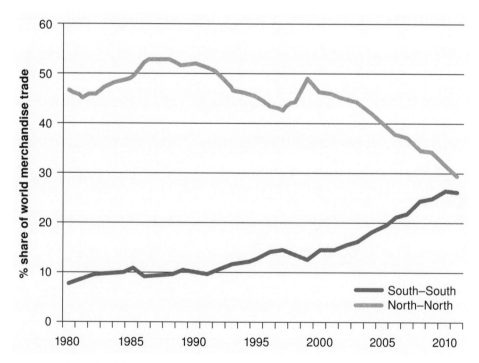

Figure 17: Share of world trade North vs South.
(Source: *Economist*)

this rumour with a senior member of the German banking system and asked if it was indeed true. His reply? 'We would be very unwise not to.'

Whatever happens with the euro as a currency, Germany will remain the primary power within the EU over the next ten years. Overall, however, the continent's influence will be eroded by its internal problems, such as the UK's destabilising 'Brexit' vote or the ever-present chance of a 'Grexit'.

Bridging Europe and Asia, but some way yet from being an economic superpower, lies Turkey. In a conversation in New Delhi with the Bank of India, Turkey was described as Europe's China – an interesting perspective and one not overtly agreed with in Paris. Since the establishment of a Customs Union with the EU in 1996, Turkey's exports to Europe accounted for nearly $70 billion, or 43.5 per cent of its total exports, in 2014. Whether the description of Turkey as 'the world's most progressive Muslim state' will still hold in 2025, its influence on the regional and global economy seems set to grow, as does – given its geopolitical location – its sway on global trade.

Things, though, are not looking good in Russia. It is suffering from declining population, poor access to secure water and food supplies (previously supplied by former Soviet Union neighbours) and a corrupt economy dominated by quasi-state firms whose revenues depend on political contacts rather than economic efficiency. GDP growth averaged a paltry 2.4 per cent from 2011–14 despite high oil prices and renewed access to credit markets. Most economists believe that things will likely get even worse in the next decade. This will not deter Putin, keen to bolster his status at home, from maintaining a presence on the world stage.

Wherever you go in the Middle East you find some elements of commonality, but also many areas of difference – especially concerning competition and conflict between Sunni and Shia, the financing of ISIS, the changes afoot in Saudi Arabia, and Iran's ambitions to create a new Persian empire in the future. The USA's influence is declining, for economic and political reasons. Many OPEC (Organization of the Petroleum Exporting Countries) economies need to increase diversification: not only do they face the climate change challenge, but they potentially will need to act as a growing, pivotal gateway for China and India, not just to the Middle East but significantly (in the long-term) to Africa.

Few forget the scale of the African continent (a land mass greater than India, China, the USA and Europe combined), with its workforce set to be the world's largest by 2040, or its resources. With a collective GDP of $2.6 trillion by 2020 and $1.4 trillion of consumer-spending, many anticipate the impact of around 500 million new middle-class consumers. The question here is one of timescale: will there be significant changes in the next decade or, like India, will it be a longer period of transition?

India's perfect population pyramid, a massive domestic market, a growing middle class, more successful home-based multinational private companies, little interest in military expansion to secure resources, and world-class expertise in IT and process innovation, all add up to the potential for India to be a top three economy. With a highly connected Indian diaspora and a number of very progressive business leaders, many see India as a certain long-term bet. For others, India is still a tricky place to do business, with its sagging infrastructure and endemic corruption presenting huge obstacles. The government aims to double India's export of goods to $900 billion a year by 2020 and improve India's share of global trade from 2 per cent to 3.5 per cent by 2020 (Figure 18). The World Bank, Economist Intelligence Unit (EIU), International Monetary Fund (IMF) and UN all expect between 6 and 7 per cent GDP growth for the next decade. But progress on reform has been slow.

Also in the region, Singapore will continue to be a major global trade hub, and the Asian leader in GDP per head; and Indonesia will grow steadily via more progressive government polices and a strong base of raw material exports. But it is China that dominates; IMF figures show that over the past decade it has averaged more than 25 per cent of global GDP growth. Some are questioning the long-term sustainability of the Chinese economy, especially with the burden of unbalanced demographics stemming from the impact of the one child policy. If China uses more of its economic might and soft diplomacy to reshape the world order, and if the renminbi usurps the dollar as the world's reserve currency, then China could dominate world trade.

Brazil's fortunes reflect China's curtailment of the commodity boom; future growth for the next decade is projected to be less than three per cent. Other Latin America countries such as Chile, Peru and Mexico will benefit from being part of the new Trans-Pacific Partnership (TPP) trade agreement. By contrast, the more inward-looking Argentina is generally seen to be stumbling from one crisis to another.

To the North lies the USA. Whereas China has 20 per cent of the world's population and generates around one-seventh of global GDP, the USA has 6 per cent of the world's population but produces between 20 and 25 per cent of global GDP.[97] Increasingly self-supporting both in trade and energy, will the USA remain the world's naval policeman and 'guarantee' to keep global trade routes open? It may be several decades before there is a significant decline in US foreign policy and economic influence.

The world's centre of economic gravity has changed over past centuries. It began gradually, spending the first 1,000 years in Iraq and gradually reaching its westernmost point just off the Newfoundland coast in the 1950s. Since the mid-1980s, the pace of that shift, from the West towards Asia, has been increasing dramatically, at a speed of

India's Exports

2013–14 $466bn

2019–20 (Projected) $900bn

Figure 18: India's exports to 2020.
(Source: *Economic Times*)

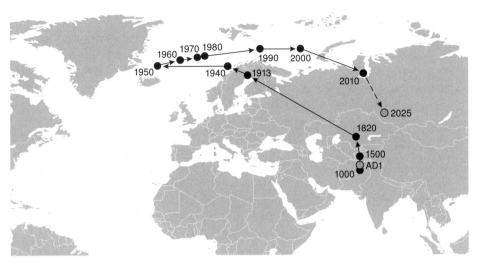

Figure 19: Evolution of the world's economic centre of gravity.
(Source: McKinsey Global Institute)

140 kilometres a year – faster than ever before in human history. A McKinsey model predicts that by 2025, with the growing impact of India and Africa, it will be near to the Russian border with China and Mongolia (Figure 19).[98] Change is on the cards.

Rise of the Cult of China

As China's economic influence on the world continues, there is a rise in the 'cult of China' in popular imaginations elsewhere. Myths of both hope and fear will proliferate as China's cultural influence increases.

It is a platitude to say that China is going to be important over the next decade; the more interesting question is: how? To some, China is a land of promise; to others it is an unwieldy behemoth, blighted by heavy-handed governance, outdated ideology and selfish insularity. The point perhaps is this: it does not so much matter where the truth of these views lies (reality will always lie somewhere in the middle anyway), but the fact that China is being viewed through such extreme lenses. It seems China will either save the world – or doom us all.

The trend in this kind of thinking seems set to continue as more industries, more governments and more people become aware of the influence of China (or Chinese things) on their day-to-day lives.

The importance of Chinese consumption is already apparent. Apple's stock rises and falls based on its Chinese sales figures, Uber says that China accounts for 30 per cent of all Uber journeys, Chinese drinkers now consume more fine whisky than the Scots, and Chinese film-goers can now determine the success or failure of Hollywood films, with *Fast and Furious 7* making more than $180m in three days in China alone.

For smaller companies, the Chinese market can quickly become a major source of sales as Chinese consumers turn their attention to products like Dutch Edam cheese, Spanish chorizo or Brompton's folding bicycles. These figures are driven by the sheer scale of the Chinese population; in 2015, the number of 'middle class', or 'relatively affluent', consumers in China overtook the equivalent number in the USA.[99] That gap is only going to grow in China's favour.

Accordingly, many companies (large and small) located outside China now see the Chinese market as the pre-eminent (and sometimes 'only conceivable') opportunity for growth over the next decade.[100] China is presented as an Eldorado, promising riches to those successful in penetrating its borders. The flipside is that the fortunes of many Western companies are now inextricably linked to the slightest movements in Chinese consumption, and fluctuations can lead to a slew of panic-stricken analyses. For every visionary who sees boundless opportunity, there is a naysayer who points to fickle, unfathomable Chinese consumers, opaque debt, property and stock market bubbles, and a Chinese state that intervenes cack-handedly in markets.

But China is not just a consumer of value-added products. Its rapid economic rise has only been possible thanks to an equally rapid scaling-up in consumption of natural resources. Unsurprisingly, China is the largest emitter of carbon, driven in part by its massive production and consumption of coal, and is also the world's largest consumer of precious (and not-so-precious) metals (Figure 20).[101] And – while we are at it – add to that list fresh water, livestock, and phosphorous (a finite resource

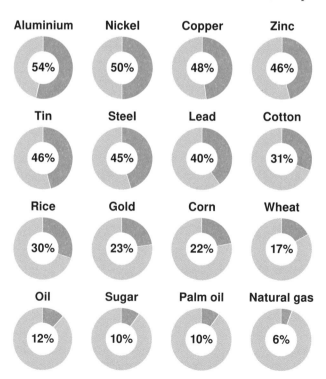

Figure 20: China's share of global resource consumption, 2014. (Source: WEF)

essential to agriculture). On the other hand, China is also the world's largest investor in renewable energy technologies. It has broken new ground (literally) in exploring the limits and possibilities of hydroelectric power, most notably through the Three Gorges Dam project, and is now the world's largest producer of both photovoltaic solar energy and wind energy. While China may indeed be causing natural resource problems, it is also, for some, the most likely source of immediate solutions – especially as its eco-civilisation initiative takes hold.

In 2005 few Western consumers would have consciously been aware of any consumer-facing Chinese brands. That was the year that Lenovo acquired IBM's personal computer business – one year later, Lenovo dropped the IBM brand and became the first familiar Chinese brand on Western high streets. Today, Western consumers will be familiar with (even if they are not yet personally buying into) brands such as Huawei, Tencent, Alibaba, Xiaomi, Haier, Air China, China Eastern Airlines and China UnionPay. Tencent (especially through its instant-messaging service WeChat) and Alibaba are leading the way in the technology sector, but there are many others set to follow, from personal care, through to clothing and home appliances, retail and food.

Further, China has significant financial reach (Figure 21). Chinese capital and investment now sit behind many large Western companies, from Pirelli tyres, to Barcelona's Espanyol football club and Smithfield Foods in the USA. This is in addition to the increasing role that Chinese finance and expertise plays in global property markets and national infrastructure projects, from railways in Gabon to nuclear power in the UK.

For some, China's shift in role from workhouse churning out goods for overseas companies, to innovative producer competing on its own terms, is a worrying sign. Anti-competitive practices, copyright theft, patent infringement and protectionist state policy all make it difficult to compete for access to the Chinese market. But for

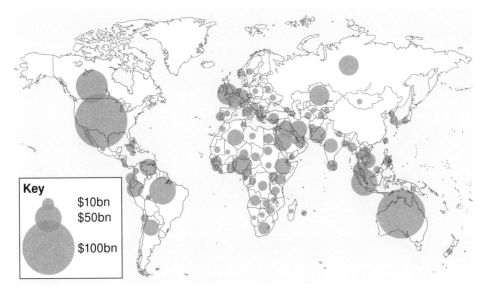

Figure 21: China's worldwide investments, 2014.
(Source: Heritage Foundation/American Enterprise Institute)

others, a new player on the global scene – driving innovation, bringing fresh ideas to the table, investing imaginatively and challenging existing multinational oligopolies – is exactly what the world needs.

The rise of China as a political force (backed by military might) is, for many, something to be feared. They point to an increasingly expansionist posture (especially in the South China seas), threats to cyber security and data privacy, a poor record with respect to upholding human rights and a 'let them eat cake' attitude to resource consumption. Others highlight China's enlightened attitudes to the care of the elderly, its supposedly dedicated work ethic, its relatively insular approach to foreign policy – and see a more benign influence on the world.

If, crudely speaking, the 20th century saw the political and economic encounter between China and the rest of the world, the next few years are likely to give birth to the cultural one. With Chinese economic dominance growing steadily (at least for the foreseeable future), the challenge of understanding the ideas that drive it will rise to the fore. Expect to see fevered commentary on the actions and behaviours of the Chinese state, attempts to decode the meaning of 'socialism with Chinese characteristics' and Confucian policy ideals, and confused diatribes about the 'Chinese mindset'.

For many of us, however, the most immediate encounter with Chinese culture will come in the form of having to learn new business etiquettes (such as 'guanxi capitalism') or coming face-to-face with emboldened Chinese travellers demanding Chinese food and signage, while looking incredulously at our ageing infrastructure and peculiar religious beliefs. In return, our fascination with this infamously inscrutable nation will come to resemble the world's 20th century love-hate obsession with the USA.

Africa Growth

With a land mass bigger than India, China, the USA and Europe combined, few doubt the scale of the African continent and its resources. However, until recently, only some have seen it as the growth market that it is fast becoming.

As a continent, Africa has, on average, grown its economy by at least five per cent per year over the last decade. Already as urbanised as China and with as many cities of more than 1 million people as Europe, and a steadily growing population heading towards 2 billion, the coming years will see the impact of around 500 million new middle-class consumers (Figure 22).[102]

However, clearly there are many 'Africas', with varied economies: from the oil exporters of Nigeria, Angola, Libya and Algeria to the already more diversified economies found in Egypt, South Africa and Morocco, there is a host of nations already with GDP per head of well over $2,000. Elsewhere on the continent there are many countries such as Kenya, Tanzania, Ghana and Cameroon making the transition from agricultural economies.

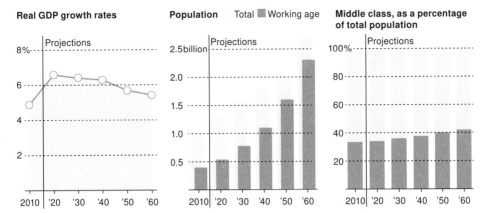

Figure 22: Africa's growing population.
(Source: African Development Bank)

For years, Africa's growth has been shaped by commodity prices – the continent has a third of the planet's mineral resources, 10 per cent of the world's oil reserves and produces nearly 70 per cent of the global diamond trade. While this has clearly been good for growth in the past, the dependency on a few key commodities, and hence their global price, has led to high levels of market uncertainty – especially around many of Africa's currencies: at least 10 African currencies, for example, lost more than 10 per cent of their value in 2014. Although prices are volatile, oil and gas will continue to be an important factor in the future: Africa will remain an important producer, probably still accounting for 10 per cent of global oil and 9 per cent of natural gas production in 2035.[103]

In a bid to diversify away from resources, several nations have been pushing hard to grow other sectors of the economy. To date, manufacturing, services and tourism in particular have all shown progress (although, whether as a result of Ebola, localised terrorism or national political change, growth from tourism is volatile). For example, while Nigeria is still very much an oil-exporting economy, its service sector now accounts for 60 per cent of its GDP and 'Nollywood', its $3bn film industry, is now the second largest in the world, bigger than Hollywood and just behind Bollywood in Mumbai. Likewise, in Angola, Africa's second largest oil exporter, growth in the fishing, agriculture and manufacturing sectors now means that a third of government revenue comes from non-oil sources. Some African states, including Kenya, Nigeria, South Africa and the Democratic Republic of Congo, are now seen as world leaders in adapting mobile technology and social networks to deliver life-changing new platforms, particularly in financial services and health care.

Although the growth is occurring across several key economies, including Nigeria, Ethiopia, Kenya, Angola, Ghana, Zambia and Mozambique, there is little doubt that South Africa continues to be a major driver in the region. It is the country that many see as economically representative of the continent as a whole – or at least Sub-Saharan Africa. However, South Africa is not a proxy for the way that Africa as a whole will play out. South Africa's GDP growth has fluctuated and averaged around two per cent over the past decade and is likely to continue on a similar trajectory for the ten years.

Other experts highlight issues such as life expectancy, infant mortality and energy consumption, instead of focusing on GDP growth. With global life expectancy averaging 70 for the last decade, in Africa as a whole there has been major improvement with a more than 10 per cent rise from 49 to 55, including significant change in countries such as Zimbabwe where, despite economic turmoil, average life expectancy has risen from 37 to 46 (Figure 23). By 2030, across the continent it will have climbed to 64 years. Meanwhile, infant mortality remains high at 81 deaths per 1,000 population (compared to a global average of 42), but this has dropped from 177 in 1990. At the same time, energy use per head has grown significantly, from 500 kWh (kilowatt-hour) in 1990 to around 600 KWh per head in 2014. This, a key metric, is not far behind Asia but still at only 20 per cent of Europe's use.

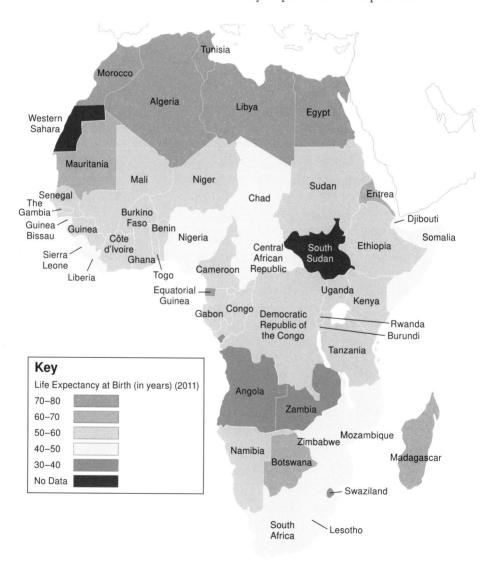

Figure 23: Life expectancy at birth in African countries, 2011.
(Source: CIA Factbook)

Despite long-standing commercial ties with Europe, Africa now conducts half its trade South–South with other developing economic regions. China has doubled its share of trade with Africa to 17 per cent over the last decade, and wider connections across Asia, South America and via the Middle East are all being developed. India has a 6 per cent share of Africa's trade and Brazil 3 per cent;[104] both are expected to increase significantly and, with rising concern over China's business practices, may take over a chunk of China's land-grab. In addition, many note the significance of increased intra-African trade. Bilateral agreements between nations, with differing political standpoints but common growth agendas, are linking with emergent cross-continent agreements, the growth of trading zones and increased investment in infrastructure. True, some African nations remain flawed democracies or authoritarian regimes, but over the next few years, a number of breakaway countries will show economic and political progress, and barriers to trade will be lifted as infrastructure is improved.

By 2030, Africa will be increasingly urban with half the population projected to live cities. The continent's top 18 megacities will have combined consumer spending of around $1.3 trn. This in turn will boost productivity, demand and hence investment. Half of the region's population is under 25 and each year between 2015 and 2035 there will be 500,000 more 15-year-olds in Africa.[105] The challenge will be to transform this youth bulge into an opportunity. Africa will most likely become one of the world's primary growth markets. The question is one of timescales. Despite years of steady economic growth, Africa's middle class is still relatively tiny. The central question is, therefore, will there be significant change over the next decade or, like India, will there be a period of longer transition?

Declining Government Influence

> *National governments' ability to lead change comes under greater pressure from both above and below by 2025. Multinational organisations increasingly set the rules while citizens trust and support local and network-based actions.*

Moving back to the West, many believe that government and governance itself is in a state of flux. The 20th century move towards greater democracy seems to have halted; the majority of governments are feeling less influential on a global scale and are seeking to collaborate more, whether as part of trade alliances, military pacts or multipolar groups. After the global financial crisis, the power and influence of the IMF, G20, the World Bank and the Asian Infrastructure Investment Bank (AIIB) has come to the fore, and multinational trade agreements such as the TPP and the Transatlantic Trade and Investment Partnership (TTIP) are now seeking to control pivotal standards and protocols that will influence future economic growth. Other intergovernmental organisations such as the WHO, Food and Agriculture Organization (FAO), IPCC, OECD and International Energy Agency (IEA) are all variously seeking to influence future global directions. Within regions, the EU,

Association of Southeast Asian Nations (ASEAN), Gulf Cooperation Council (GCC), African Union and Organization of American States (OAS) are, at different levels, also aiming to set the future agenda.

For some, it feels like sovereignty itself is being given away, and several national governments find that global, non-elected bodies that sit above sovereign states are deciding regional imperatives. This suits some, particularly in the West, where trust in national politicians and the political process is in decline. Perhaps it is no coincidence that the shift to democracy seems to have halted. From having only 11 democracies in the middle of the Second World War, by 2000, US think-tank Freedom House classified 120 countries – 63 per cent of the world's total – as being democracies. Yet today the EIU sees that we only have 20 full democracies – the USA, Canada, Australia, New Zealand, Japan, over half of Europe plus Uruguay and Costa Rica (Figure 24).[106] These are followed by 56 flawed democracies including in their number the likes of Taiwan, Indonesia, Greece, Israel and Mexico. Underneath them in the democracy index are 39 hybrid and 52 authoritarian regimes.

	Rank	Overall score	Electoral process and pluralism	Functioning of government	Political participation	Political culture	Civil liberties
Full democracies							
Norway	1	9.93	10.00	9.64	10.00	10.00	10.00
Iceland	2	9.58	10.00	9.29	8.89	10.00	9.71
Sweden	3	9.45	9.58	9.64	8.33	10.00	9.71
New Zealand	4	9.26	10.00	9.29	8.89	8.13	10.00
Denmark	5	9.11	9.17	9.29	8.33	9.38	9.41
Switzerland	6	9.09	9.58	9.29	7.78	9.38	9.41
Canada	7	9.08	9.58	9.29	7.78	8.75	10.00
Finland	8	9.03	10.00	8.93	7.78	8.75	9.71
Australia	9	9.01	9.58	8.93	7.78	8.75	10.00
Netherlands	10	8.92	9.58	8.57	8.89	8.13	9.41
Luxembourg	11	8.88	10.00	9.29	6.67	8.75	9.71
Ireland	12	8.85	9.58	7.50	7.78	9.38	10.00
Germany	13	8.64	9.58	8.57	7.78	8.13	9.12
Austria	14	8.54	9.58	7.86	8.33	7.50	9.41
Malta	15	8.39	9.17	8.21	6.11	8.75	9.71
United Kingdom	16	8.31	9.58	7.14	6.67	8.75	9.41
Spain	17	8.30	9.58	7.14	7.22	8.13	9.41
Mauritius	18	8.28	9.17	8.21	5.56	8.75	9.71
Uruguay	19	8.17	10.00	8.93	4.44	7.50	10.00
United States of America	20	8.05	9.17	7.50	7.22	8.13	8.24

Figure 24: The 20 full democracies in the world, 2015.
(Source: EIU Democracy Index)

Challenges for those who think democracy is the best option for government are threefold. First, some of the countries that either jumped ahead as part of decolonisation, or had democracy forced upon them, are evidently struggling: South Africa, Pakistan and Ukraine just as much as Iraq and Libya. Secondly, some of the long-term shining lights for democracy seem to be in paralysis: Washington and Brussels are both viewed elsewhere as perpetually struggling with consensus and gridlock. In addition, other non-democratic countries, whether benevolent dictatorships such as the UAE or the Chinese Communist Party are doing quite well. Public support is shifting: twice as many Chinese as Americans are very satisfied with their country's direction, while voter turnout has fallen by a third across the EU in the past 30 years, with participation in parliamentary elections in France, Britain and Germany now nearly as low as Russia and the USA.

Meanwhile trust and confidence for state- or city-level types of governance is on the increase. Citizens are becoming more confident that people like them can do something significant about the issues that are most present. With the C40 helping mayors around the world share best practice, the power and influence of mayoral offices has increased, almost universally in tandem with public support. Whether in New York, London, Paris, Quito or Istanbul, support for greater city level powers is growing.[107] Similar support can also be found for state level governors. At an even more local level, the rise of the real sharing economy and more community level collaborations is helping to cement responsibility and leadership closer to home.

One of the consequences of governments, and particularly cities, making more of their data open has been great empowerment of communities and networks. London leads the world in making data public – so seeding multiple platforms for new innovations and efficiency improvements. At a country level, an interesting combination of Taiwan, the UK, Denmark, Colombia and Finland are the top five in the global open data index.[108] It is envisaged that open public and private data will together drive transparency from the bottom up; citizens will be able to access and use their public data and share what they wish of their private data to collectively co-create better ways of using social resources.

At the same time as engagement increases, so crowdsourcing of policies and decision-making may well further reduce the need for politicians while increasing the roles of platform designers and facilitators of discussion. If this direction is followed, the more connected citizens will arguably become the most empowered. Looking ahead, reduced influence of national government is probable, along with greater decentralisation. Singapore for one sees that decentralised service provision at the hyper-local level can help to reduce inequality.

At the same time, governments and regulators have to play catch-up with business. Innovation is currently in the hands of organisations, many based in Silicon Valley, with greater financial muscle and power than most nations. As technological change meets social need, people often look to leading tech firms for signals of what may be on, or just over, the horizon. Today many eyes are on Alphabet (Google) and Apple. While Apple is notoriously secretive about the projects it has under development, many are now aware of its Car project (Titan), as well as activities in augmented and virtual reality. For Alphabet, there is more transparency of what is under development (Figure 25). As well as its own driverless car and VR projects, it is busy in many other fields. Project Wing is its drone programme, competing with Amazon to change 'last mile' delivery, while Verily is its active contact lens project – smart lenses that that are solar powered and collect biological data about the wearer such as body temperature and blood-alcohol content. Project Loon reflects Alphabet's desire to bring connectivity to two-thirds of the world's population using Internet-beaming hot air balloons. According to the *Wall Street Journal*, Google X is designing tiny magnetic nanoparticles that can look for signs of cancer and other diseases in the human body, while Boston Dynamics is creating robots inspired by animals to aid in military use: the Cheetah Robot is the fastest robot in the world and can already get to a speed of 29 miles per hour. There is also a project run by Calico looking into extending the average lifespan by investigating genes that correlate to longer lives in certain people. While these organisations may not be the sole sources of new technological change, the level of focus and resource available within the big Silicon Valley tech firms is certainly giving many a view of what may soon be part of our world – and the organisations that will control the systems. Where is the nation state in all this – controlling the technology, channelling the resources? Increasingly, businesses such as Google and Apple are demonstrating – through their own practices – the irrelevance of governments.

Lastly, in this world of more top-down and bottom-up strain on influence at the national level, some also see governments facing greater challenges from NGOs (non-governmental organisations) and religious groups. As the third sector has grown, a host of NGOs have gained in reach and influence. Oxfam, Amnesty, World Vision and Greenpeace have now been joined by the likes of Doctors Without Borders (MSF),

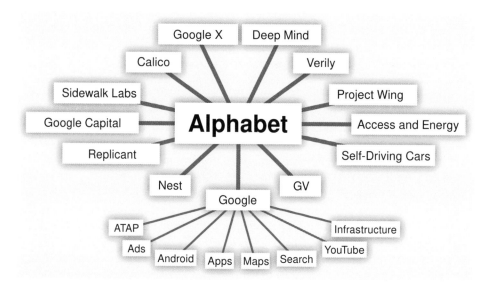

Figure 25: Alphabet activities, 2016.
(Source: Arstechnica)

Save the Children, Ashoka, Grameen Bank and the Gates Foundation.[109] These have seats at the table not only to deal with national issues but often also at an international level, and are just as much part of the Davos entourage as many governments. Together all these varied organisations are evidently filling a growing gap and, in many cases, are driving change more than governments. In a few areas, however, there is pushback.

Influence and trust has shifted significantly over the centuries. As we move forward the question will be whether there are new cross-society bodies that take the next step, or whether we take advantage of our increasing connectivity to follow and give more influence to groups from the past and the present that resonate most – be that local communities, regional leaders, religious groups, NGOs or networks. Whichever direction we take, it looks as if in many countries a steady decline in national government influence is on the table.

Everything Connected

More than one trillion sensors are connected to multiple networks: everything that can benefit from a connection has one. We deliver 10,000 times more data 100 times more effectively but are concerned about the security of the information that flows.

By 2020, there will be more than 50 billion SIM cards in use, we will have digitised all of our archives, and new information will be being created at such a rate that some see us doubling the volume of our total data set every month.[110] Much of this will come from machines talking to each other as well as to us. By the end of the decade, pretty much everything that can have a connection will have one. By 2025, IBM, Nokia and co, all predict that the IoT will bring more than one trillion sensors into the world,[111] all connected to each other and multiple networks, delivering 10,000 times more data 100 times more effectively.[112] Everything that could benefit from an Internet connection will, by 2025, probably have one, be that fridges, toasters, driverless trucks or T-shirts. This digitisation of the world has the potential to provide us with previously unknown levels of information and insight; equally, it could open the doors to unpredicted risk.

Today, more than 3.3 billion of us are connected to the Internet globally. We are currently adding another billion every three years and within the decade pretty much all of us will have the capacity to be online, wherever we may be. Smartphones and other devices will be a primary driver of change; with 2.6 billion already in use, Ericsson states that there will be 6 billion by 2020 (Figure 26). It and firms such as Nokia and Huawei are planning for a doubling of data traffic per user every 18 months, to a point where each of us can access 1GB of information every day. Facebook and Google are looking at vast fleets of balloons and drones to bridge the digital divide, providing connectivity to those currently without coverage. With Africa and Asia accounting for more than 80 per cent of new connections, total mobile subscriptions by 2020 are now expected to number over 9 billion.[113]

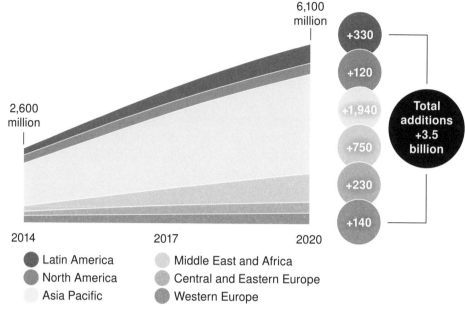

Figure 26: Smartphone subscriptions per region by 2020.
(Source: Ericsson)

As of 2015, some countries are already very connected. In terms of the number of devices per head, Germany, Sweden, the Netherlands, Switzerland and the USA had already passed the 20 threshold, Denmark was over 30 and South Korea was touching 40, while fast accelerating up the league tables was China with six. Given the investment taking place, a global average of a little more than ten devices per capita by 2020 certainly seems credible.[114] However, many of these devices will not be owned or used by us: the vast majority, maybe 30 to 40 billion of them, will be embedded in machines. Most of the digital information will be stored in the Cloud, with users expecting instant access anywhere, any time, and thus testing the physical limits of networks. Networks will have to become programmable to create capacity on demand, heralding the advent of self-optimising and cognitive networks, able to handle complex end-to-end tasks autonomously and in real time. The concept of interconnected networks of physical objects, machines, buildings, infrastructure and devices is already a focus for companies such as Cisco and IBM as part of the vision for a Smarter Planet.[115]

Arguably even more data will be generated from passive tags and sensors. Miniature sensors are now entering the marketplace that can be placed anywhere – on food, in clothing, within packaging, inside components and in animals to highlight a few. These will be activated by a multitude of different energy waves from a reading device, and provide location, temperature, orientation, movement or biological information to be read remotely, hundreds at a time.

While the benefits are lauded in terms of the opportunities to improve efficiency, reduce waste and find out new things that were previously unknown, there are concerns about the risks involved. Some argue that we are jumping into connecting everything without thinking through the consequences, especially as the data protection on some devices is very low. A connected kettle could become the back door to your Wi-Fi network that bypasses all passwords and so an open door to your personal data.

When everything is connected, not just kettles and laptops but power stations, traffic systems and medical devices, then the concern shifts from privacy to security. Cyber attacks are already happening on a regular basis, targeting not just databases but also machines and systems. As we move forward with everything being linked online, the potential for harmful hacks rises significantly. This is especially true of the billions of passive tags and sensors that do not have the power to support high levels of encryption.

What will happen when everything is tagged and connected, through the Cloud, to systems analysing everything? One of the key concepts within the film *Minority Report* is the idea of being able to predict crime, so-called 'precrime'. While this Philip K. Dick story features the three 'precogs' – the psychic women in the flotation tank – who enable prediction, in today's world the police are using big data analytics.[116] While there is much hype over how we can mine all the data being made available to us, the reality on the streets of Los Angeles is that an element of prediction is already possible. Using multiple data streams from public and proprietary sources, the Los Angeles Police Department is able to send a policeman to the scene of a crime *before* it has happened. 'The algorithm at play is performing what's commonly referred to as predictive policing. Using years – and sometimes decades – worth of crime reports, the algorithm analyses the data to identify areas with high probabilities for certain types of crime.'[117] It takes information on where crimes have happened in the past, and where criminals are, and overlays with that information such as weather patterns, sports events and other large group gatherings. Running real-time analysis, it identifies where crime is likely to happen. '*Minority Report* is about predicting who will commit a crime before they commit it. This is about predicting where and when crime is most likely to occur, not who will commit it.'[118] The results? Around 20 per cent of probable crimes are prevented by police presence in the vicinity. Although not yet near the 100 per cent target of the movie, in such a large city this level of success is a strong indicator of the future capabilities of big data analysis that we will soon take for granted. Data, and the so-called digital transformation, is having significant impact in many areas. Future power will increasingly be aligned with those who have ownership, or preferential access, to the most relevant data.

Privacy Regulation

The push towards global standards, protocols and greater transparency is a focus for many nations driving proactive regulation, but others choose to opt-out of international agreements and go their own way.

Some suggest that the EU's consensual style of politics is poorly placed to deal with the privacy problem – it is too protectionist, focuses too much on controlling the data and not on managing the users. Others point out that this is because regulators are obliged to deal with legacy legal systems and governance structures bound by geographic borders when the world has moved on. Certainly the current European model is designed to help existing market leaders adapt to change and collaborate with challengers. Brussels is taking a tough stance on privacy, increasing fines, placing requirements on organisations to obtain consent and creating a 'data protection by design' obligation. The USA, on the other hand, is more open to creative disruption. China and India veer to the European approach. In a multicultural, multilingual environment there is a lot to be said for this, as only the well-established companies can afford the time, money and resources to work with regulators to identify the challenges and opportunities ahead.

Despite some important differences, the privacy frameworks in the USA and those countries following the EU model are both based on the Fair Information Practice Principles. The European approach, based on a view that privacy is a fundamental human right, generally involves top-down regulation and the imposition of across-the-board rules restricting the use of data or requiring explicit consent for that use.[119] The USA, in contrast, employs a sectoral approach that focuses on regulating specific risks of privacy harm in particular contexts, such as health care and credit. This places fewer broad rules on the use of data, allowing industry to be more innovative in its products and services, while also sometimes leaving unregulated potential uses of information that fall between sectors.[120]

It is time that regulation caught up with technology. Existing data protection emerged in the 1970s and 1980s in response to the developments of the time. The assumption was that data processing would always be a complex and resource-intensive activity, and therefore would be the preserve of large, well-resourced organisations. Mistake: more than 500 million photos are now uploaded and shared every day, along with more than 200 hours of video every minute. The assumption therefore no longer holds true. Beyond this, the volume of information that people create themselves, including voice calls, pales in comparison with the amount of digital information generated about them every day.[121] The technical capabilities of big data, in its myriad forms, have already reached a level of sophistication and pervasiveness that demands careful thinking on how best to balance the opportunities it affords with the social and ethical questions these technologies raise.

In addition to what happens within national boundaries, many governments are concerned about how their citizens' information makes its way in and out of other countries' jurisdictions. Catalysed by the Snowden revelations, some, including South Korea, Russia, Indonesia, Vietnam and Brazil, are now pushing forward new data localisation laws. These, in theory, ensure the privacy and security of citizens and enable domestic growth within the technology sector. But, given the decentralised structure of the Internet, these requirements alone will not prevent information from flowing across borders. Indeed, some authoritarian regimes seem to be using the policies to achieve other goals, such as enhanced domestic surveillance, or to reduce competition for domestic Internet companies through localisation regulation. While this may be successful in boosting the economic future of local data centres, it will have costly implications for other domestic businesses that rely on foreign Internet companies and cheap technology such as Cloud computing. In the future, a global agreement on standards seems a more pragmatic solution.

There is a basis to work from. The United Nations Guiding Principles on Business and Human Rights states that every country has a duty to protect individuals from abuse by business and other third parties. In addition, the UN General Assembly adopted Resolution 68/167 which expresses deep concern at the negative impact that surveillance and interception of communications may have on human rights, and affirmed that the rights held by people offline must also be protected online. It called upon all states to respect and protect the right to privacy in digital communication. However, although it is not hard to agree with these principles, their application is far more difficult.

With the 2016 example of the FBI requesting Apple to change its core code being just one of several data access cases, the regulation of data to allow it to be commercialised while maintaining privacy will become an increasingly hot topic. A key issue will be how we modernise the legal framework to make privacy regulation global and how we raise customer awareness. The legal definition of what constitutes public consent will be key, as this will define the practical reality. Currently there is a distrust of corporations, amid a general belief that they already use private customer data for profit rather than to improve customer service. Trust in Internet infrastructure will decline; at the same time, there will be growing concern about the existence of bulk, or historical, data that could be mined without permission.

Standards Driving Trade

International regulation is progressively aimed at freeing up trade and making it simpler and less bureaucratic – but there are a number of agreements, standards and protocols that some are seeing as increasingly constraining.

Also increasingly digital, the balance of power in global trade, too, is experiencing significant transformation. Removing regional trade barriers could increase GDP for India by 15 per cent and for Bangladesh and Sri Lanka by 17 per cent. The World Bank estimated that 'automating customs processes can save as much as $115 per container'.[122]

As the world seeks to optimise global trade flows, there are high and low points emerging that may well influence future regulatory direction and support. Much of the development in global trade has been led by the USA, which, in the eyes of some, means that, while enabling global trade to develop significantly, it has also gained more than others. For instance, for the past decade or so the vast majority of international transactions have had to go through US clearing banks (even those not in US$), which can lead to transfers being blocked due to flagging triggers set up as part of the US anti-terrorism regulations. Some see this as deliberate and unnecessary interference. As the Indian Ocean becomes as important for trade as the Pacific, questions are being raised as to how the USA will maintain its leadership and control – and the role that standards will play in this.

The TPP[123] links together 12 Pacific countries, including Japan but excluding China, that collectively account for 44 per cent of US goods exports and 85 per cent of US agricultural exports. Its stated ambition is to build a fully integrated economic area and establish the rules for major future growth of services and hence capital flows across the region. Critics are suspicious that this favours US technology companies and banking institutions, and will further cement the role of the dollar in international trade. Supporters maintain that it will raise governance standards for many of China's trade partners and so put pressure on China to adhere more closely to international standards.

The potentially more controversial TTIP links the USA and the EU. Supporters speak of an 'economic NATO' that cements the world's democratic powers at an unstable time. However, several foresee a number of risks. As the USA does not regulate all new types of genetic engineering of plants, animals and microbes, the argument goes that the TTIP will open the back door for such foods to enter the EU, bypassing current strong regulation and standards. The ability, for example, of individual countries to inspect food for pests and diseases they say will be reduced, and the freedom to introduce higher local standards, which often raises the quality bar for everyone, will be reduced.

Some in Asia are keen to create an alternative, non-US driven agenda, believing that their needs are better met through the Regional Comprehensive Economic Partnership (RCEP), a separate free trade agreement (FTA) which brings 16 countries together, not including the USA.

One important relationship that may shape future geopolitics is that between Russia and China. The partnership is already complex, sturdy and deeply rooted and, since the demise of the Soviet Union, the two countries have continued to work together with 'mutual respect for sovereignty and territorial integrity, mutual nonaggression, non-interference in each other's internal affairs, equality and mutual benefit, and peaceful coexistence'.[124] In 2011, China became Russia's largest trading partner. In the early 1990s, annual bilateral trade between China and Russia amounted to around $5 billion; by 2014, it came close to $100 billion. Moscow initially worried that China was competing for influence in its neighbourhood, and so hesitated to support Beijing's Silk Road Economic Belt initiative, but ultimately embraced it in 2014. The two countries are now cooperating on new multinational financial institutions, such as the Asian Infrastructure Investment Bank, the New Development Bank BRICS (Brazil, Russia, India, China and South Africa), and the BRICS foreign exchange reserve pool.

Free trade areas such as the EU, North American Free Trade Agreement (NATFA) and potentially both the TTP and TTIP[125] all restrict the use of tariffs to tax international trade, so alternative ways for countries to protect their own interests have gained ground such as quotas, licences, anti-dumping regulations, standards, import credits, export subsidies, etc. Such customs procedures, technical standards and labelling/packing requirements are not directly aimed at restricting trade but add to administrative bureaucracy, so lead to the same result.

Securing the safety of the global supply chain is a priority shared by governments regulating the cross-border flow of goods. It requires a dual focus: to promote and facilitate legitimate commerce, while simultaneously mitigating supply chain risks. The processes that enable government agencies to balance these dual priorities rely on data, cross-border standards, widely embraced policies and cutting-edge technologies that are dramatically changing the global economy.

The adoption of automation, along with the growth in the use of sensors and other M2M (machine-to-machine) mobile technologies, is helping to make trade more frictionless. There are increasingly better information flows not just between different governments but also between trading partners across manufacturing, shipping and trucking, which streamlines processes. However, this greater connectivity requires higher security and therefore standards and protocols also play a major role here. Those setting the standards not only set the rules but, by implication, also define the landscape. Those who want to gain from increasing automation and system efficiency have to join in, so this becomes another lever to bring them inside the tent. With the promise of greater efficiency from predictive analytics, which make the global trade system safer and more secure, the case for joining in is compelling.

The key benefits of increased automation will include reduction of paperwork and lower transaction costs. As different parties all agree the standards for exchanging data, enabling the sharing of data will more effectively release cargo across borders. Matching internal and independent third-party data sets via trusted trader platforms will, it is hoped, give border agencies real-time access to the most up-to-date information and so ease international trade. The days of stamping paper documents is fast being replaced by electronic verification via RFID (radio frequency identification) and other M2M and IoT platforms.

But to make this work there need to be clearer, recognised digital standards that enable all parties to collaborate. Here again the USA is very much in the driving seat. Sector or regionally focused consortiums such as the Industrial Internet Consortium (IIC) formed by AT&T, Cisco, General Electric, IBM and Intel are a key step forward but the aim is to achieve global standards across all industries – and, as unsurprisingly proposed by risk-management company Dun & Bradstreet, all probably using a global unique entity identifier.

While some argue that it is the global and regional mega agreements that are setting the future trading landscape, it is clear that, underneath these, varied standards are actually driving trade. Whether safety standards for food, cars or services, or communication and data standards for increased automation, they are the gateways for many imports and exports. They are being used positively to enable better, faster and safer trade, but they are also used negatively, especially as non-tariff barriers to restrict trade. Going forward, standards will increasingly be used as the tactical response to defend domestic markets, manifest change in target export markets and maintain a degree of control over importers. Without them there might be a completely level playing field and few nations really seem to want that.

Open Supply Webs

> *The shift from centralised production to decentralised manufacturing drives many to take a 'smaller and distributed' approach: global supply chains are replaced by more regional, consumer-oriented supply webs and networks.*

Moving things is clearly big business. Estimates vary, but around 80 per cent of everything we use or consume has, at some point or another, been on a ship, either as a finished product or a component or ingredient. Whether importing cocoa from Côte d'Ivoire, sending LCD (liquid crystal display) items from Seoul, or exporting T-shirts from Bangladesh, the need for companies to plan, manage and execute timely provision of products worldwide has been a major source of competitive advantage for many years – and one that is both strategic and long-term as well as short-term, operational and tactical. For some, logistics prowess has altered the basis of competition: 'Companies don't compete – supply chains do.'

Over the past few decades, the investment made in setting up and optimising global supply chains has been considerable. With multinationals manufacturing products in multiple factories across the globe, to supply to a growing yet dispersed consumer base, supply chain management has become a core corporate USP (unique selling point). Whether in relatively simple food produce or complex automotive products, companies have set up complex supply chains across multiple tiers. Tier 1 suppliers – such as Bosch – provide myriad finished components, from air-conditioning units to fuel injectors to car brands globally, but they, in turn, acquire components from Tier 2 and 3 suppliers around the world. As companies have sought to ensure continuous availability of products to customers globally, the ownership and control of supply chains has become pivotal to success.

However, changes are happening fast – from digital marketplaces and 3D printing to mass personalised distributed local supply – and they are challenging the status quo. Digital marketplaces are not only improving efficiency and access for more organisations, they are also significantly increasing transparency in terms of consignment location tracking and cost of shipment, making what was previously hidden within the organisation visible to all.[126] Although still searching for mass-market applications, 3D printing is redefining the means of product delivery. It has already had a significant impact in the aerospace sector and is now moving across to other industries. Rather than shipping products halfway round the world, we may soon be able to print off components in our home – obviating the need for a supply chain, except for the metal and plastic material and the 3D printer itself.

More companies are offering local finishing, whether for the final assembly of consumer electronics to meet customer specifications or locating option fitting for a BMW at a local dealership. Hence elements of end production are becoming more distributed and therefore undertaken in smaller batches. Amazon has already filed patents for installing printers in delivery trucks, thus taking the concept of real time to a new level.

This agility now extends to the need to increasingly hedge options – not only against different production costs and currency exchange, but also against supplier risk. As the age of the vertically integrated corporation has started to recede, so new, more fluid alternatives have begun to emerge. Companies are moving from running supply chains to establishing supply webs where the democratised flow of information, mostly in the Cloud, enable a complex, three-dimensional network of partners, customers and suppliers to operate across a web rather than a chain.

When shipping lanes clog, infrastructure fails, currency exchanges fluctuate or a factory shuts down, impacting on component supply, organisations can gain from a more responsive, flexible network of different options to maintain product delivery to their customers. At the same time, a more transparent supply web allows low-level suppliers to monitor their positions and so compete on a more level playing field than before. According to Deloitte, a consulting firm, supply chains have evolved into value webs that span and connect whole ecosystems of suppliers and collaborators.[127] These webs can be more effective in many ways – by reducing costs, improving service levels, mitigating risk, and driving learning and innovation. Moreover, as new technologies generate more data and so provide greater transparency, the move to the web approach may well accelerate.

In an open, shared web, operational efficiency is improved by opening space and assets to other companies' short-term needs, geographic reach is extended and customers gain from fast and reliable provision from globally dispersed facilities.[128] Companies that join in to exploit a more open supply web have access to more distributed manufacturing, assembling and distribution facilities that can be used for both short- and long-term contracts – but without the requirement to be involved in large investments, long-term leasing or strategic partnerships that may need to evolve as markets change. Open supply webs could allow companies to achieve better global distribution than ever before. Enabled by the digital marketplace, driven by increasing demand for customer proximity and mass customisation, and able to provide multiple hedges, open supply webs are seen as the way forward for many manufacturers both large and small.

As we move forward, the core question will be: how will organisations seek to balance the rewards of greater efficiency from adopting the shared, and open, supply webs approach to distribution, against the apparent commercial risk of partnerships with competitors? The reality, so some say, is that the transparency and effectiveness of a more flexible approach will become the main driver in making the open supply web the norm for the future.

Energy Storage

Storage, and particularly electricity storage, is the missing piece in the renewables jigsaw. If solved, it will enable truly distributed solar energy as well as accelerate the electrification of the transport industry.

Lastly we come to the power of energy – an issue that over the last century has arguably been pivotal to geopolitical shifts. From OPEC price hikes to country invasions and industry takeovers, securing energy has been *the* essential concern for many governments. However, after years of rising prices and increasing demand, there is change in the air for energy supply, as the shift to renewables accelerates. Although there are short-term factors in matching current supply and demand in varied regions, most agree that in the long term we will move to a renewables-based energy system.

There is much optimism that substantial improvements in energy storage will be achieved over the next decade, but there are also several misconceptions. One of the most prominent of these is that, by itself, energy storage will transform the energy system overnight; in fact, it will take many years or even decades to shift from fossil fuels to renewables. The existing energy system is not designed for renewable energy – rather it is focused around fossil fuels, which simply hold their energy until ignited.

Controlling how and when energy is provided is implicitly linked to our ability to store it, especially so in locations where energy demand is not in sync with supply – whether that be from solar, wind or wave renewables, or a wider energy mix. People have been looking forward to the advent of smart energy grids for some time and having two-way transmission of electricity between supplier and consumer is a core element of this.

Meanwhile, though, the role that batteries can play in displacing other energy solutions, even with incremental change, can be significant. Battery costs are falling steadily – they have halved in the last five years. In the past, batteries were made from materials such as lead-acid and nickel-cadmium. Highly toxic, some of these ingredients are also bulky and heavy. The rechargeable lithium-ion battery helped slim them down and these batteries now power not just smartphones and laptops but also power tools, electric cars and drones. Lithium-ion batteries have been steadily getting better and, with improved chemistry and production techniques, the energy stored in them has increased by 50 per cent.

For some applications, such as electric cars, a better battery would be transformative. Until recently the battery for an electric car could cost $400–$500 per kilowatt-hour, perhaps 30 per cent or so of the overall cost of the vehicle. General Motors (itself involved in about a dozen battery storage projects) expects the battery in its latest Chevy Bolt electric car to cost around $145 per kilowatt-hour. Once costs come down to around $100 per kilowatt-hour, electric vehicles will become mainstream because they will be able to compete with petrol cars of all sizes without subsidy.

Other organisations are looking at a more radical changes in the technology. Sakti3 focuses on producing a lithium-ion battery with a solid electrolyte that offers about double the energy density; Dyson, the British inventor of the bag-less vacuum cleaner, recently bought the company.[129] As Dyson expands into domestic robotics, expect to see solid-state batteries in the mix. And, with further engineering, maybe in electric cars and grid storage too: in large volumes, such solid-state batteries should cost around the target $100 per kilowatt-hour.

Many research groups around the world are hoping for battery breakthroughs. 24M, a Massachusetts start-up, is using nanotechnology to develop a cost-effective 'semi-solid' lithium-ion battery, while in Cambridge in the UK, there is much expectation surrounding a new lithium-air cell that has overtaken current lithium-ion batteries in the amount of energy stored per kilogram. A spin-off of Carnegie Mellon University, Aquion Energy's nontoxic, saltwater-based batteries are designed to deliver high-performance storage while avoiding the expensive maintenance of competing chemistries such as lead-acid. South Korea's LG Chem is building on its experience supplying lithium-ion batteries for electric cars to providing residential, commercial and industrial stationary batteries. Alongside LG Chem, numerous other big lithium-ion battery producers, such as BYD, Johnson Controls, Panasonic, Samsung and Sony, are partnering with solar installers, inverter manufacturers and innovative product integrators.[130]

Perhaps most significant, however, is SolarCity, the largest residential solar PV (photovoltaic) installer in the USA, rolling out storage systems that rely on lithium-ion batteries supplied by electric carmaker Tesla – whose CEO and founder, Elon Musk, is also SolarCity's chairman. The duo's entry into stationary energy storage is significant.[131] SolarCity hopes to offer its solution to enable residential customers to take advantage of time-of-use rates, ancillary services and PV system interaction. It is spearheading a 200-kilowatt project to store energy from rooftop solar arrays at Tesla's factory in Fremont, with the aim of helping the company offset millions of dollars in peak-rate charges.

Tesla (with its Japanese battery supplier, Panasonic) is building a $5 billion lithium-ion battery factory in Nevada – the 'Gigafactory'.[132] A new Tesla battery, Powerwall, can be used to store solar electricity generated at home, as well as lower electric car costs.[133] This will mean Tesla is as much an energy storage company as it is a manufacturer of electric cars.

Some solar industry leaders forecast that within the next couple of years consumers will no longer be buying just solar systems, but rather a complete energy system, consisting of generation, storage, load-management and an app to oversee it all – with everything leveraged through big data analytics in the Cloud. Each consumer will take more responsibility for storage, generation and usage, but do it in such a way that is less expensive than pure utility energy, while the utility has access to what it needs to make sure that it plays well on the grid.

Tesla's Elon Musk highlights the possible network benefits of the 'system-wide implementation' of energy storage, including flattening peaks of electricity demand.

This could lead to far fewer conventional-generation power plants being required: 'You can basically, in principle, shut down half of the world's power plants if you had stationary storage, independent of renewable energy.'

Conclusion: Shifting Sands

Power in its many forms is evidently interlinked and undergoing considerable transition. From the geopolitics of superpower influence, to increasing transparency in a more digital world, to developments in energy supply, the sands are shifting.

While the US–China relationship/competition and the ongoing Middle East quagmire are always front of mind in many discussions, for me the potential future roles of India and Africa are of equal – if not greater – interest. While many companies understand that these will be important centres of influence and economic power in the long-term future, a good number somehow do not see them as significant in the next ten years. Throughout 2015, as well as running Future Agenda workshops to gain new insights, we also continued to run several for organisations looking at the implications of some of the shifts – at a regional, market or even company level. When asked to put our major trends in different groupings of high, medium and low impact, it was amazing how often India and Africa ended up in the low pile – and all because of 'time to', and not 'scale of', impact.

The multiple events we ran on the future of data, the future of privacy and specific workshops on cyber security, connected cars and their like, all continually highlighted the power of data – in the right hands. It seems that, as the big data explosion continues, we will increasingly shift from the current land grab (or trying to get hold of as much data as possible), to a more focused approach to identify the data of value, or, more significantly, the insights available from more sophisticated real- time analysis. The question, however, will be: which data are valuable? With more information being made open and shared as a necessary precursor to enable some of the much-discussed changes to take place, who will have the 'special data' is as yet unclear. Take, for example, driverless cars. To work, the whole system needs to share information, not just on the location of every vehicle but also on weather, traffic signals, etc. If all this is shared in an open data set, essentially for free, then many are asking what, and where, will the additional data of influence be – and so have most value.

What is clear is that across the many arenas highlighted, in the future, global, or even regional, leadership will be in a state of flux. As governments compete with corporations, and each other, and as networks and NGOs exert more influence, future power will be a different beast in the next decade to the one it was in the last.

Chapter 5

CHALLENGE 4:
Future Belief

> *In a world of changing priorities and shifting loyalties,*
> *who and what will set the values and norms by which*
> *we choose to live our lives to greater benefit?*

- Capitalism challenged
- Nature's capital
- Full cost
- Human touch

- Changing nature of privacy
- Truth and illusion
- Ethical machines
- Keeping the faith

Perhaps more than at any time in history, the nature of what, who and why we believe in one thing over another is in transition. With the rise of religious fundamentalism, the stumbling of capitalism and the ever more pervasive online maelstrom, it is not surprising that questions are being asked.

Over dinner in London, a philosophy professor offered the view that *who* and *why* we trust, and hence *who* we believe, is at a point of potential inflection. Looking back over the millennia, he suggested that we first followed tribal leaders and kings then, as beliefs consolidated, religion gained the upper hand. While religious movements have remained dominant, in some regions we also have seen the rise of national allegiances and governments, as exemplified in Europe from the Renaissance through to the late 19th century. Then, in general terms, in the 20th century we moved onto having more faith in organisations, companies and, in many regions, the capitalist system. Today, as confidence in some companies and governments is waning and questions are being raised about established religions, a divergence is taking place. Some of us have effectively lost confidence in formal systems and instead are turning to people we have an association with – even if it is via social networks. Others have become disillusioned and are choosing to eschew 'modern' religions and go back to a more fundamental faith based on a direct interpretation of religious belief.

Most of our discussions in 2015 were focused on concrete issues such as energy, data, cities or health, but throughout there were multiple references to the shift in belief. In order to gain alternative views, in Mumbai and Singapore, we delved deeper, looking into the future of faith, identity and how the media influences behaviour.

This chapter, *Future Belief*, seeks to make connections to understand why we adopt certain views. We examine the paradigm of capitalism, the predominant 20th century mantra in the West, to the emerging challenges around social behaviour in a fast-changing world. It seeks to share some of the shifts that we heard. In no way a validated view in the future of faith or trust, it is nevertheless a playback of a number of discussions from around the world.

Capitalism Challenged

Unable to shake issues like inequality, capitalist societies face cries for change, structural challenges and technology-enabled freedoms. Together these rewrite the rules and propose a collaborative landscape of all working together.

Kicking off at the systemic level, the current manifestation of capitalism is being challenged. Many believe it contributed to the global crisis, while providing no solution, and there is a desire to see a fairer system take its place. It is inequality that is at the heart of this backlash. Thomas Piketty, author of *Capital in the Twenty-First Century*, is convinced that rising inequality is a nut that will never be cracked by capitalism. His particular emphasis is on wealth inequality, which in Europe and the

USA is roughly twice that of income – the top ten per cent possess between 60 per cent and 70 per cent of wealth, but only 25 per cent to 35 per cent of income.[134] In the USA the top 0.1 per cent have as much of the total household wealth as the bottom 90 per cent (Figure 27). Economies with greater inequality suffer adverse consequences in areas like health, violence, drug addiction and lifespan. With no resolution in sight, some darkly predict social unrest – so tackling it makes good economic sense.

When founders Ben Cohen and Jerry Greenfield sold their ice cream business in 2000, they asked the buyer, Unilever, to continue the organisation's Social Mission programme. Unilever not only agreed but responded by asking the duo to identify appropriate social metrics to measure success, and thus a high-profile Multi-Capital Scorecard was piloted.[135] Another example is the successful UK retail partnership John Lewis, where an official pay ratio is in effect and no one person can earn more than 75 times the average pay.[136]

Contrast this with a workshop with some bankers in New York, where we were discussing inequality and why the banking sector seems to have such a problem getting its collective head around public sentiment. While the banks are keen to tell the media the average salary ($30,000) and bonus ($10,000) across the whole organisations, few wanted to reveal the top tier pay – which in this group clearly went into the multi-millions. One particular sticking point was whether or not bank staff should have their remuneration linked to benchmarks outside the sector, or stick to paying what is competitive within the industry. To test this, we picked a well-known person doing an important job – the secretary general of the UN, with a salary around $230,000 a year plus expenses and living costs – more than the US president, although probably without some of the fringe benefits. Acknowledging that banking is a competitive market, we suggested that maybe capping bankers pay at say 20 times that of the secretary general would be a good start – one that at least had some sense of comparable worth and benefit to society. The response? 'Don't be so naive' – why should a bank reduce its competitive positioning by putting

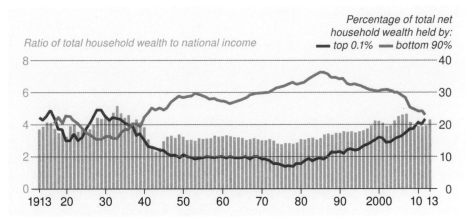

Figure 27: Total share of net wealth held in the USA.
(Source: Piketty)

such a limit on pay for the top talent, as they could go elsewhere? 'How about as an industry-wide ceiling?' we suggested. 'It would never work,' was the reply. Maybe we were naive but wouldn't it be good if what we suggested had some traction?

In an era where the public voice is easier to access and harder to suppress, it becomes more difficult to generate support for new initiatives without taking public views into account. As a simple but important example, remuneration is a core issue. Perhaps we should take a more holistic view of capital.

Nature's Capital

In the Anthropocene, humankind is presiding over the Earth's sixth major extinction. But as biodiversity declines, nature becomes increasingly valued and valuable.

We are living in the Anthropocene, the proposed epoch that began when human activities start to have a significant global impact on Earth's geology and ecosystems.[137] Many scientists are calling it the Earth's 'sixth mass extinction event', a period defined as a loss of 75 per cent of species.[138] According to *Nature*,[139] a staggering 41 per cent of all amphibians on the planet now face extinction, while 26 per cent of mammals and 13 per cent of birds are similarly threatened. Put simply, as humans degrade and destroy habitats, so the species that live in them die. In the end this will also affect humans; as Stanford ecologist Paul Ehrlich put it, 'In pushing other species to extinction, humanity is busy sawing off the limb on which it perches.'

The case for preserving and enhancing nature's biodiversity can be made along three dimensions. First, the moral obligation that we should protect nature for its own sake; why do we have the right to destroy it? Second, the social benefits to health and well-being that nature provides; numerous studies have evidenced the benefits of nature to our psychological, physiological and cognitive, social, aesthetic and spiritual well-being[140] Third, and seemingly increasing in importance in our capitalist world, are the economic benefits – the so called 'eco-system services' provided by nature. These ecosystem services are typically grouped into four broad categories: *provisioning*, such as the production of food and water; *regulating*, such as the control of climate and disease; *supporting*, such as nutrient cycles and crop pollination; and *cultural*, such as spiritual and recreational benefits.

Many ecosystem services are now being assigned economic values. As UN Secretary General Ban Ki-moon puts it: 'It is time to recognize that human capital and natural capital are every bit as important as financial capital.'[141] The global initiative TEEB (the Economics of Ecosystems and Biodiversity),[142] led by Pavan Sukhdev, seeks to 'make nature's values visible' through incorporating the values of biodiversity and ecosystem services into decision-making at all levels. Its approach to valuation helps decision-makers to recognise the wide range of benefits provided by ecosystems and biodiversity, demonstrates their values in economic terms and, where appropriate, suggests how to capture those values in decision-making. More broadly, as our understanding of the social and economic value of nature evolves, new means of measuring the costs and benefits of nature are being developed, for example, through natural capital accounting. According to estimates, the total annual global value of ecosystem services is in excess of $125 trillion, more than total global GDP itself.[143] Importantly, however, the valuation of eco-services (in whatever units) is not the same as commodification or privatisation. Many eco-services are best considered public goods or common pool resources, so conventional markets are often not the best institutional frameworks to manage them. However, these services must be (and are being) valued, and we need new, common asset institutions to better take them into account.

Looking forward, as these values become better understood, both governments and corporations will seek to enhance nature's capital or reduce their impact on it. A number of governments are developing plans for enhancing long-term natural capital, for example, the UK taking forward the recommendations of the Natural Capital Committee.[144] Similarly, growing recognition of the economic value of ecosystem services will lead to core business considerations that recognise their explicit value.

Natural capital will therefore become more commonplace in accounting systems, and will impact on the way in which leading organisations choose to operate and report (for example, Unilever's Sustainable Living Plan).[145] Within this context a core element raised in our discussions is that we should – and will – soon start to take a more holistic view of the true cost of our actions.

Full Cost

Increasing awareness of society's reliance on nature will intensify requirements for business to pay the true costs of the resources provided by 'natural capital' and so compensate for their negative impact on society.

In many of today's commercial activities, decisions are often taken on the narrow basis of profitability and performance. However, increasing transparency, provided by technology and a growing understanding of supply chain impacts and dependencies, is shifting opinion towards a re-evaluation of accounting practices to include 'whole value chain' costs and benefits – in other words, taking the social and environmental impacts and benefits to people and the planet into account as well as profit. Instead of simply providing financial returns for shareholders, and ignoring any negative impacts on stakeholders such as exploitation of workers or degradation of societal well-being or the environment, shared value will be created for and pooled between customers, employees, shareholders and wider society.

This move towards a 'net positive' position will necessitate businesses understanding and accounting for the full costs of negative impacts, as well as the benefits, often termed 'externalities', brought to staff, supply chain communities and wider society, as well as traditional customers and shareholders.

From an economist's point of view, a positive externality may arise from things such as inventions that are then widely used, or investments in infrastructure, such as a road that creates access opportunities for housing, shops or leisure activities. Negative externalities occur in communities when, for example, a factory is closed down, but are more often associated with the environment in relation to free 'goods', produced or provided by nature and available to everybody, such as air, rivers, lakes and ecosystems. This can be thought of as a 'liquidation of natural capital' where nature is degraded to be turned into goods and services for human benefit – man-made capital.

Estimates suggest that the world's top 100 environmental impacts cost the global economy around $4.7 trn per year (Figure 28). Of these 100 externalities, the majority of unpriced natural capital costs are related to free usage of ecosystem services and natural resources, such as the greenhouse gas emissions to the atmosphere (38 per cent), water use (25 per cent), land use (24 per cent) and air, land and water pollution (12 per cent).[146] In some industries, the damage actually outstrips the value of products created.

Going forward, we will see the rise of accounting methods and practices that aim to recognise these externalities and bring greater transparency to business operations. The Natural Capital Protocol, and the SDGs agreed by the UN at the end of 2015, are being adopted by businesses as a framework for what 'good' looks like. Triple bottom line accounting, including financial, environmental and social factors, is being developed into integrated reporting by the International Integrated Reporting Council (IIRC), a global coalition of business, investors and regulators. Global businesses such as Puma have calculated their environmentally extended profit-and-loss accounts to support their decision-making.[147]

As accounting methods start to shed light on these hidden costs, it becomes more apparent that they are paid for by wider society, while the profit from using these free services is largely enjoyed by private individuals or companies. The issue of balancing the private and public good, and who pays the cost, has been with us for a long time and the debate will escalate in the next decade.

Similarly, both energy producers and users benefit considerably from the 'free' carbon sink services provided by the atmosphere, while the cost of disruption from the build-up of carbon in the atmosphere is borne by global society. Several efforts have been made by governments to assess the 'social cost of carbon' to illustrate the

Rank	Sector	Region	Natural capital cost, $bn	Revenue, $bn	Impact ratio
1	Coal power generation	Eastern Asia	452.8	443.1	1.0
2	Cattle ranching and farming	South America	353.8	16.6	18.8
3	Coal power generation	Northern America	316.8	246.7	1.3
4	Wheat farming	Southern Asia	266.6	31.8	8.4
5	Rice farming	Southern Asia	235.6	65.8	3.6

Figure 28: Top five major costs of natural capital.
(Source: Trucost)

true costs of producing and using fossil energy. Some argue that this (true) higher price of carbon (estimates range from $37 to $220 per tonne) should be incorporated into carbon trading schemes, although, as yet, there are no mandated schemes which use these alternative figures.[148]

The use of water is also subject to externalities. Variability in water availability is highly localised and it could be naturally expected that pricing would reflect its availability. Such variability might be geographical (water-stressed areas versus water-abundant areas) or seasonal (between wet and dry times of year). But this is often not the case, and the price of water may be influenced by cultural and political issues rather than availability (Figure 29). Although not lacking in rainfall, Singapore has been dependent on importing water from its neighbour Malaysia, which fixes the price. With water harvesting, low-cost desalination and grey water reuse, Singapore has kept the costs at around $1 per cubic meter. By contrast, in the UAE – where most water comes from desalination plants – water costs some customers nearly $3 per cubic meter, while for Emirati nationals, just like energy, it is free. Trucost, an environmental consultancy, says, 'Based on current production locations, if water were to be priced according to its availability, 27 per cent of profits would be at risk across the world's largest companies.'

In addition, the wider social costs of depleting a water source through overuse are often not included in water pricing. The development of tourism infrastructure (such as hotels and golf courses) in water-stressed areas means that local communities have reduced access to water for their everyday activities – another case of privatising profits while socialising losses. There is an inevitable link between this and the inequality issue, exacerbating the situation where one per cent of the global population owns nearly 50 per cent of the wealth and the least well-off 80 per cent only own 5.5 per cent. This has the potential for the poor to be priced out of access to those public goods intrinsic to progress.

Environmental issues have historically been treated as add-ons to business practices. With the growing realisation that the wealth created by business is heavily reliant on natural capital assets, however, there is now a palpable move towards embedding the true costs of nature at the core of business strategy and operations. Some experts point out that better measuring and costing externalities are only interesting when there is an intention to act; simply knowing the rate at which we are depleting natural capital, and attempting to put a price on it, does not address the fundamental issue that we are approaching – or in some cases already breaching – the limits to growth imposed by planetary boundaries.

While this understanding has been growing in the West for some years, China and much of Asia are playing catch-up as the realisation dawns that managing resources and climate risk are fundamental to long-term success in wealth creation. If we're to start properly measuring progress, at a time when GDP growth has run its course, how do we establish alternatives?

Besides overall GDP growth, GDP per capita and national debt, the current defaults for checking how well we are doing include a diverse mix of issues such as trade

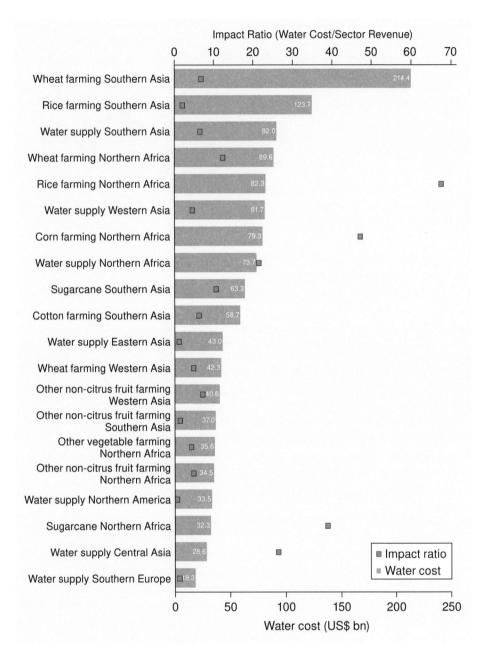

Figure 29: Ranking of 20 sectors and regions with greatest water costs, 2013.
(Source: Trucost)

growth, salary growth, infrastructure spending, stock market shifts, oil and other core commodity prices, household debt and inflation. Refined over the years, many analysts see that these hard numbers collectively provide us with a multitude of different ways to measure whether a year has been better or worse that the last.

At a time when more are starting to look at nature's capital and take a more holistic view of integrated reporting, a question often raised is: what will be the primary monthly numbers that we focus on? At a global level, will it be global warming and CO_2 levels (or the UN's SDGs that form the scorecard) or will we still be looking at OECD and IMF views of world GDP? It seems clear that we are entering a state of transition; however, until we have more clarity on the right things to measure and agreement on how to do this consistently and accurately, we may well default back to the standard fare for some time to come.

Human Touch

As service provision and consumption becomes ever more digital, automated and algorithmic, those brands that can offer more emotional engagement and human-to-human contact become increasingly attractive.

Moving from a more human view of socio-economic metrics to personal experience, some also detect change afoot for many brands. As the world becomes ever more automated, there is increasing nostalgia for a human voice at the end of the line or, better still, with a real person supporting a physical purchase. Despite the efficiency of machines, the brands that can offer more emotional engagement will become increasingly valued.

Since the Industrial Revolution, the world has become more automated. Broadly speaking, in the 19th century, machines, from looms to the cotton gin, helped to remove the dirty and the dangerous, relieving humans of onerous manual labour. In the 20th century, they took away the dull and the repetitive, with automated interfaces relieving humans of routine service transactions and clerical chores, from airline kiosks to call centres. Today, a world increasingly awash with connected and artificial intelligence and with virtual reality emerging quickly, machines are taking away and making better choices than humans, reliably and faster (for example, Google Now).[149] This is a glimpse of what our tomorrow will look like.

People are becoming increasingly distant from each other in many aspects of life, and this is perhaps most noticeable when you consider how some of us shop. Driven largely by the digitisation of customer service channels, digital automation and connectivity has enabled consumers to self-serve. Many of us like this: 72 per cent of customers prefer to self-serve when supported by an appropriate contact-centre experience. Web chat and social media interactions can often be automated so the customer is signposted to the help they need without a human being involved at all. The leaders in automation, from Google to Amazon and Alibaba, make it extremely difficult, if not impossible, for us to meet or speak to a real person. With this trend set to continue, it is expected that, by 2020, more than 85 per cent of customer relationships will have no human interaction at all. Automation will be the norm, with machines responding to humans themselves responding to machines. Average latency is the time it takes for a computer to respond to a human and so mimic natural speech. Amazon's Echo product has managed to get this down from three seconds to one – nearly at human-to-human levels.

From a commercial perspective, this is all good. Automation and intelligence can increase the functional outcome of an interaction, thereby improving speed or accuracy. It also reduces the service cost per customer which ultimately results in a lower price point for consumption – or an opportunity for profit margin gain.

It is not just retailers that are benefiting. In Singapore's Marina Bay Sands hotel, a three-tower building with a curved swimming pool deck on top, there is a notable focus on automation – its ability to improve efficiency and reduce the number of tedious, repetitive jobs. With more than 3,500 rooms, a 24/7 upscale shopping mall packed with brands not even available on Bond Street or Madison Avenue, a huge conference facility and a vast casino, the Marina Bay Sands has been attracting understandable attention. Providing more than 20,000 meals every day and handling more than 1,000 guests checking in each afternoon is no easy task and it is one that is increasingly become a platform for automation.

Whereas in most countries large hospitality complexes are significant employers that attract a good proportion of low paid labour, in Singapore the desire to pay higher wages and continue to raise GDP per capita provides a challenge for employing large numbers of cooks, waiters, cleaners and bell-boys. Developments already underway include robots folding the 20,000 plus napkins used every day and automated delivery of drinks to the casino tables. Coming soon are the prospects of automated delivery of guests' suitcases to their bedrooms, collection of laundry, delivery of room service and parking of cars. Replacing humans for these repetitive and time-consuming tasks, it is argued, will free the staff up for more value-adding (and hence better-paid) roles. A concierge on every floor would interact with guests, answer questions and make sure that the robots deliver and take the right stuff to and from the right rooms. Marina Bay Sands may be outside the norm for the hospitality industry, but many of the approaches being piloted here may well become part of the wider global hotel experience in years to come.

These benefits come at a price, however, namely the cost to a customer's emotional experience of contact with the brand.[150] People enjoy interacting with other people. Recent research confirmed the importance of personal service in a large study of the hospitality industry. Those customers who interact more often with service staff, and with a broader cross-section of that staff, reported greater satisfaction. A brand, so the phrase goes, is only as strong as the next engagement.

Automation can only go so far. It is hard, for example, to imagine automating the service provision of a funeral director. What is needed is an appreciation of where human interaction can be applied to make a positive difference to the overall customer experience. This might be in functionally complex problem-solving or perhaps giving assistance in intuitive or more emotional situations or being an integral part of a competitive strategy to stand out with a differentiated level of service. Consider Apple's use of in-store Genius's providing service and reassurance, something its competitors could not afford to match.

Adding a human touch will provide fertile opportunities for brands to engage with their customers and build a deeper sense of connection, relationship and affinity. In a world of digital marketing and consumption, consumers may increasingly prefer those brands that can offer more emotional engagement and real contact. The new model for organisations is to treat customers not merely as consumers but as the complex, multi-dimensional human beings that they are.[151] Customers, in turn, have been choosing companies and products that satisfy their deeper need for participation, creativity, community and idealism. A human touch assists in delivering this, even though it comes at a cost in terms of recruitment, training, wages and management and compliance overheads.

As a result, the provision of a good service is likely to be associated with greater human contact and more premium or luxury offers, and made available first to those who can afford it. It will also be judiciously used to differentiate brand and service experience: premium grocery retailers like Whole Foods or Waitrose are investing in more store and checkout service staff; Webchat and Facetime are also augmenting users' online service. It is true that while personal service is celebrated as warm, friendly and helpful, people are also more likely get it wrong too – it is what makes us human, after all. Mercifully, we also possess a wonderful, innate, self-correction mechanism that is difficult to replicate in machines – people can apologise when it all goes pear-shaped. A core component of 'human touch' staff training is to ensure that they know how to say sorry when mistakes happen.

Cosmetics company, Sephora, already uses social media and community engagement to increase human interaction for customers online, but doesn't miss the opportunity to sell products at the same time. Siri, Cortana and Google Now are proactive digital personal assistants,[152] bridging the gap between humans and automation. Apple programmers have even hidden 'easter eggs' in Siri that trigger 'her' sense of humour.[153] In Japan, robots are already tasked with relieving the burden on caregivers and in 2015 Hasbro introduced its 'Joy For All' line of robotic cats designed to provide companionship for the elderly.[154]

Where will it all end? Ray Kurzweil, futurist and author of *The Singularity is Near*, says that technology changes at an exponential rate.[155] This means that we always misunderstand just how much technological change will take place over a given time span: 'We won't experience 100 years of progress in the 21st century – it will be more like 20,000 years of progress (at today's rate)'.[156] So who really knows?

Looking forward, leading organisations are seeking ways to avoid making a trade-off between automated transactions and managing proper customer relationships. Intelligent self-service is likely to continue to transform customer experiences in the years ahead, with conversational IVR (interactive voice response) becoming the new standard for automated phone experiences, reactive virtual assistants becoming proactive virtual advisers, and self- and assisted-service converging. The human touch, however, will always be valued and, as machines step up to the plate, it will increasingly provide the differentiation in experience – or so many hope. Others see different patterns emerging.

Changing Nature of Privacy

As privacy is a public issue, more international frameworks seek to govern the Internet, protect the vulnerable and secure personal data: the balance between protection, security, privacy and public good is increasingly political.

In 2015 the privacy conversation is still rather low key – primarily a debate taking place in a closed community comprised primarily of academics, lawyers, regulators and security executives. This will not last. Privacy will transition from being considered a dry legal matter to one that is more widely understood and debated both commercially and by consumers. The new opportunities presented by big data, balanced with the increasing risk of data breaches, will ensure it climbs up the public agenda, becoming an important political issue along the way.

Currently the main international reference frameworks used for privacy and data protection are the OECD guidelines, the European Union Data Protection Directive and the Asia Pacific Economic Co-operation Privacy Framework. However, each organisation's approach to privacy differs: some data protection regimes apply equally to those processing personal data, while others apply different rules to specific sectors such as the health sector, types of processing entity such as public authorities, or categories of data such as data about children.

Up until now, personal data have driven the digital economy, but the IoT adds a rich new information source that can be collected, transmitted and stored online at comparatively little cost. In order to maximise the opportunity this presents, technology companies will have to tread carefully. Citizens may push back against the notion that their personal data can be used, seemingly without consent or direct benefit, for corporate profit, while governments, increasingly concerned about cyberterrorism, will demand more immediate access to personal data as a matter of national security. The challenge will be to satisfy both requirements, separating the practical from the ideological, while at the same time ensuring long-term profitability. Matters will become even more complicated when the networks are faced with the management of the expected torrent of new data from the myriad 'Things' which will soon generate their own digital footprints.

Awareness of both the opportunities and risks this presents is growing as commercial organisations, governments and, increasingly, people, all vie to maintain control. It raises the question: are we witnessing the emergence of new business models that threaten to disrupt not just the default Internet business model, but, more broadly, the assumption that the *organisation* is the natural and legitimate point of control and ownership of personal data? Some certainly think so. Given the global nature of data, several suggest there is a need for global consensus around regulation alongside an independent arbiter that can monitor activity and offer judicial support. But how can this be delivered?

One option put forward by Sir Tim Berners-Lee, founder of the Internet, is the creation of a 'Magna Carta for the Web', to ensure the Internet remains open and neutral by enshrining key principles in a global constitution. He states there is a need to 'hardwire the rights to privacy, freedom of expression, affordable access and net neutrality into the rules of the game',[157] and warns that if we are not careful, lack of awareness and general apathy might lead to a gradual erosion of an individual's right to privacy by large organisations. Action should be taken to prevent this. However, there is a lack of agreement about what this should realistically be, and the result of this impasse seems to be inactivity. Research by the UN Conference on Trade and Development (UNCTAD) found that, by 2013, only 107 countries had developed legislation to secure the protection of data and privacy, while another 33 draft bills were pending enactment. Many of those privacy laws have been developed on an ad hoc basis and are often bitty, disjointed and seemingly incapable of keeping up with the very technology they are designed to influence.

Like it or not, in order to function effectively, personal data, codes and locations are now shared across multiple jurisdictions by operators, manufacturers, developers and even users themselves. Differences are increasingly regional: in the USA, every state has its own definition for what constitutes an adequate standard. If a global regulatory framework is possible, it is likely that, although the principles will remain consistent, implementation will be localised and diverse, so the idea of privacy having borders will become a reality.

In the meantime, technology is driving relentlessly onwards, and we are now witnessing the emergence of new business models designed to circumvent third parties and put the individual back in control of their personal data. Tech companies provide consumers with increased encryption options, thus absolving themselves, to some extent, of the responsibility of data protection. As the recent Apple vs FBI case has shown, this has created problems for law enforcement agencies, as 'strong' or end-to-end encryption makes it almost impossible for the companies that process or carry the data to unscramble it. Despite this, it is becoming the norm; for instance, IBM has licensed its server chip technology to Chinese manufacturers in a way that gives them control over encryption.

The issues of data privacy cut right through the Internet. With approximately one-third of Internet users aged under 18, adult regulation struggles to protect the young while giving them authentic expression – few of those under age have a voice in how they are monitored; in-built defaults and sophisticated assessments seek to mitigate risk but with no major shift. In addition, cultural differences about the interpretation of privacy also need to be addressed; there is no standard for anonymisation, for example. The European ruling on the 'right to be forgotten' was described as 'disappointing' in the USA, where the idea of deleting information from the Internet is interpreted by some as a threat to freedom of speech.

Meanwhile, the regulated press and unregulated Internet continue to push the boundaries of information sharing. Everyone's personal information is in the public domain. As people react to more surveillance, some simply choose to 'go dark', which presents a huge challenge for many established Internet businesses whose default model is based on mining and repackaging data.

The speed of technological change is making it difficult for governments to keep up. Lack of understanding among politicians is delaying much-needed privacy regulation to protect both consumers and business. Perhaps emerging markets, where Internet take-up was initially slow, are particularly challenged as to how to respond. An UNCTAD report showed that out of 38 countries in Africa, Asia, Latin America and the Caribbean, 75 per cent of government representatives have difficulties in understanding the legal issues related to privacy, a figure reduced to 68 per cent when understanding cybercrime.

The establishment of clear principles around privacy does help but, such are the complexities, it is difficult for legislators to identify a specific body or organisation that can take overall responsibility, and in particular create standards around privacy that would be acceptable to all even at this stage of the game. In the next ten years it is hoped that harmonisation will take place; the key question will be how this can be achieved, and which organisation will take the crown and establish the global standards. Privacy will become an increasingly political issue and will also challenge us to question what is, and what is not, real.

Truth and Illusion

The Internet has democratised knowledge and changed the nature of who we trust and why. As confidence in large organisations declines, the search for trustworthy alternatives evolves. What we believe is changing how we behave.

What we believe is changing how we behave. Such is the influence of the rising data swirl that 'truth' may well become what the online crowds agree to – a world where 'crowd truth verification' is prioritised over search and results.

If pushed, most people would agree that we have always lived in a world of smoke and mirrors, where it is difficult to separate what is true from what is not – generations of historians, journalists and politicians have forged careers out of unravelling fact from fiction and explaining it to the masses. Looking ahead, however, it seems that, despite having (almost) perfect information at our fingertips, life is becoming increasingly ambiguous. It is ever more difficult for us to decide what is true and what is false, and who or what is best placed to help us interpret meaning. Instead of providing clarity, vast mountains of data have made it almost impossible for individuals to distinguish between fact, accuracy, misinformation, reinterpretation – and plain old-fashioned lying. Access to opinion and counter-opinion on every conceivable subject is now available to us all. Interpreting it is increasingly tricky, and deciding who or what will help with this process is trickier still.

Public faith, battered by revelations of corruption and mismanagement, has become wary of the establishment. A global opinion poll by Edelman in 2015 showed that, although trust in government has increased slightly, driven by big gains in India, Indonesia and, interestingly, Russia, overall, governments are distrusted in 19 of the 27 markets surveyed (Figure 30). The media does no better, distrusted as they are in 60 per cent of the countries; while trust in business leaders is at a record low, with less than 50 per cent of respondents trusting chief executives in most markets. Finally, although NGOs continue to be the most trusted institutions, overall faith even in them is in decline, from 66 to 63 per cent. Where do we go to get the 'right' answer?

Online reviews from seemingly like-minded individuals and comments on social media help consumers see a product or belief's underlying merits and demerits, not the image that its makers are trying to build around it. We take careful note of what our social networks say about quality, or value, or truth about an extraordinary range of products, services and ideas. But whereas historically it has been relatively easy to know the background of those we take advice from, in a time-stretched, instant-action society, few of us stop to think about whose recommendations we are really taking, particularly when that advice is found online. At the same time, some argue we are becoming self-referential, turning mainly to friends and family – people who think the same way we do.

Our modern economy depends heavily on free movement and trust. Looking ahead, many long-established, heavily advertised but mediocre products may lose consumers who have grown savvy to their flaws and will be unwilling to pay premium prices. However, for those firms that get the product right and have a genuine story to tell, the rewards will still be huge. The textbook example of this is Apple, whose devices' superior design and ease of use make it a powerful brand in a commoditised market.

One reason for our decreasing levels of trust is because the Internet has made it easy for anyone to publish an opinion, and is based on the premise that other contributors will verify accuracy. For big issues this generally works, but not even Wikipedia can get it right all the time. And some Internet publishers, either individuals or larger organisations, have little to lose from printing untruths – and plenty to gain in notoriety – if the story they put out is sensational enough. Faking an Internet page is easy, as is faking an online review.

Thanks to the democratisation of information via the Internet, alongside high-profile revelations of greed and incompetence among corporate and government institutions, and rising income inequality, trust in the status quo can no longer be taken for granted. As alternatives to media-trained career politicians and big brands, there is a growing appetite for plainspoken authenticity and a tendency to trust small companies. From a political perspective this may well explain the rise of more extreme phenomena such as Donald Trump in the USA and Marine Le Pen's National Front in France. From a business point of view, big corporates are trying to match the mood by boasting about the provenance of their products and latching onto 'authentic' brands (see Coca Cola's purchase of Innocent Drinks).

Understanding whether or not someone is telling the truth is, of course, not only a problem for individuals. A well-executed cyber attack has the potential to destroy

2015	
GLOBAL	**55**
UAE	84
India	79
Indonesia	78
China	75
Singapore	65
Netherlands	64
Brazil	59
Mexico	59
Malaysia	56
Canada	53
Australia	52
France	52
USA	52
Germany	50
Italy	48
S. Africa	48
Hong Kong	47
S. Korea	47
UK	46
Argentina	45
Poland	45
Russia	45
Spain	45
Sweden	45
Turkey	40
Iceland	37
Japan	37

TRUSTERS from 30% to 22% in 2015

DISTRUSTERS from 33% to 48% in 2015

Figure 30: Trust index.
(Source: Edelman Trust Barometer 2015)

a business with the click of a mouse. It is entirely feasible that, unless truly robust solutions are found, some might prefer to go off-line. Michael Lynton, chief executive of Sony Pictures, whose private emails and credit card details were hacked, has revealed that, since then, he writes sensitive messages by hand and sends them by fax. He is not the only CEO to do this.

Looking ahead, maintaining trust will become ever more difficult. Whether a brand or a politician, really delivering on promises has never been so important. Technology, far from making our lives easier, has added another layer of complexity. We have to work harder across multiple platforms to get a clearer picture of the truth. With everything becoming more automated, how many of us will really have the time or the inclination to do this? Moreover, as human actions give way to AI decisions, some see an even greater shift taking place.

Ethical Machines

Automation spreads beyond trading and managing systemic risk. As we approach technology singularity, autonomous robots and smarter algorithms make ethical judgements that will have life or death implications.

In ten years' time, driverless cars may fill our roads, machine-learning algorithms will combat disease and drones will deliver our shopping. Rapid advances in machine learning, visual and voice recognition, and neural network processing mean that computers are getting better at perception tasks. This puts AI, once the mainstay of science fiction writing, at the forefront of the next generation of computing.

AI brings extraordinary benefits, particularly around disease diagnosis, while doing a lot of boring but useful tasks, like recommending a book for online shoppers. Despite this, many thoughtful people – Stephen Hawking, Bill Gates and President Obama among them – are concerned about the impact that AI will have, not only from a social and economic perspective, but on the future of humanity itself. Hawking, for example, warns of the 'technological catastrophe' that could follow if artificial intelligence vastly exceeds that of its human creators.

Certainly data generated by the IoT will enable intelligent machines, as they crunch their way through it all, to increase their accumulation of knowledge exponentially. Algorithms are now designed to learn from raw perceptual data, understand language and recognise images, meaning that computers build on the knowledge they amass, learn more skills, understand nuance and, ultimately, gain what we term common sense. As they become more adept, they can also self-improve, building better versions of themselves without human involvement. The impact of this is not lost on Google, rumoured to have paid up to $400 million for DeepMind, a UK-based AI start-up. Facebook and Amazon are also making huge investments in this area.

This presents both a threat and an opportunity. On the one hand, greater AI and automation will threaten jobs, both low-skilled and managerial/administrative roles; on the other, it will offer individuals more control, allowing them to better manage their health, safety and privacy.

Some argue that AI is not replacing people, rather that it is augmenting their abilities and in so doing making them more effective. Certainly more efficient computers will make some firms much more productive, but most likely at the expense of human capital. In the short term, concerns about AI surpassing its creators are low but what seems certain is that it will soon take over some of the tasks that until now have formed the basic activity of many traditional professions. For a long time now computers have been better at analysing complicated data more effectively than people: supermarket and factory workers have already found this to their cost. These days computers can read handwritten notes, write and translate reports and even respond to conversations. Despite initial installation costs, they have the added benefit of not getting tired or fed up, and are unlikely to demand a pay rise. It is no surprise that they are gradually replacing their less flexible human colleagues.

AI's transformational role is already impacting on the automation industry. 'Swarm intelligence', the collective behaviour of decentralised, self-organised systems, is now being used to improve safety; when one car's brake sensors register icy conditions, for example, the information is shared with other vehicles on the same road through the Cloud. Cars are, therefore, becoming more intelligent and the next generation of vehicles will have thousands more sensor-connected computers to build on this. When all of this is taken collectively, cars will be able to monitor themselves, their environment and even keep a weather eye out for passengers.

Widening this out, mesh networks and ubiquitous mobile connectivity will soon be able to offer totally automated highways that will improve safety, increase road capacity and reduce congestion. Pretty soon driverless cars will become an accepted norm. We are almost there: Google's autonomous vehicles have already covered two million miles and, with only 14 accidents in that time, have an impressive safety record. Safer and more efficient roads will in turn change how risk is managed and shared, as insurance shifts from the individual and their car to whole fleets and, ultimately, the entire system. There will be challenges. Insurance companies will also have to work out how to deal with drivers who refuse to hand over control to managed systems: will those drivers pay a higher premium to remain 'free', while subjecting everyone else to a level of risk that the system will have to handle?

Realistically, however, accidents do and will continue to happen, particularly in built-up areas. Autonomous vehicles will, therefore, have to make some difficult ethical decisions and there are questions around how they will do this. Getting it wrong has huge legal implications that may well vary across jurisdictions. In Germany, for example, it is illegal to weigh up the value of one life against another, making it almost impossible to programme human life to a value that could be processed by an algorithm – whereas the USA is not so rigorous in this regard. Should rules governing autonomous vehicles emphasise the greater good, the number of lives saved, without putting value on the individuals involved? At the moment there seem to be more questions than answers.

Google's DeepMind[158] and others are busy writing the code for the AI systems that will replicate the good human values and behaviours we all need to be in place, before regulatory approval for the widespread adoption of driverless cars can happen. For example, one tricky challenge is the question of how you code a car to potentially kill the 'driver' rather than a pedestrian or a child on a bicycle, and it is one that came up again and again. Isaac Asimov's famous three laws of robotics[159] start with 'a robot may not injure a human being or, through inaction, allow a human being to come to harm'. The question is, however, when does an autonomous car, going at speed, swerve away from its chosen route so as not to hit an obstacle – and is the response different if it is a sheep in the road, or a child?

In Abu Dhabi, we were talking with very senior members of the government and the future of autonomous cars inevitably came up. Explaining the technology vs ethical issue was met with blank looks. 'Why would you swerve?' they asked. 'You can just keep going.' We explained that elsewhere people seem to think that this is a big issue. 'Not here – *Inshallah*,' was the reply. 'If there is a child in the road, then God wills it and there is no need for the car to swerve and potentially harm the "driver". It is the same when someone is drowning – you don't try and save them in case you put yourself in danger.' We cannot look at the future only through our own values; what we think is right and wrong is clearly different in other cultures and so thinking through the local, as well as global, implications of the ethics of driverless cars has to include the unexpected angle. One more challenge for AI?

Of even more concern than this to many is the use of AI in warfare. As highlighted in the recent film *Eye in the Sky*, remote drones are already distancing fighters from the fighting; soldier robots and autonomous weapons are perhaps the next step. In the next decade or so, algorithmic intelligence may well have the potential to surpass that of its human creators, identifying who to target and why – and the implications of this are frightening. Some argue that AI might be a better judge than, say, extremists. But what if such AI were in the hands of extremists? As with the Internet, once created it will be impossible to pull the plug on AI weapons. The UN now convenes regular meetings to discuss this and the matter is of such concern that over 1,000 AI experts have already called for development to stop. This is unlikely to happen: perhaps the best we can hope for is a postponement, while more consideration is given to regulation and constraint. One proposal is to ensure that the first generally intelligent AI is 'Friendly AI' which will be able to control subsequently developed AIs. It seems rather fanciful today, but perhaps in ten years this will be normal?

Historically, the ethics of technology has been mainly about its responsible and irresponsible use. In the future, deeper consideration will need to be given to the behaviour of machines towards human users and other machines. Trust in the system will increasingly drive success, so organisations will seek to make data ethics a focus. In the short term, regulation is needed to determine whether the designer, the programmer, the manufacturer or the operator is at fault if something goes wrong –

whether that is a car on a motorway, or robot in a warzone. It all seems a bit sci-fi, but science fiction is often the precursor of reality. We really do have to consider what will happen when machines become smarter and more adaptable than their creators.

Keeping the Faith

> *As people move they take their beliefs with them. For many, religion is one of the few remaining aspects of their previous lives, key to their identity and stronger than the citizenship of their adopted country or the nation they left behind.*

Lastly, with all the technology-driven change taking place, what will happen to our inner beliefs? The 21st century has dawned with millions migrating across countries, across continents, across the globe. As people move, they take their beliefs with them.

In addition to this movement, the world's religious landscape is changing, thanks to differences in population structure such as age and sex, as well as demographic processes such as fertility, mortality and, of course, religious conversions between different groups. Increasing migration has meant that many countries are becoming more religiously diverse. This is most evident in major cities, as they are often the first port of call for new arrivals. More than eight out of ten people around the world identify with a religion and are, to a greater or lesser extent, influenced by it. For many it provides a sense of belonging and definition in society, both in terms of behaviour and orientation, and influences everything from trade patterns, female employment levels, legal and banking systems to societal structures – how you are born, who you marry and how you die.

Christianity covers most of Europe, the Americas and large swathes of central and southern Africa, while Islam is mainly centred in North Africa, the Middle East and Asia. How these different faiths co-exist will have a profound effect in the coming decade. Projections from recent research is that, over the next four decades, Christians will remain the largest religious group, but Islam will almost equal their number around the world by 2050 (Figure 31).[160] If current demographic trends continue, the world's population is expected to increase by 35 per cent by 2050; over the same period the Muslim population is projected to increase by 73 per cent, simply because of its comparative youth and high fertility rates. Young religious people in the developing world as a group contrast sharply with ageing and increasingly secular Westerners (content to keep their families small), so expect the number of religious believers in developing countries where there is a high birth rate and declining infant mortality to grow more quickly.

The *Yearbook of International Religious Demography* measures the inter-religious diversity of a particular country or region's population.[161] Among the six regions analysed in this study, the Asia-Pacific region has the highest level of diversity, followed by Sub-Saharan Africa. Europe and North America by comparison have moderate

	2010 Population	% of World Population in 2010	Projected 2050 Population	% of World Population in 2050	Population growth 2010–2050
Christians	2,168,330,000	31.4	2,918,070,000	31.4	749,740,000
Muslims	1,599,700,000	23.2	2,761,480,000	29.7	1,161,780,000
Unaffiliated	1,131,150,000	16.4	1,230,340,000	13.2	99,190,000
Hindus	1,032,210,000	15.0	1,384,360,000	14.9	352,140,000
Buddhists	487,760,000	7.1	486,270,000	5.2	−1,490,000
Folk Religions	404,690,000	5.9	449,140,000	4.8	44,450,000
Other Religions	58,150,000	0.8	61,450,000	0.7	3,300,000
Jews	13,860,000	0.2	16,090,000	0.2	2,230,000
World total	**6,895,850,000**	**100.0**	**9,307,190,000**	**100.0**	**2,411,340,000**

Figure 31: Projected growth of major religious groups.
(Source: Pew Research Center)

religious diversity, while the Latin America-Caribbean and Middle East-North Africa regions have low religious diversity. Unsurprisingly, perhaps, non-religious people tend to live in religiously diverse places, as do Christians – the number of whom are living in religiously diverse countries has increased by approximately 50 per cent over the past century. The opposite is true for the Muslim faith; a century ago 20 per cent of all Muslims lived in countries with low religious diversity, but by 2010 this had increased to more than 30 per cent.

Although still a key aspect of many Western societies, there has been a gradual separation of religion and state in many Christian nations. However, this is not the case for Islam, and more so in the case of some countries than others. Saudi Arabia does not tolerate any form of overt religious practice other than the officially approved interpretation of Sunni Islam, whereas Indonesia and Malaysia, countries with Muslim majorities, have a tradition of syncretic Islam that is more tolerant. There is growing concern across the globe that the stricter forms of Islam imported from the Middle East are seen as more modern and correct, and are gaining popularity. At its most extreme these are the ultra-conservative views of Wahhabis, which form the basis for ISIS.

For me some of the most revealing conversations of the Future Agenda programme took place in unusual locations beyond the traditional London–New York–Brussels–Dubai–Singapore–Mumbai–Hong Kong–Sydney centres of focus. One of these was in Beirut where I had lunch with several academics. In the workshops we covered a number of important topics, including water supply, the role of women and the problems of waste disposal, as well as the global influence of the 20 million Lebanese diaspora, and the challenges of having 2.5 million refugees from Palestine and Syria hosted in a country with a population of 4 million (which puts Europe's 1 million refugees in perspective).

Over lunch, our discussions inevitably covered Syria and the wider conflicts and politics across the Middle East. A complex, contentious and conspiracy-laden conversation took place, but one of the points that struck me was the role that the minority Christians play in Lebanon. If this country is a microcosm of the Shia vs

Sunni rivalry that dominates the Middle East, a place that lives under the shadow of Israel and Syria, and is a tangible focal point for the external powers of the USA, Europe and Russia, the political positioning of the Christians is quite unusual. They essentially keep the balance of power between Sunni and Shia in check, and, as the power of Iranian-backed Hezbollah has grown while that of the Syrian army has declined, play a bridging role to maintain stability. Moreover, as refugee migration into Lebanon is reducing the influence of Christians – and hence their moderating influence – the need for their active future involvement in the political processes is seen as pivotal.

Many Christians hold French passports but continue to stay on in the hope of a better future for Lebanon. 'Why stay?' I asked one of those I met, 'especially when your children are already in New York and Paris?' The answer – 'If I move to Paris and am shot there, I will be just another body in the morgue. Whereas if I am blown up here, I will be seen as a martyr and so help keep us in political prominence.' On such fine judgements hang the fate of nations.

Increasingly, the concept of religious freedom, a human right, is being challenged. The latest US State Department report points to terrible violations of basic freedoms in dozens of countries.[162] This is not, it says, due to cruel governments, but more to the kind of forces that step into a vacuum when legitimate authority collapses: warlords, racketeers and terrorist groups. On the Syrian-Iraqi border, ISIS is reported to have 'forcibly displaced hundreds of thousands of people, conducted mass executions, and kidnapped, sold, enslaved, raped and or forcibly converted thousands of women and children...'. ISIS is not the only fanatical organisation implicated; in its quest for religious domination, Boko Haram has been similarly barbaric in Nigeria, Niger, Chad and Cameroon.

Some expect that the rise of Islam in Europe, boosted as it is by immigrants from North Africa, Turkey and South Asia, will challenge the secular nature of state governance and may well reshape the balance between religion and state. Some consider that Western democracies lack the mechanisms for dealing with the powerful transnational ideological forces of extreme Islam, and may well struggle to maintain a balance between the desire to maintain a society which upholds the right to religious freedom, and adherence to a common set of values on which all can agree. There are also fears that countries such as Indonesia and Malaysia will retreat from diversity and cede greater control over beliefs, customs and freedom of expression to a dominant orthodoxy.

The next decade will see different countries approaching religious freedoms in different ways. France, much like the USA, has a clear constitution with a specific set of founding principles, and it expects all citizens to accept them, including the idea that universal education should help to reinforce these principles. Britain, though, lacks a specifically written constitution, and has taken a different approach, allowing immigrant sub-cultures to develop and accepting faith-based (including ultra-conservative Islam) schools. Germany, keen to avoid any fanatically professed ideology, religious or secular, has always supported religious education and is making room for Islam through its classrooms.

On the issue of radicals returning home after life under ISIS, Western governments will have to tread carefully to manage their response – and the Paris and Brussels bombings brought this very much to the fore. Muslim migration and population growth in Europe is resulting in increasing political influence for this group. Muslim communities will react against harsh penalties such as prison for young men and women coming back. In the future, community-based programmes designed to divert young people from extremism may well be the only solution.

Against this backdrop, Christianity drifts South. There are 277 million adherent Christians in Sub-Saharan Africa and 250 million in Latin America. That has moved the centre of Christianity (calculated by taking the Christian-adherence weighted-average latitude and longitude of countries' capital cities) to Niamey, the capital of Niger. Should the Vatican follow?

Conclusion

Belief has always ebbed and flowed – albeit at different speeds in different regions and in different communities. How far things will change by 2025 is hard to call. Pew Research shows that the USA, for one, is becoming less religious, particularly among the millennial generation, who say they do not belong to any organised faith (Figure 32). The same may not be true elsewhere.

The 20th century saw many events that challenged and changed our views of what was right and wrong: two world wars; the Great Depression; Bretton Woods; the Russian revolution; the Cold War; the Chinese Communist revolution; Chinese economic reform; apartheid; the Rwandan genocide; secular states; CNN; and the creation of the Internet to name just a few. To date, it looks like the 21st century

	Silent generation (born 1928–1945)	Baby Boomers (born 1946–1964)	Generation X (born 1965–1980)	Older Millennials (born 1981–1989)	Younger Millennials (born 1990–1996)
Religious Behaviours					
They pray daily	67	61	56	46	39
They attend services at least weekly	51	38	34	27	28
Religious Beliefs					
They believe in God	92	92	89	84	80
With absolute certainty	71	69	64	54	50
They believe in heaven	75	74	72	67	68
They believe scripture is word of God	69	64	61	50	52
They believe in hell	57	59	59	55	56
Religion's importance					
Religion is very important in their lives	67	59	53	44	38

Figure 32: Religious affiliation in the USA, 2014.
(Source: Pew Research Center)

could well chalk up a good number too: 9/11; Al-Qaeda and ISIS; climate change; the 2007/08 financial crisis; an increasingly Muslim Europe; social media; and Edward Snowden are just some of the candidates. The nature of whom, what and why we trust in one thing over another is changing as fast as ever.

We cannot predict the catalytic incidents that will shape our future belief and who or what we trust, but we can certainly anticipate that over the next decade or so there will be a good number. However, from the evidence we gathered from our multiple discussions, it looks as though our world is simultaneously becoming more connected and more fragmented. Globalisation driven by GDP growth may well be peaking and giving way to a more holistic view of progress in some regions, but not in all. Big data, digitisation and a transformation of many systems together are fundamentally changing which information we have access to, which we don't and what we consequently think about what we see, read and hear. As different faiths and beliefs vie for attention and new networks emerge for the non-believers, we can at least be sure of one thing: change.

Chapter 6

CHALLENGE 5:
Future Behaviour

As more of us recognise the core issues and constraints
for the future, how do we adopt more efficient attitudes
and change our behaviour to protect what matters?

- Key resource constraints
- Data ownership
- Digital money
- Food waste
- The real sharing economy

- Urban obesity
- Education revolution
- Caring for those left behind
- Still being stupid?

As we look forward, there are several shifts on the horizon being driven by technological advances: autonomous cars, data marketplaces, personalised medicine, for instance. Equally, some changes, such as those associated with privacy, trade and retirement, are awaiting regulatory progress. However, there are a good number of changes that do not require major external adjustment to take place, but rather are more dependent on how we see, understand and act around certain issues. A good proportion of them are linked to the environment, but others are simply about our attitudes to some very basic and core topics – what we do, what we value and how we behave, either individually or collectively.

In the group linked to the environment there are items such as resource use and management of waste, which are common around the world but sometimes different in nuance. In September 2015 in Beirut, garbage had not been collected for weeks and was piling up in the streets – not because anyone disagreed that garbage should be collected, but rather because the different Sunni and Shia Muslim factions in Lebanon could not agree in whose area a new landfill site should be sited. In Vienna, at our venue for a discussion on the future of food, there were no less than seven different coloured bins to sort waste into – paper, non-recyclable waste, organic waste, plastic, clear glass, drinks cans and stained glass). The same core issue, but a different response: while the systems and circumstances are evidently dissimilar and very much driven by a cultural as much as a political viewpoints, the underlying behaviours and attitudes to waste may not be so different. If waste was seen as a resource by us all, and not just a few, what we throw away, where, why and how may well change quickly.

In a separate field, as the world becomes ever more connected and digitisation continues to transform parts of our lives, how we treat our digital footprint is one area of growing debate. While some advocate a more proactive stance on data ownership, others are less concerned. But as the value of our data becomes more visible to more of us, a good number of the experts we talked to felt that our personal behaviours around data sharing may alter in the years ahead. Some think that these behaviours will change more across different demographics than different geographies, others that a number of major events, such as what was described as a 'Privacy Chernobyl' in Washington, would alter the global stance.

In other discussions around the world, people raised and debated potential changes that are emerging in and around education, separated families, obesity, mental health and deeper partnerships. The changes being discussed are not new and have been debated at length in public.

For many, these and their like are the changes that should and could take place quickly, but somehow they don't. They are connected to issues that many of us recognise, some of us understand but few of us seem to actually be doing anything about. This chapter, *Future Behaviour*, explores some of these topics and asks what will make us change our perspectives and hence our actions.

Key Resource Constraints

Economic, physical and political shortages of key resources drive increasing tension between and within countries. As we exceed the Earth's natural thresholds, food and water receive as much focus as oil and gas.

Globally, more people are increasingly concerned about the environmental impact of humans continuing to consume more resources than the Earth can naturally replenish; we currently consume the equivalent of 1.6 planets a year.[163] The picture is itself complex but consistent: while we are not necessarily running out of things, access to many important resources is increasingly constrained – be those physical, economic, political or environmental. As a result, over the next decade, many resources are going to become more difficult to get hold of and may become more expensive. And as we deplete these resources, countries with supplies will seek to hold on to them and their prices will increase.

At current rates of consumption, we have around eight years' production left of antimony, a key ingredient in batteries; 12 years of iridium, important for solar panels; and only 17 years of silver and zinc. We have around 30 years' worth of copper and 45 years' of titanium left.[164] Other resources are in more plentiful supply but are under pressure politically, environmentally or economically (Figure 33). We have between 40 and 80 years' supply left of coal, but given its impact on carbon emissions, it is little surprise that its use is being restricted on environmental grounds. Gas and oil, the other two major fossil fuels, are also under pressure but with different emphasis. Less well-known, but essential for fertiliser, phosphate rock is found only in a few countries (the USA, China and Morocco); we have around 75 years' supply left. Phosphorous cannot be replaced by something else, nor can it be artificially manufactured; it can only be recycled through organic methods.[165] Demand is directly linked to us wanting more efficient food production. With peak-phosphorous usage estimated around 2030, it will increasingly feature on news bulletins over the next decade as another key resource of concern.

Importantly, water – a resource neither running out, nor becoming more plentiful – is increasingly under pressure. While we have the same amount of water today as we did 10,000 years ago, the challenge today is how we use it. Globally, around 70 per cent of all fresh water is used for agricultural purposes – while, depending where you live, the other 30 per cent is split between domestic purposes, manufacturing and waste in the system[166] (Figure 34). Managing the water needs of ten billion people with the same amount of water as worked for one billion is no easy task. Nevertheless, today few regions value fresh water and have little idea of its true cost. Going forward, we can expect the challenge of water supply to be more widely recognised.

Globally, we also face more of a problem in net food distribution than food supply, at both local and regional levels. With more people increasingly living in places where

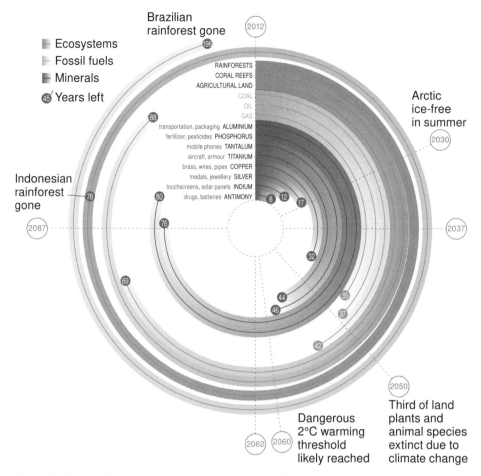

Figure 33: Estimated remaining world supply of non-renewable resources, 2014. (Source: BBC)

food is not plentiful, transporting good quality food to them at affordable prices is already a challenge. Add in future population growth, more uncertain weather patterns (hence less predictable harvests) and food as a resource will become the subject of more political as well as economic interest. Over the next decade, maintaining global food security will become much more difficult as the population increases.[167] Solutions include changing our diets, eating less meat, improving yields and the wider adoption of GMOs (genetically modified organisms). Some of these may work in some cultures, but not all. The challenge, therefore, is how to manage an increasingly constrained food supply at the same time as we add another billion mouths to feed into the system.

Linked to producing food for more people, but also driven by mass urbanisation, is the amount of arable land available. Per head this has already dropped from 0.45 hectares in 1960 to 0.25 hectares today, and is set to decline further. More efficient farming has helped manage this transition over the past 50 years, but there are concerns about the next 50. If 2010 was the year in which the land available for agriculture peaked, in future we are going to need to produce more food from less

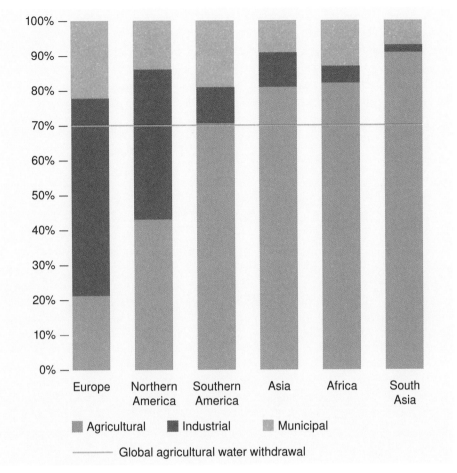

Figure 34: Water use globally.
(Source: Globalagriculture.org)

land. As such, many see that to feed more people we must double food production and hence productivity over the next decade – in a sustainable manner. Others say perhaps not – maybe there is a simpler alternative?

Food Waste

We waste 30–50 per cent of our food either in the supply chain or in consumption and could feed another three billion people. Optimising distribution and storage in developing countries and enabling better consumer information in others could solve this.

The statistics are shocking: one in four of the calories we create is never eaten; every day, consumers in the West throw away as much food as is produced in the whole of Sub-Saharan Africa; globally, the two billion tonnes of food wasted each year are equivalent to around $1 trn of financial loss.[168] If we are to support another billion or so people on the planet this century, with limited land and water resources, reducing this massive wastage is perhaps the most significant shift we could make to help us to feed the global population. By using data to optimise distribution and storage in developing countries, and enabling better consumer information in others, we could feed another three billion people every day.

Depending which region you are in, the nature of food waste shifts from production and storage to distribution and consumption. In developing counties, 40 per cent of the loss occurs post harvest, storage and in processing, while in developed nations 40 per cent of the losses are in retail and with the consumer (Figure 35).[169] In China, losses of rice are at 45 per cent of total production and in Vietnam it is 80 per cent. In India, Delhi has Asia's largest food produce market but no cool storage facility, meaning that in soaring temperatures fruit and vegetables cannot stay fresh for long. In South Africa, 50 per cent of mangoes are damaged in the first mile of transportation, while in India 20 million tonnes of wheat, equivalent to the entire production of Australia, are lost every year due to poor storage. Improving storage with simple, low-cost methods (such as using crates rather than bags and sacks) could drastically cut food loss.

Productivity around the world varies: India overall is half as productive as global averages – whereas US farmers produced 11 tonnes of food per acre, in India the figure is 3 tonnes. These inefficiencies of production occur because 90 per cent of Indian farmers do not use animal feed and therefore miss out on easy ways to improve yields. Given that pretty much all arable land is in use, along with urbanisation and climate change fast shifting the balance, higher productivity per hectare is a major theme in the food industry.[170]

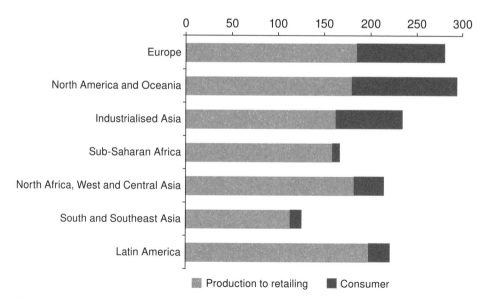

Figure 35: Per head food losses and waste (kg/year).
(Source: FAO)

One obvious option is to adopt more GMO approaches. However, although these are embraced in some regions, in others, such as the EU, they are demonised. The GMO actions that gain the greatest support are for the introduction of drought-tolerant and salt-resistant crops, thus many would argue that the problem can be solved without taking too many steps towards more GM (genetically modified) food produce.

Also significant in the list of areas for improvement is water supply and irrigation: as agriculture consumes 70 per cent of our fresh water, reducing food waste frees up more water. In the USA, where 30 per cent of purchased food is thrown away, this means that half of the water used to produce food is wasted. Globally, shifting from flooding and spray irrigation to drip-and-trickle feed can improve productivity by more than a third.

In the Western world of retail, quality standards and obsessions with food appearance are the major issues driving food waste. In many developed markets, around 50 per cent of some vegetables harvested do not make it onto the shelves because they do not look right. No one, apparently, wants a wonky carrot. Labelling issues also matter: in the UK, about 20 per cent of food is thrown away because consumers incorrectly perceive it as being out of date. This has led to calls for the wider use of just the 'use-by' date, now being piloted by Tesco across Europe. Meanwhile, networked smart fridges and storage cabinets that interact with food packing to track supplies, use-by dates and link to online delivery firms, thereby minimising the purchase of unnecessary goods, are another option.

Considerable waste also takes place worldwide in hotels and catering, where 80 per cent of food waste is attributed to events such as parties, conferences and weddings. Because they are cheaper to provide than plated service at tables, hotels typically favour buffets to feed lots of people. Although cost-effective in terms of labour, they are incredibly inefficient in terms of the ratio of food consumed to that prepared, especially so with banquets. In Singapore, a typical Chinese wedding may expect 1,000 guests, and hotels usually cater for an extra 10 per cent in case people bring a friend. However, in a culture where RSVP is anathema, sometimes only 500 people turn up, and so 55 per cent of the food may be thrown away.

Another option is to redistribute food that is not sold. While, unfortunately, in many countries food safety regulations forbid the reuse of food, firms like Pret-a-Manger have made a point of giving unsold products to organisations for the homeless. Individuals are joining in by using apps such as the US's Leftoverswap which links people with leftover food, and in Australia Secondbite redirects unwanted food to community food banks. In many US cities, food can no longer be sent to landfill and instead is turned into energy – anaerobic digesters are popping up all over the place, turning food scraps into gas. In the UK, Waitrose is just one of the supermarkets that has already diverted all its shop-generated waste from landfill to anaerobic digestion. France has passed a law banning supermarkets from destroying unsold food.

If we could reduce current food waste by just a quarter, that would be enough to feed all of the world's hungry; reduce it by half, and we will have freed up enough to cope with an extra billion or so people on the planet. By 2050 the world will need 60 per cent more calories every day to feed nine billion people; cutting current food loss and waste levels in half will shrink the gap by 22 per cent – a relatively simple solution to one of the world's major problems, some would say. While improving supply chains, refrigeration and farmer training in many emerging economies will take some effort and hence time, changing our attitudes to food and its labelling, as well as its value, globally could certainly have an impact very quickly.

Urban Obesity

Mass urbanisation, reduced activity and poor diets are accelerating the rise of obesity. Levels of obesity in most cities are growing fast and the associated health-care burden will soon account for five per cent of global GDP.

Linked to food consumption, and over-consumption in particular, is a chronic disease that, despite all the warnings, is still getting worse year on year. The obesity epidemic has been a major concern for a number of years, and half the global population is expected to be overweight by 2030.[171] Many governments see obesity as the main driver of a health-care funding time bomb.

The average American is 11 kg heavier today than in 1960. Not even including the significant loss in economic productivity each year, by 2030, health-care costs due to obesity are projected to add an extra $550 billion and so account for 16 to 18 per cent of total US health-care expenditure.[172]

Globally, the nations with the highest ratios of overweight and obese populations continue to be found in the Pacific Islands, followed by many of the Gulf States such as Kuwait, Qatar, Saudi Arabia and the UAE, and then the more populous USA and Mexico (Figure 36). However, although much of Asia and Africa are, on average, well under half the US level of obesity of 35 per cent, things are changing quickly, especially in the cities. In both India and China, the prevalence of urban obesity is three to four times the rate in rural areas.[173]

In China in 2014, more than 25 per cent of the adult population was overweight or obese; 11.6 per cent of Chinese are now diabetic, almost as high as in the far-fatter USA. The obesity rate for boys is around 7 per cent, twice that of men. In India, urban men and women have higher blood pressure, dyslipidemia and pre-diabetes than rural men, while the rates of obesity and diabetes are more than double in urban Indians than rural Indians. In Africa, the issue of rising urban obesity, especially for the poor, is evident. Across the continent, urban obesity is running at nearly three times the level found in rural areas – more than a third of Africa's urban population is overweight or obese and most of the recent increase has been in non-educated poor women. Given that obesity has a higher incidence in disadvantaged households, it also imposes a disproportionate burden on these already struggling households in terms of health-care costs.

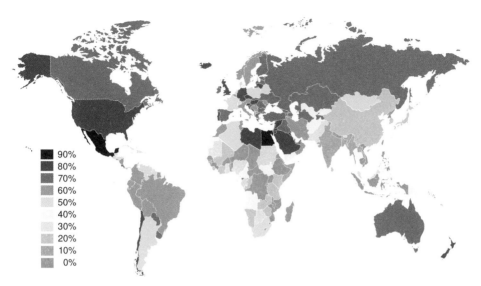

90%
80%
70%
60%
50%
40%
30%
20%
10%
0%

Figure 36: Overweight and obesity patterns (BMI>25) for adults, 2013.
(Source: Institute for Health Metrics and Evaluation)

Cities around the world are coming up with initiatives to combat this. In Paris, car ownership has dropped by 50 per cent since 2001, while in London twice as many people now ride a bike as they did at the turn of the century. Taipei has encouraged many women to take up cycling via its YouBike sharing scheme, while New York has joined London and Paris is expanding its bike-sharing programmes, while simultaneously reducing speed limits for cars. Following on from the success of Bogata's *ciclovia*, where 120km of streets are closed on Sundays and holidays and given over to cyclists, many other cities have followed suit: Gurgaon's equivalent since 2013 is called *Raahgiri*, and similar initiatives can now be found across Brazil and, with its *Paseo de Todos* (monthly massive night ride), in Mexico City. The challenge for fast-growing cities in developing countries is to emulate this shift – or come up with their own way to get citizens off their bottoms.

Inequality does not help. According to the CDC, childhood obesity in the USA has been directly linked to both the education level of the head of the household and also lower-income families: obesity among children whose adult head of household completed college is approximately half that of those whose adult head of household did not complete high school, while obesity prevalence is also highest among families with an income to poverty ratio of 100 per cent or less.[174]

With the prevalence of severe obesity globally expected to increase by 130 per cent over the next two decades, what was once seen as a rich-country problem has become the top health concern worldwide. Alongside the ageing demographic, it is seen as a primary driver of increased and unwarranted health-care spend which few nations can afford. In the UK, it has the second highest social impact after smoking, already accounting for three per cent of GDP. Although some believe that we may be reaching peak-obesity in some countries, in others the trend, especially in cities, is clearly upwards. With mass urbanisation adding millions more people to cities, food becoming cheaper and cheaper, and one in 12 of the global adult population now having diabetes, the social and economic burden of urban obesity is, like many waistlines, getting bigger and bigger. Most of us now understand this issue, and if we do not, then governments and health-care organisations are very busy telling us more and more about it. We can comprehend the connection between that extra portion, extra weight and increased risk of diabetes, but still, many, even in the health-care profession, continue to act in way driven neither by our heads or our hearts – just our stomachs.

Plastic Oceans

There are increasing high levels of man-made pollution in many of the world's seas and little actually disappears. By 2050 there will be more plastic than fish in the world's oceans.

Similarly related to food, but also covering a wide range of other areas, is our behaviour around packaging and other waste and its journey towards many the world's seas. While some have historically assumed that the oceans are so big that they can absorb and break down our garbage, the reality is that little actually disappears. And yet, the volume of plastic waste entering the oceans is set to double in 10 years.[175]

We live on a blue planet; the world's oceans cover three quarters of the Earth. They contain 97 per cent of the Earth's water and are currently absorbing around a third of the CO_2 being produced by our activities, so help by acting a buffer for some of the impacts of climate change. Carbon dioxide from human activity released into the atmosphere dissolves into oceans, resulting in the creation of carbonic acid. Ocean acidification is therefore a rising concern. The average pH balance is dropping and as a result the growth of calcifying organisms such as corals and shellfish is being reduced. Acidification alone, though, is not the only pollution problem faced by the world's seas, and others are escalating at an even faster rate. The implications are huge and growing.

Around 80 per cent of marine pollution comes from land-based activities. Waste runs or is dumped into drains and rivers and hence the seas. Oil, fertilisers, sewage, plastics and toxic chemicals are all part of the mix. Oil spills are less frequent now, but in many countries without an established recycling system, used oil is thrown down the drain or poured directly into rivers. Nutrients in fertiliser run-off from farms and lawns produce algae, depleting dissolved oxygen and suffocating marine life, and have caused dead zones in places such as the Gulf of Mexico and the Baltic. In many regions, untreated sewage still flows into the seas – 80 per cent in the case of the Mediterranean. A recent addition to the challenge is the role of desalination plants, cropping up in areas of water stress from the Middle East to Australia and California. As a core by-product of their water purification process, they add salt into the seas, so increase salinity and hence toxicity.

While all of the pollutants are having severe negative impact, perhaps the most visible – hence one that will drive the biggest change in the next decade – is plastic. Around 275 million tons of plastic waste is generated each year; between 4.8 million and 12.7 million tons is either washed or dumped deliberately into the sea.[176] The World Bank expects the planet's municipal solid waste to double within 15 years, and much of this in the form of single-use plastic items. Bottles, bags, balloons, packaging, shoes – all take decades to break down. This waste is ingested by pretty much every marine animal including fish, dolphins, seals, turtles and seabirds. So far, plastic has been found to be blocking the digestive tracts of at least 267 different species.

Although this is a global problem, the epicentre of plastic pollution is clear. Today 60 per cent of the plastic waste in the ocean comes from just five countries – China, Indonesia, the Philippines, Thailand and Vietnam. The media already talks about the Great Pacific Garbage Patch.[177] By 2025, plastic consumption in Asia will have increased by 80 per cent, surpassing 200 million tons; some are calling for specific interventions in these five countries. Regionally, the EU is aiming to halve plastic bag use by 2018, but this is not an international standard. Industry experts expect that by 2050 we will be producing three times as much plastic as we do today; on a volume basis, the World Economic Forum (WEF) predicts that by 2050 there will be more plastic than fish in the world's oceans.

However, plastic pollution is not alone as an increasing danger to the world's seas. One politically sensitive issue now is associated with dredging and land reclamation. Whether in the South China seas, where China is creating islands built on coral reefs, or in Indonesia, where sand mining has been providing Singapore with the resource to add 130 square kilometres of artificial 'reclaimed' land in the past 40 years, mining has evidently moved from land to sea.

With all the consequences of our actions now becoming apparent, the question is: what will change going forward? Has ocean pollution become such a significant issue that there will be tangible change within the next decade? Some think so. The UN has included as its 14th SDG the ambition to 'conserve and sustainably use the oceans, seas and marine resources'. A core 2025 objective is to prevent and significantly reduce marine pollution of all kinds, especially land-based activities, including marine debris and nutrient pollution.

Unfortunately, much of the world's oceans are not part of any one country's territorial waters. More than 40 per cent of the planet's surface (80 million square miles – seven times the area of the whole African continent) is ocean that belongs to everyone and no one – and hence is largely unregulated. While fishing, environmental, tourist and defence policies all unite to seek to protect and manage the sea close to a nation's shoreline, beyond a notional 12–200 mile limit, it is largely a free-for-all. This is where the fish, dolphins and plankton are taking the hit. No one is setting the global rules and few agree on a better way.

When will the balance tip? When will the negative impacts on our environment, the ecology and, most significantly from a financial perspective, a good share of our food resources start to change attitudes? Some are putting their faith in China to set new standards, but these may only apply locally. At a global level some believe that a rethinking of the value of the 'blue-economy' is required. The Global Ocean Commission, for one, has called for adoption of an ambitious, long-term goal of zero plastic waste into the marine environment. This will require partnerships and behaviour changes that simply do not exist today, and the end of Europe and the US shipping its waste to Asia. If we start to see waste as a resource in the next decade, will perceptions – and maybe behaviours – shift?

Whether seeking to protect food supplies or looking to fulfil UN development goals, bringing order to the high seas is seen as critical for the future. We have already overshot the planetary limits on biodiversity and nitrogen: as the consequences become more apparent, can we avoid the same for ocean pollution?

Data Ownership

Individuals recognise the value of their digital shadows, privacy agents curate clients' data sets while personal data stores give us transparent control of our information. We retain more ownership of our data and opt to share it.

Moving away from resources and waste, one of the fast-growing areas of further potential behavioural change lies around how we see, value and share our personal data. Until recently, people mostly felt relaxed trading elements of their personal life in return for better online services, to assist with health research or traffic surveys, but the removal of personally identifiable information such as names, date of birth, addresses do little to cover our tracks. These days, the ability to compare databases makes it almost impossible to ensure anonymity is maintained. The Internet has created value in ourselves. We are not, after all, paying for products such as social network services, so by default connectivity has turned us all into a commodity that needs to be managed and controlled. Personal data is controlled by suppliers and government, and used by them for their benefit, rather than to solve your problems or for your benefit. As was reiterated in a privacy workshop we ran inside Windsor Castle: 'If you are not *paying* for a product, you *are* the product.'

This, combined with a growing awareness that companies are benefiting disproportionately from the collection and sale of personal information, is driving the desire for greater individual control of personal data. It has also created a dilemma: how best to balance the benefits and conveniences that open data undoubtedly provides with the desire to retain personal power and control.

Total privacy in a connected world may be an impossible goal, but there are alternative ways to use the Internet without having to sacrifice everything to corporate search engines. The IndieWeb, for example, is a set of software utilities aimed at securing individual ownership of all the information you post, including photos, status updates, blog posts, comments and so on – and all this without being cut off from the rest of the Net. It paints a vision of a world where easy-to-use open source software makes publishing possible, while keeping your own data private.

By 2025 there will be a seamless border between the digital and real world, where the digital truth becomes the real truth, suggesting that we should increase awareness of our digital shadow and become 'masters of our data'. At the same time, consumers will be more aware of the power of their personal information and therefore want more control over how it is used.[178] One suggestion is that it will be possible to retain full ownership of personal data in a machine-readable format but outsource its management and distribution to professional curators, 'privacy agents' or brokers acting as intermediaries, who will ensure that appropriate policies are maintained and, under instruction from the owner, will be prepared to trade personal data in return for benefits. Individuals will control their data (personal, identity and transactional data) and be able to selectively permit others to access it to solve problems and provide other benefits. Some will even hire 'personal information managers' who will operate in the same manner as financial advisers do today, in order to make the process easier still. Developments in authentication systems will create new personal data platforms that will utilise universally accepted credentials that can be shared with multiple brand partners for marketing purposes.

It is understandable that many citizens around the world regard the collection of personal information with deep suspicion, seeing the data flood as nothing more than, at best, state and/or commercial intrusion into their privacy.[179] However, as yet there is scant evidence that these sorts of concerns are causing a fundamental change in the way data are used and stored. Data analysts, however, should have a care: as public understanding increases, so will awareness – and therefore concerns – about privacy violation and data ownership.

The length of time that companies are able to hold on to data remains a thorny issue as, although the principle of the 'right to be forgotten' has now been established, the process is still evolving and is complicated. Some decisions – such as the removal of links to revenge porn – seem straightforward; others are not so, for example, news reports of violent crime allegedly committed by someone later acquitted. For most of us it seems the Internet has a long and unforgiving memory. This will be addressed in part through the development of services that promise to limit the time they hold data; the market for this will grow as customer awareness increases.

Of course, there are positives. The mobile Internet is doing for medicine what the printing press did for learning, giving us unprecedented control over our health care. With smartphones in hand, we are no longer beholden to an impersonal and paternalistic system in which 'doctor knows best'.[180] Computers will replace physicians for many diagnostic tasks, citizen science will give rise to citizen medicine and enormous data sets will give us new means to attack conditions that have long been incurable. Massive, open, online medicine, where diagnostics are done by Facebook-like comparisons of medical profiles, will enable real-time, real-world research on massive populations. There is no doubt the path forward will be complicated: the medical establishment will resist these changes, and digitised medicine inevitably raises serious issues surrounding privacy. Nevertheless, the result – better, cheaper and more human health care – will be worth it.

Moreover, there is of course a world beyond the familiar Google, Facebook and Amazon. The Dark Web is epitomised by the encrypted world of Tor Hidden Services, where users cannot be traced and cannot be identified. But brands and organisations will fight harder for their customers and at some point those 'going dark' may be expected to pay for the privilege. In the meantime, the mainstream Internet will certainly be a big market for privacy products, as companies attempt to limit the risk of a mass migration of their customers – they may well find that privacy itself becomes a useful marketing tool. Meanwhile, regulation has yet to catch up with the growing number of digital assets that are stored on shared servers, some in different countries to their users.

If we were given access to all our data, would we know what to do with it, and do we as citizens really understand the value of the data we share? When we talked to a number of students in different universities around the world, several suggested that in the future we might well expect to pay more for our privacy than the data we share. However, while we may see things differently in the future, and change our behaviour accordingly, other, more systematic applications of digital technologies may add alternative ways of doing things that have previously been implicit.

Digital Money

> *Cash continues to be gradually replaced by digital money, providing consumers with more convenience and choice – and organisations with lower cost transactions. Wider adoption enables new offers to proliferate.*

The sum total of money in the world is about $60trn, of which about 10 per cent is held as coins or bank notes;[181] the remaining 90 per cent is held as digital money on computer servers. The vast majority of transactions by value are executed by moving electronic data from one computer file to another, without any exchange of physical cash.

Why are people turning to digital money?[182] Mainly because it is cheaper to handle than cash: cash costs society as much as 1.5 per cent of GDP. Digital money benefits from reduced administration costs, reduced security costs and reduced costs from saving time or transportation. Enabled by the growth of mobile and fixed line networks, and underpinned by maturing technology standards and protocols, it increases financial inclusion where there is a lack of a banking and cash infrastructure. And with so many people on the move, whether through migration, in mass transit or using Uber, consumers are seeking more convenient ways to pay. In addition, it plays a huge role in cross-border commerce, which is growing faster than domestic commerce, increasing threefold to $85trn by 2025, and so will become more important and influential.

As banks and payment schemes struggle to cope with legacy technology and sometimes stifling regulation, new entrants have arrived. Square, Paypal, Stripe and their competition are aiming to reduce the cost of accepting digital money or making digital payments. AliPay and ApplePay seek to offer more convenience to consumers while increasing the firm's share of the financial transaction. The most disruptive new entrants may prove to be the crypto-currencies, for example, Bitcoin, and the associated underlying and decentralised blockchain technology.

Alongside commercial innovations, both governments and central banks are accelerating moves towards digital money, largely because of its inherent ability to carry a negative interest rate, something which it's not possible to do with cash. Additionally, it will ensure that taxes will be paid and only legal transactions will take place, putting pressure on both the informal and black economy.

Conversely, a downside of the shift to digital money has been the enormous growth in fraud. According to Nielsen, the cost of global payment card fraud reached $16 billion in 2014.[183] The theft of $450 million from Mt. Gox, the world's leading Bitcoin exchange, in 2013 provides another example of the downside potential of digital money. So, while many have hailed the 'end of cash', its death appears premature: physical money has been with us for thousands of years for a reason. It is essentially untraceable, it is easy to carry, it is widely accepted and it is reliable when the power goes out. There is, arguably, simply no alternative system of payment that is as convenient, reliable and anonymous. Libertarians are also at pains to point out the benefits of retaining economic privacy, of not having digital money transactions surveyed, of giving neither government the ability to block payments, nor central banks more power. The result, as can be seen in the USA, is that the absolute value and volume of cash in circulation has continued to grow.[184]

Looking ahead, we'll see further growth in non-traditional financial institutions seeking to control the payments interface and developing their own financial services (Amazon Payments, Amazon Lending Programme) and retail offers (Alibaba, Google Shopping). To enable this, there is also likely to be further collaboration between organisations (device manufacturers, telecoms players, industry associations, banks, Google and co). There will also be growth in alternative currencies and money networks, and the first state-issued flat digital currencies.

In the next decade, consumers will continue to choose digital or contactless payment over cash; digital wallets will start to eclipse the physical wallet. Checkouts will move from place to device, as payments continue to shift from an active to a passive process (as exists today in paying for your Uber ride). To combat fraud, and keep transactions simple and safe, multi-factor authentication will become the norm (for example, growth in real time geo-tagging, biometrics and tokenisation), with more appropriately authenticated transactions taking place.

Cold hard cash will not disappear completely any time soon, but the wider availability of digital money has the capability to bring about increased socio-economic mobility, increase the ability for itinerant workers to live and work in a new country, and enable millions more people to be financially included within ten years. Accelerating at different speeds across varied regions, the associated changes in our relationship with money may well add an extra, deeper social change over the next decade.

Education Revolution

> *Broader access to improved education acts as a major catalyst for empowerment, sustained economic growth, overcoming inequality and reducing conflict. We need an education system fit for the digital revolution.*

Another area seen as ripe for digital transformation is how we learn. The current education system is increasingly seen as being outdated, having been designed to fit the needs of the last century – or even the one before.[185] In schools and institutions across the world questions are being asked about how to make education fit for purpose, from both a supply and a demand perspective. On the supply side, the problem is around quality and quantity; there is a global shortage of qualified teachers and those who are in the profession are often obliged to deliver an inflexible curriculum with an over-dependency on exams not fit for purpose. On the demand side, students are often underqualified in the core social skills required for later life and ill-prepared to adapt to a more flexible and analytical professional environment. The shift from factual learning to learning how to work on projects and better meet the future business environment is an issue frequently raised, providing both a challenge and an opportunity for change.

It is no surprise that getting every school, and ideally every child, connected to online resources is a high-profile ambition for many. Whether via technology firms like Google and Facebook (using balloons and other solutions to provide connectivity to remote areas), or governments investing in fixed and mobile broadband infrastructures, the opportunity for every child to have access to the world's information is a pivotal and potentially transformational shift. Yes, some will get left behind at first, but the digital divide will, it is argued, be reduced and sometime in the next decade every school should be connected.

While Internet connectivity has a major role to play, many are also focused on fixing some of the basics, believing that although technology can help improve education it is not a silver bullet. It should be integrated with traditional education techniques which allow young people to develop holistically and become responsible citizens. Moreover, in order to achieve widespread success, all teaching approaches have to be sustainable, replicable and scalable.

Foremost in terms of global impact is tackling the access challenge. Improving quality and access to education is seen as a common need in many countries and not just developing ones. In several Western countries the imperative to engage more students in better education is seen as pivotal in mitigating the risk of a disenfranchised next generation. Not surprisingly, universal support for enhancing female education is growing and getting input, from the UN and governments through to foundations and NGOs.[186] The social, economic and political benefits of making sure girls get the same opportunities as boys is driving a host of initiatives. Some are addressing basic needs (making sure that girls make it through to secondary education) and this means not just supporting the cultural shift of valuing daughters as much as sons but also in providing sanitation – the lack of toilets is still highlighted as a reason why so many girls stop going to school when they reach puberty.[187] In other areas the net benefit of reducing population growth by delaying the age of having children is seen as directly linked to supporting girls in education for longer.

Across most parts of Africa, India and Asia there is a strong movement supporting better access to education as a means of helping to empower and enable people to drive progress. Improving the level to which children are educated means they become more economically productive and so live better lives. But it can also help societies to have more informed views and so hopefully reduce conflict and inequality. Within this context, in some regions we also need to address other basics. Inequality in many education systems may continue until common standards are adopted across all schools, both public and private.

The delivery of education also faces upheaval, and using practices from outside education will completely revolutionise the experience. If we can give every child access to the best content, whether delivered via a MOOC (massive open online course) or curated YouTube videos, then we are no longer dependent on a teacher transferring standardised knowledge in largely the same way as 300 years ago. Why provide average face-to-face teaching when everyone has access to the Massachusetts Institute of Technology (MIT)?[188] For some this becomes an extreme of children being enabled to self-learn, remote from teachers and via peer-to-peer networks, while for others it's an opportunity to reinvent the way children learn – and how teachers teach, to decouple them from content delivery. If learning can be project-based rather than about pure content acquisition, then not only are we better prepared for the real world but also the role of teachers changes to being coaches, mentors and catalysts for change. And if *everything* you need to know will be available online, it is vital that there are ways of filtering and curating this overwhelming wealth of information in a way that is simple, intuitive and valuable – a natural role for teachers. Whether online in the Cloud or in schools physically, many see this freeing up of teachers as one way of addressing the supply–demand imbalance. The reality for the next decade will probably be a hybrid of face-to-face and online learning, but a change in the nature of education is underway.

Additionally, as we enter a world where education for many does not stop at graduation, it is thought of as an increasingly non-linear process, a lifelong activity where skills and knowledge are updated and upgraded both formally and informally throughout a working life. We may also move from placing all the value on IQ to a system that values emotional intelligence and learning from risk-taking, innovation and entrepreneurship. If we are to have a smoother transition from education to work, then maybe we need to make education more aligned with the future of work.

In some select schools, new approaches are in development or have even been put in practice, but by 2025 few believe that we will have changed the whole system at a national, never mind global, level. There will be pockets of innovation around the world, testing, enhancing and so proving the new approaches. If we can crack the access challenge and so give every child greater opportunity, then the potential to turn the dial on how and what we learn is certainly on the cards for the next decade.

Mass Engagement

> *As the public voice becomes easier to access and harder to suppress, leaders seek to engage, develop, secure and maintain legitimacy for their initiatives and policies – so further reducing their hierarchical power.*

Ever since homo sapiens first appeared some 200,000 years ago, communication and engagement styles have continued to evolve. When we lived in small groups, one-to-one communication and gossip was enough. The agricultural and industrial revolutions enabled larger groups to form – from organisations to cities and countries. Leaders, and those in or wanting to keep power, needed to be able to speak to, and often control, the masses. To do this, broadcast media developed: from town criers, to, following the invention of the printing press, pamphlets, books and newspapers, to radio, TV and now to the digital era. Adjacent to this has been an evolution of engagement. In the past, engagement rarely happened on a mass basis, it was atomised (for example, writing a letter to a newspaper, which may or may not be published). The mass engagement that did exist was typically limited by geographical access (that is, the ability to join a meeting, a protest, a march) or through physically collated initiatives (for example, petitions).

In the digital world the rules have changed. From a Tweet or Facebook post, to joining a campaign orchestrated by Change.org[189] or 38Degrees[190] ('38 degrees is the angle at which snowflakes come together to form an avalanche – together, we are unstoppable') or a charity, mass engagement has become easier. It has enabled dispersed individuals and communities to engage and ensure their presence is heard and felt. Digital engagement can easily be made public, visible to a large audience and no longer limited to those present. Further, as the transaction cost of engagement has continued to fall, engagement can now occur on micro as well as macro issues (such as enabling the Arab Spring).

The power dynamic has shifted, placing power in the hands of everyone. As a result, in this digital era where the public voice is easier to access and tougher to suppress, it becomes harder to generate support for new initiatives without taking first public views into account. Those in power are more easily held to account and less in control of the message. Their hierarchical power is weakened. So to create, develop, secure and maintain legitimacy for their initiatives and policies, leaders in all fields will need to engage to maintain public and political support.

It is worth noting that digital mass engagement varies widely across a number of dimensions. It can occur at a transactional (for example, join X) or a conversational (for example, what do you think about Y? Which direction should be taken?) level. It can also be active (for example, here is my input on X) or passive (for example, I allow you to access data on my location to help build a better understanding of, say, travel within a city). The strength of engagement can also vary (for example, a 'like' on Facebook or a 'follow' on Twitter or WeChat vs signing a petition to a government or making a donation on JustGiving). Leading brands are now shifting from measuring exposure and impressions to 'expressions'.[191]

In his book *Trust Me, PR is Dead*, Robert Phillips, the former president and CEO Europe, Middle East and Africa of PR firm Edelman, argues that centralised communications can no longer be a fig-leaf on trust or a cover for the real actions of leaders. As Phillips writes, 'In an age of individual empowerment, power is shifting from state to cities; employer to employee; corporation to citizen-consumer. Power and influence have become asymmetrical. Trust is forever fragile and attempts at control futile'.[192] Managing the message simply won't work in today's complex and interconnected world. Or, as Margaret Hefferman puts it, for organisations, 'Instead of talking themselves up, companies should just start doing the right thing – for real. Employ people on decent wages. Eschew stupid bonuses. Pay taxes. Care about customers. Listen. Share ownership. Stop spinning. Don't say you will – do it for real. Trust isn't a message; it's an outcome and the only way to win it is to earn it.'[193]

In this world, leaders may need to move beyond politics, profit maximisation and adherence to top-down hierarchies and centralised communication. Embracing mass engagement by providing citizens and consumers with the opportunity to participate in decisions enables different, better, more understood solutions to be envisaged and created, going beyond top-down, orchestrated answers. Different approaches to business and politics, adapted for this era, will need to emerge.[194] 'In this era of social and mobile technology, customers, employees, suppliers and partners are in direct communication with one another. Those personal networks, and the brands they're passionate about, influence their decision-making and their spending.'[195]

These new forms of digital mass engagement may also facilitate faster change (for example, cultural change within a population[196]) and enable new ways for research to be carried out (for example, citizen science projects). Of course, digital mass engagement is not a panacea. Micro-failings, mistakes or miscommunication may have consequences blown out of all proportion[197] and there are examples where the speed and scale of engagement are unwarranted, misplaced or misused.

Going forward it is clear that leaders and initiatives will be more easily and more readily held to account, and will need to maintain popular support in order to retain legitimacy with their audience. Autocratic leadership will become harder to sustain. There is likely to be an increase in demand for and occurrence of public engagement (for example, referenda and single-issue votes such as that for the UK to leave the EU) or vested party participation and interference (for example, shareholder activism).

More mass engagement is likely to require an increased willingness and ability of all parties to enter into sustained dialogue, and may also lead to a growth in trusted and validated networks for mass engagement to protect against fraud. It will also need to actively design and cater for those who are not engaged or who are left behind (for example, those on the wrong side of the digital divide).

Caring for Those Left Behind

Although significant progress has been made, positive change has limited reach. Millions of people continue to be left behind mainstream progress, especially the young, the poor and those who are disadvantaged.

Progress has always been a pretty bumpy journey; the next ten years looks as if little will be done to improve the ride. Although for some, access to better medicine, education and employment will be transformational; for others, life will just get worse. It may also *feel* worse as the chasm between the haves and the have-nots is widening, and some expect that it will become progressively difficult for anyone to hear the voices of those left behind.

Consider the plight of the children who stay in the countryside while their parents head to the city. In China, where more than 270 million people have left their villages to look for work, they are named *liushou ertong*, or left-behind children. According to the All-China Women's Federation,[198] there are around 61 million of them, only 10 million less that the total child population of the USA. China is not the only country whose children suffer as a result of urbanisation, but given the one child policy, and its enormously distorted sex ratio, this mass abandonment may fundamentally alter an entire generation.

Not that there is a significant 'urban advantage' for the poor living in informal townships; UN Habitat estimates that one in six people in the world lives in deprivation in urban slums and squatter settlements.[199] Given the demographics of poor countries and communities, with their relatively high numbers of children, we can estimate that one out of every four children in the world currently lives in urban poverty. As more people migrate, the chances are this number will grow. Slum children's lives are frequently challenged from the get-go. Their parents are often unable to register their births, limiting their access to basic services, like education and health. Reliant on the informal economy, many poor urban households are also obliged to push their children into labour.

On the surface, things look a bit better in the countryside, but not by much. In many cases farming productivity is pretty woeful; in India, roughly half the population – 600 million people – depend upon growing crops or rearing animals to survive. Volatile prices, poor access to markets, outdated regulation, limited access to finance and stringent land ownership rules all combine to make it almost impossible for many to earn a reasonable wage. Low productivity is a bigger long-term problem. One cause of this is the shrinking size of cultivated plots; as India's population expands, the average plot size has fallen from nearly 2.3 hectares (5.7 acres) in 1970 to less than 1.2 hectares today. Oxfam states that 216 million people – a quarter of rural India's population – live below the poverty line.[200]

A search for a better way of life for a population of this magnitude is never going to be possible via migration to the cities so, looking ahead, many see that much could be done to improve the lot of farmers. The high rate of suicides among Indian farmers has already drawn widespread media attention, and it is believed that an overhaul of regulation would help. Current restrictions on the storage of commodities such as onions and wheat actively discourage farmers from investing in cold storage and warehouses; leasing land is famously hard, since strong tenancy rights discourage owners from renting out fields; state marketing boards restrict trade in fruit and vegetables, often making it easier for traders to import from abroad.

In addition to advocating a regulatory review, some point out that small changes could make fundamental differences. In Bangalore, for example, only those who have no other choice become truck drivers – which explains why there are so many road accidents. The International Road Assessment Programme[201] estimates that, in India, there are 76,000 deaths and serious injuries every year, with most casualties being male and under 30. Often the breadwinner, their deaths have a huge emotional and financial toll, plunging families into generations of poverty and costing the government around US$ 2.8 billion. Licensing and improving the working conditions of drivers would, it is argued, make a difference. In towns, giving pedestrians a safe place to walk would help too.

You do not have to be poor, and living in an emerging economy, to slip through the system. Rich countries face challenges too, not least in the care of their mentally ill. This accounts for more suffering and premature deaths than heart disease and strokes put together, or than cancer; in many nations it costs around three to four per cent of GDP in treatment and lost productivity. Some argue that the USA in particular is ill-prepared to cope, leaving prisons and police officers to deal with the effects of untreated mental illness. However, across Europe, 40–70 per cent of prison inmates are also mentally ill. In the developed world, the WHO estimates that only about half of all people with depression are diagnosed and treated.[202]

Because of the heightened attention now being given to the impacts of urbanisation, rural need and mental illnesses, there are indications that change is on its way. The UN has already declared 2011–20 the Decade of Action for Road Safety and the one of the new SDGs includes an ambitious target to halve road deaths by 2020. Governments are becoming more proactively involved, while small donors make a sizeable difference. Indeed their contributions vastly outweigh those of billionaire philanthropists and their foundations, although the Gates Foundation in particular has done a lot to reduce child mortality and improve agricultural activity. Around 200 countries have approved the WHO's Mental Health Action Plan, calling for better treatment by 2020. In the UK, the NHS has pledged to invest more than £1bn a year by 2020 to help more than a million extra people with mental health problems. Within the corporate world, companies are adding mental illness to their diversity initiative, with Accenture recently launching its Mental Health Allies programme.

And yet, the most telling moment in any workshop is often the casual comment just before a coffee break. On one such occasion a well-meaning participant observed that nothing would change over the next decade because mostly bad things happen to poor people or to those living on the peripheries. Too comfortable and too distant from the reality of others' lives, many of the well-off are unprepared to sacrifice their high quality of life to change the status quo. No one disagreed. Let us hope they are wrong.

Conclusion: Still Being Stupid?

Despite a better understanding of the long-term challenges we face, we – individually and collectively – continue to make decisions that may make sense in the short term, but do not lead to better longer term consequences.

What, then, are the disasters we are trying to avoid? The climate change challenge, cyber attacks, geopolitical instability, water crises, food shortages, constrained economic growth, weaker societal cohesion, increased security risks, the global refugee crisis and the threat of nuclear attack – none of these is a new issue. As a society we have long known that we are teetering on the brink of potential global disaster, yet despite this, and despite the wealth of innovation, technology prowess and sheer talent at our disposal, we seem incapable of doing anything about it. Why?

One reason may be the sheer size and complexity of the problems we face and the need for extensive collaboration to drive change, not to mention the need for huge investment. There is also the need for time for solutions to take effect, with the possibility of extreme change/disruption if left unresolved. Some say that we are already too late to crack the problem, or that the correction needed would require too significant a change from our current way of life, so corrective traction will never willingly occur. Others are even more direct, pointing out that many of the challenges we face need to be addressed in corners of the world that simply do not have the necessary infrastructure to deal with the problem, are too poor to carry much weight on the global stage, and so find it hard to get the necessary support. Sometimes consumer/citizen awareness is robust, but there is a belief that nothing can be done – many believe that disease, hunger and poverty will always be with us, for example.

Collectively, it seems we lack understanding of the complex nature of the issues, we disagree on how to address them and, even if we do achieve consensus, we struggle with capacity-building to do anything impactful. In addition, we have little or no global coordination, few frameworks and regulation often behind the curve. Our institutions such as the World Economic Forum, the UN and WHO work hard to make a difference and are successful at maintaining awareness, but they are unwieldy, consensus-driven and usually have to follow the path of least resistance to achieve anything. Often their actions are in response to a crisis, not because they were not aware of impending problems but simply because they cannot get political traction for things that might not happen for a while, or indeed might not happen at all. The recent Ebola crisis and the current migration crisis in Europe are both good examples of how, despite previous warnings, the global community failed to act in time to avert disaster.

Avoiding catastrophe requires swift, collective action. It needs 'whole party' participation with new corporate forms and multi-capital success measures that genuinely value people, society and nature alongside traditional assets. Also needed is a shift in perception where humans become more connected to nature, social development and legacy thinking as well as focused social movements, such as the emerging fossil fuel divestment activity today.[203] While there is a vast array of all of the above in place already, at the time of writing this does not seem to be enough. As was stated in many different countries, we need to start to behave as conscious stewards.

Chapter 7

CHALLENGE 6:
Future Business

By 2025, organisations driven solely by profit will not be sustainable. How will they evolve to address new challenges, develop opportunities and contribute to society?

- Speed-to-scale
- Companies with purpose
- The value of data
- Dynamic pricing
- Creative economy
- Sometimes nomads

- Autonomous vehicles
- Optimising last-mile delivery
- Organisation 3.0
- Deeper collaboration

An optimist would say that business is entering a time of unparalleled prospects; opportunities are growing, while obstacles decline. Markets are opening up in all corners of the globe almost as fast as technology is unlocking new doors, while at the same time a widening pool of talent is emerging to supply not just new ideas and stimuli but an increasingly able workforce. What is more, individual governments, with their outdated ideas about taxation and regulation, are no longer the major force they once were. Economies are freer. All of this combined makes it a golden time for businesses.

A pessimist, on the other hand, would retort that business is in trouble. The shutters are coming down; those holding the purse strings are tightening them. Complicated trade agreements and fractious international relationships are driving a wedge between companies and those who want to use their products and services. Worse, many people are now so distrustful of large corporations that they are returning to local markets and other off-line enterprises. New technology, far from delivering a pot of gold, simply wipes out margins and bottom-line profits. Add to this the growing lack of skilled workers, endless regulation, increasing cost of production – not to mention the unsettling gulf between rich and poor – and we are witnessing the death throes of traditional business practice. Whatever's next?

Companies with Purpose

As trust in 'business' declines, the structures and practices of large corporations are under scrutiny. Businesses come under greater pressure to improve performance on environmental, social and governance issues.

The truth, of course, lies somewhere in between. The Internet and, more recently, innovations around production and delivery are not only changing business models, but they are also driving fundamental change in business philosophy. It is time for the corporate world to adapt.

Like it or not, success is currently judged by return on investment, particularly by the financial institutions which are unlikely to risk funds without being confident of good monetary rewards. The same can be said of executives – many of them paid in stock options incentivising them to extract financial value, sometimes at the expense of, rather than the betterment of, the wider community. But as awareness of this grows, and the increasingly excessive salaries of some turn the spotlight on the expanding inequality gap, the view that businesses should do more for their money, for example by improving their performance on environmental, social and governance issues, is growing.

One way to achieve this is for companies to adopt a broader definition of success, a better balance between short- and long-term profits and increased social involvement. Far from being philanthropic, this pragmatic shift is motivated by growing pressure from a connected, networked and informed community using its collective voice to influence and drive change. Growing political support for this is encouraging regulatory shifts intent on blurring the boundaries between organisations and society. Companies such as Puma, Patagonia, Lego and Unilever are already actively pursuing strategies around climate change, social innovation and corporate responsibility, but change needs to go further than action by individual organisations. There is a growing consensus that fundamental issues around societal and environmental stress, resource constraints, forced migration and urbanisation means that commercial organisations can no longer stand aside and let governments and NGOs deal with the problems on their own. In order to prosper, business will have to be prepared to take greater responsibility and support the wider community.

Some organisations will need to work hard to rebuild public trust, sorely tested in recent years. Successful demands for greater corporate transparency mean that NGO and media campaigns have been able to raise concerns across a variety of issues, from executive pay, supply chain anomalies and environmental abuse, to the political influence of global organisations. They have also played a strong role in galvanising public response to the steady stream of high-profile incidences of corporate tax avoidance (Starbucks, Google and Facebook) as companies aggressively manage their tax affairs. Accountants and CFOs (chief financial officers) can no longer claim that non-payment of tax is merely 'efficient' and expect public support. Indeed, in some countries, such is the public outcry (and government need) that the OECD has already taken action to develop an agreement on rules against complex tax avoidance.[204] The EU is potentially following suit – but how quickly change may come is still unclear. At the very least, new reporting and transparency procedures will lead to significant changes in the systems within which many companies currently operate. Wider consumer awareness and the assimilation of different working models will continue to influence this.

Disgruntlement at some corporate behaviour has also seen the birth of the Social Enterprise movement. Organisations such as B Corp are providing a process and certification for benefit companies or companies with a purpose (that is, B Corp is to business what Fair Trade certification is to coffee). Started in the USA, B Corp was launched in Europe in 2015. While many benefit companies are small, the influence of the approach is being felt in wider business, and organisations focused on delivering community value are on the increase – by 2016, 10,000 community interest companies were registered in the UK.

In addition to identifying and creating business value out of solving social problems, there is a call for longer-term thinking around the creation of value. Unilever's progressive move away from quarterly reporting in 2011 has not yet been widely copied, but it appears not to have harmed the value of a business. Furthermore, large listed companies with dispersed shareholders may well want to debate whether the concept of growth, traditionally defined by rising profits, is enough; or whether consideration should be given to how 'shared value' will not only provide a sense of collective purpose, but can be developed as part of a corporate strategy that drives profits while having a societal benefit. With this in mind, global business organisations such as the World Business Council for Sustainable Development (WBCSD) are already transforming the UN SDGs into a framework for action and a number of corporates are using them to help transform their approach; Unilever, for example, states its purpose to be 'to make sustainable living commonplace'.

The changing geopolitical environment is also testing established business models. Overall, Western markets are weakening compared to the new opportunities from emerging economies. Asian countries, benefiting from a youthful workforce and rising middle class, are beginning to influence world trade and play a greater role on the diplomatic stage. Most organisations in Africa and South America have yet to make a significant impact but it won't be long before they do. With a wealth of natural resources at their disposal, we should see change in the next ten years. Look out for established African companies such as SAB Miller, BHP Billiton and Anglo American being joined on the world stage by the likes of the First Bank of Nigeria, Dimension Data and Orascom Group.

Globally, partially as a result of the balance-of-power reshuffle, and because the incumbent powers have been lackadaisical in their support, it looks like the structures set up in the wake of the Second World War to support global business may no longer be fit for purpose, and many are lobbying for institutions such as the World Trade Organization to be restructured. As the US appetite to act as overall arbiter diminishes and Europe faces its own constitutional challenges, change is in the air.

Given the transitions we are beginning to see, national, corporate and individual loyalties will shift and influence the way that markets react to each other. Like-minded people are connecting online and building new networks that extend well beyond national borders. New currencies and different payment platforms are beginning to challenge seemingly invincible institutions, the third-party intermediaries in particular. Goods will always need to be designed, built, bought, sold and moved from one place to another, but new alliances are developing and old associations are becoming less relevant.

In order to address this, a number of international organisations and NGOs are keen to adopt a global consensus around how business practices should develop, in the belief that better collaboration will help to accelerate positive change – the success of many of the UN MDGs is testament to this. But as we see an increase in protectionism between nations, increasing fragmentation and inequality shaping the geopolitical environment, some fear that that the appetite for consensual behaviour is weakening, to be replaced with greater division, little real alignment around goals and the corporate focus reverting to short-term growth. There is an irony in this, given that we now live in a world that is more interconnected than ever before.

Speed-to-Scale

Greater global connectivity, growing consumer wealth and broader reach all combine to accelerate the time to gain a billion customers and a $10bn valuation for start-ups and new corporate ventures alike.

Looking ahead, as we move from 4.5 billion to 7 billion mobile phone users and reach 99 per cent connectivity globally, many are expecting multiple new industry disruptions (first Napster, now Airbnb and Uber) to occur. Whether in banking, retail, logistics or transport, the ability to use data analytics and ubiquitous connectivity in different ways is driving a plethora of new business models, most based on achieving scale quickly. Reaching 100,000 customers within the first year is increasingly considered to be conservative. Why not 1 million, 10 million or even 100 million?

But is this realistic? How quickly are we speeding up and what levels of scale are credible? In the first decades of the 21st century we have seen that the iPod, launched in 2001, took 12 years to reach 500 million users; Gmail, launched in 2005, took seven; and Facebook and Twitter both took six years. Following the launch of the iPad in 2010, though, it took only three years for the tablet user base to reach 500 million. For some, this acceleration is down to the fact that the global Internet infrastructure is now largely in place and so a major barrier to scale has been removed; others argue that with far greater competition and multiple new businesses being launched, the achievement of reaching 500 million users is no mean feat. If it was simply down to connectivity, then by now surely Skype would have surpassed its 300 million active user figure, Tumblr would be over its 420 million and LinkedIn would have exceeded its 400 million current user base. Yes, there is the access issue – but there is also the all-important proposition and support.

In terms of financial support, a common theme in the investor community is associated with the signals from so called 'unicorns' – start-ups whose value exceeds $1bn.[205] Some are questioning whether we are in a second Internet bubble and so are seeing inflated valuations, but others suggest that the speed at which such valuations are being achieved is another indicator of how quickly scale is possible for the right proposition. Certainly, the number of start-ups hitting the $1bn threshold is rising. In 2011/12 there were 17, including the likes of Square, Spotify, Dropbox, Evernote, Pinterest and Airbnb; within the following two years there were more than 70.

Looking beyond the unicorns to 'decacorns' – companies valued at more than $10 billion – we can again see strong evidence of acceleration. Elon Musk's Space X was founded in 2002 and has taken 13 years to reach a $10bn valuation; both Dropbox and Flipkart were founded in 2007 and went on to reach the $10bn threshold within eight years. The following year saw the launch of Pinterest and Airbnb, which hit $10bn valuation seven and six years later respectively. Launched in 2009, Uber got to the same point within five years and, more recently, Chinese electronic company Xiaomi rocketed ahead to become the world's fourth largest smartphone manufacturer and hit a $10bn valuation within three years of its 2010 launch – an achievement only matched by Snapchat, launched in 2011.

What makes this escalating speed-to-scale so significant for some is that the physical size of the organisations seems to have been decoupled from their reach and value – there is no longer a link between size, most often seen as number of employees or other resources, and scale. Whereas Uber has nearly 200,000 contractor drivers in its ecosystem, it actually employs fewer than 4,000 people; Airbnb has only 1,600 employees. Corresponding valuation-to-headcount ratios have been spiralling (Figure 37). Consider: a successful company like Nike has 44,000 employees and is worth more than $110 billion, so it has a ratio of $2.5m per employee; Microsoft, by comparison, comes in at just under $4m per employee. In the lead today is Snapchat; with only 300 employees and a 2015 valuation of $15bn, it has a valuation-to-headcount ratio of $50m, double that of Facebook, Airbnb, Pinterest and Uber, five times the likes of Google, more than ten times that Microsoft and 20 times that of Nike.[206] Many are questioning whether this can be sustained.

In the past, value was largely linked to a combination of brand and tangible assets such as resources and facilities. Recently, as the speed at which companies can scale has risen exponentially, the valuation of some companies has become increasingly linked to intangibles. Equally, for established companies, creating new ventures at a significant scale is no longer a decade-long target. In Mumbai, the conglomerate Reliance Industries created a new company, Reliance Jio, a mobile and fixed telecom business, launched in December 2015 with the aim of having 100 million customers within 100 days.[207] Based in the same city, Tata Group's 2025 ambition is to be in the top 25 companies globally by market capitalisation, and to reach 25 per cent of the world's population.[208] Already India's most valuable group and accounting for 8 per cent of the Bombay Stock Exchange's total market capitalisation, that means doubling its current value and adding 1.1 billion new customers within 10 years.

Looking ahead, we might see a world where many of its most valuable companies are maybe less than ten years old (Figure 38). The top 20 may have an average age of 20.

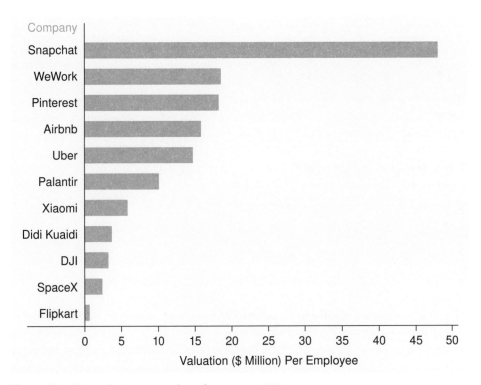

Figure 37: Highest valuation per employee for start-ups, 2015.
(Source: Forbes)

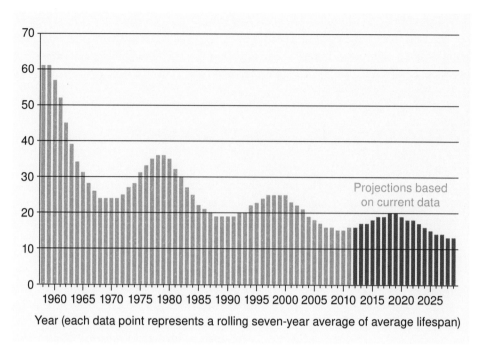

Year (each data point represents a rolling seven-year average of average lifespan)

Figure 38: Average company lifespan on S&P500.
(Source: Innosight)

By comparison, today the top ten companies are, on average, 75 years old. While this includes Google (17 years old), the Industrial and Commercial Bank of China (ICBC) (31), Apple (39) and Microsoft (40), it also has companies such as Wells Fargo, Johnson and Johnson, Exxon Mobil and Novartis, some of which go back up to 160 years. Whether making it to $100bn or just $1bn, what is clear is that we are living in an era of faster scaling, where the case studies need rewriting every year and where new data-driven models have upended the traditional rules for company growth.

The Value of Data

As organisations try to retain as much information about their customers as possible, data become a currency with a value and a price. It therefore requires a marketplace where anything that is information is represented.

For many companies, customer understanding and easy access to market is key to growth; this is why data have now become the new raw material for business, with an economic input almost on a par with capital and labour. As the capabilities of digital devices soar, and prices plummet, it is becoming progressively easier to collect and store information and use powerful algorithms and analytical tools to create meaning and add value. People and connected objects will soon generate tens of trillions of gigabytes of data which will reveal things about us, and the objects around us, that were previously unknown – and unknowable. This is transformational for every sector, with innovations in productivity, improved health-care delivery and environmental savings all bringing efficiencies and cost savings, but also entirely new service possibilities.[209]

In this land grab for information, it may also be worth noting that what is technologically possible may not be culturally acceptable. To retain trust, business and regulators need to be careful about how they manage the data they gather, creating a new legal understanding of the balance between the right to privacy and the use of data for the public good. Different countries have different standards of what data counts as personal information; Germany, for example, forbids marketing to specific ethnic groups, but the USA does not. Unravelling this – creating consensus around what information is and is not appropriate to share – will be the key to unlocking the promise of big data.

Looking ahead, the health-care industry will have to be particularly alert to public sentiment. Big data sets may help both companies and researchers synthesise patient information to allow for a more targeted approach for new drugs and diagnostics, but they could also give insurers the chance to trawl through personal information, thereby identifying tomorrow's cancer patients or accident victims. How to maintain public confidence will be key. To address this, should governments be encouraged to take the same approach as many have done for their organ donation programmes? Will citizens have to proactively opt out of sharing their personal information, rather than automatically being opted in to do it? This would make it possible for health data to be shared for the common good. Public and private data sets could be aligned in order to provide a holistic view of the individual and, at the same time, feed in to giant databases exploring key areas of significance, such as global epidemics and population flows.

To fully exploit its potential, business and government will have to tread carefully to establish an understanding of, and create a balance between, the social benefits of aggregated information and individual or corporate privacy. Data marketplaces will help to achieve this and may well become established in many sectors, allowing individuals or, indeed, their appointed advisers, to buy and sell personal data. The focus will not necessarily be about privacy but about building a collective understanding of products and outcomes – a shift in favour of the consumer. Businesses may have to get used to the idea that in the future they will have to pay for information once gathered for free. Equally, they may well find that what was previously proprietary data becomes free and open to enable shared systems to interact. Properly managed, a market will increase the value of data, using financial models that, in turn, encourage further sharing. A marketplace will also allow existing information silos to be connected via trusted third parties able to unify, mine and discover new insights.

However, maximising the opportunity that big data analytics presents will be a slow and uphill task. Some consider that personal data is already being over-exploited;

this is where the thin ribbon of trust between consumers and business is stretched. Organisations already have an abundance of information about consumers and are equipped with the necessary mechanisms to interrogate it, while consumers suffer information scarcity and possess few tools to make any sense of their own data, let alone look in the context of others.[210] The World Wide Web Foundation 2014–15 Web Index, an annual report measuring the Web's contribution to social, economic and political progress, highlights this imbalance: 'We stand at a crossroads between a Web "for everyone" – one that enables all people around the world to improve their life chances and reduces inequalities both between and within countries – and a "winner takes all" Web that further concentrates wealth and political power in the hands of a few.'

The key to all of this is to give consumers both the ability to understand how their personal information is being used and the right for them to refuse others access to it if they so choose. In 2015 the value of one person's annual data – if taken as being the same as Google's ARPU (average revenue per user) – was around $45. As technological efficiencies become more mainstream, the next decade will see a change in how business reacts to the desire for greater transparency. Supported by an overlay of predictive analytics, flexible business models and more data, better matching supply-and-demand and improving yield is becoming possible in a host of new areas. While standard profit maximisation will remain a primary driver, this also has the capability to help improve resource utilisation, reduce waste and optimise system efficiencies. For the consumer, this allows greater choice, while for business, margins and yields will increase as automated algorithms optimise pretty much everything.

Dynamic Pricing

> *The algorithms of Amazon and Uber cross over to affect more businesses, from energy use to parking. Real-time transparency allows better purchasing, at the same time as margins and yields are automatically enhanced.*

Today, perhaps the area where most of us have experienced value optimisation most directly is in booking flights; dynamic pricing is all the rage in the online travel industry. Using Expedia, we see a host of different fares and choose the one we want, only to find that the cost has changed when we return to the site a few minutes later. On their own websites, airlines, and especially low-cost flyers, track the IP address you are using and use that to nudge prices at the key moment in the booking process. As we found out, you can get round this, if you use a VPN (virtual private network) app. You can obtain different prices for the same flights just by looking at websites pointing at different countries. Expedia.com can be half the price of Expedia.co.uk for exactly the same flight. The same principles are true in the hotel sector, although less obvious.

Less well known, but more widespread, is the way that companies like Amazon have embraced dynamic pricing in a big way. Not only does the company alter its prices more than 2.5 million times a day, but it also changes the price of around 20 per cent of its total inventory every 24 hours. Wal-Mart can, by comparison, currently only change the price of 50,000 products per month. As well as, allegedly, showing higher prices to Mac users than PC users, Amazon monitors customers' behaviours to determine the best time to raise or lower prices to get the sale, and amend prices by what else is already in a customer's basket.

Currently only a few companies have the ability to combine data collection and analytics in such a way, but others – so-called pure-play analytics companies – are providing the capabilities across the board with the aim of benefiting both consumers and suppliers. For example, Qcue focuses on providing analytics for pricing of sports events; ticket prices may be adjusted on a real-time basis, either upwards or downwards, based on market demand. Rather than having a set price, tickets for less popular games drop in response to demand, while those for others rise, allowing the teams to fill their stadium to capacity.[211]

Transit systems are also increasingly connected and will soon be able to use variable pricing via apps to nudge users onto, for example, the next train to decrease congestion. In several cities, smart parking is being rolled out. Following successful pilots in San Francisco, parking rates are altered in real-time with the objective of keeping parking areas 60 to 80 per cent full. Rates are adjusted by time and location with the aim of offering the lowest possible hourly rates, but keeping them high enough to make sure that there is always a free space.

However, in the transport area, it is Uber that has, somewhat controversially, been one of the major adopters of dynamic pricing. Uber is, at one level, simply another Internet marketplace where prices vary against demand – just as on Airbnb and Google's Adwords platform. Changing the price of a fare to be more competitive than the competition is evidently a core part of the value proposition. The more contentious area is in the use of surge pricing.[212] At peak times, when there are more potential passengers than available Uber cars, the company's algorithms change prices to better match supply and demand. Prices go up so that more of the freelance drivers are incentivised to be on the roads and available for passengers. The balance is in having the prices high enough to attract the drivers without alienating customers; the real-time analytics that sit behind the system are key to maintaining this. Economists term this 'responsiveness to price elasticity' but Uber is pushing the dial around how behaviour changes can be orchestrated. When Uber first tested dynamic pricing in Boston in 2012, it was able to increase on the road supply of drivers by 70 to 80 per cent. Clearly there is a push back from some customers as well as from competitors who have fixed rates, but for most users, paying extra at peak times for a guaranteed car is part of the trade-off.

Moving forward, many expect that more companies, keen to optimise their business models and revenue models, will therefore further embrace dynamic pricing. For some it is clearly all about profit maximisation, but for others it is just as much about resource utilisation and sharing. While the airlines and retailers will seek to make an extra penny wherever they can, the advent of smart grids in the energy sector provide an opportunity for more socially beneficial applications. The past few years have seen dynamic pricing technologies evolve and be tested by suppliers keen to maximise profits, but smart meters connected to distributed renewable energy systems will be where the greatest overall impact is experienced.

Organisation 3.0

> *New forms of flatter, project-based, collaborative, virtual, informal organisations dominate – enabled by technology and a mobile workforce. As such, the nature of work and the role of the organisation blurs.*

Returning to the bigger picture, composed of individuals all striving for broadly the same end goal, organisations exist because they can achieve more with people working collectively than separately. Historically, the dominant organisational structure has been one of bureaucratic command and control, based on a hierarchy from shareholder owners at the top through to the board of directors, executives and then finally the workers. This has worked pretty well but recently, fuelled by changing worker attitudes and enabled by communication technology, alternative organisational structures have appeared. Middle management has been brushed aside in an attempt to reduce costs and improve efficiencies; devolving authority, decision-making and action has encouraged staff motivation. The old ways of working are simply too rigid for the millennial generation; these days, the knowledge economy, with its focus on intellectual capital, means that command-and-control techniques are viewed as counterproductive to creativity.

The idea is that knowledge workers are better able to create and leverage information through collaborating in small and agile self-directed teams.[213] Sometimes these exist in a virtual capacity only, as so many people now work remotely or are based in different countries – a recent survey by Steelcase, a furniture manufacturer and consultancy, suggests that the best way to ensure that employees remain engaged is to give them control of when and where they work. This necessitates flexibility.

Organisations now following this model, such as IBM and GE, talk about being 'flat' and allowing the legitimate valuation of multiple skills, types of knowledge or working styles without privileging one over the other. Despite their size, these organisations are generally viewed as exemplars of how established players can adapt to changing market conditions and become nimbler. Even the US military has changed: in his book *Team of Teams*, General Stanley McChrystal describes how he learned from the tactics of the insurgents during the Iraq War and reorganised his troops into decentralised and self-organising teams.

It all sounds rather too easy, but creating the right environment for a team to thrive is a real challenge. Human beings after all are individuals and are sometimes cranky;

mavericks have to be managed and slackers identified. Teams work best when everyone knows and trusts each other, and there is a strong common culture. This takes time and is hard to achieve, particularly as in many big firms, increasingly, a large proportion of the staff are contractors. A degree of management is necessary to avoid dither, delay and poor decision-making. To avoid this and prevent 'group speak', teams also benefit from being small. Jeff Bezos, CEO of Amazon, is quite clear on this issue: 'If I see more than two pizzas for lunch the team is too big.'

Some organisations are taking it all a step further and creating snappily titled 'holacracies'. These are radical self-governing systems in which authority and decision-making is distributed throughout self-organising teams, rather than being vested in a management hierarchy. Supporters believe that they bring structure and disciplines to peer-to-peer workplaces. The most well-known example is Zappos.[214] The company is so sold on the model that it is now at the forefront of developing holacracy apps for specific processes such as hiring and remuneration. Zappos CEO Tony Hsieh says, 'In a city, people and businesses are self-organising. We are trying to do the same thing by switching from a normal hierarchical structure. Hopefully, there are other companies out there that can borrow or modify our apps and then over time, there can be a whole ecosystem of switching from a normal hierarchical company to a holacracy – which enables employees to act more like entrepreneurs.'

Many people, however, believe that leadership is key. Deborah Anconda, professor of management and organisational studies at MIT, suggests that what is needed in today's workplace is collaborative or distributed leadership. Leaders must increase transparency, teach people to think with a strategic mindset and ensure lots of 'connectors' are in place.[215]

These changes have primarily come about because of the mutating relationship between the employee and the employer. Since the millennium, there has been sustained growth in freelancers and in the on-demand, or 'gig', economy[216] – through organisations such as Uber, Lyft, TaskRabbit and Elance. According to a study by Edelman Berland,[217] 34 per cent of America's workforce is already working freelance, with forecasts suggesting that number will rise to more than 40 per cent of the workforce by 2020 and more than 50 per cent by 2030. Organisations and managers in the future will need to better understand how to recruit, manage and reward workers who are not defined by the traditional employee model.

The same will also be true of governments. As Professor Arun Sundararajan at New York University's School of Business puts it in his 2016 book, *The Sharing Economy, The End of Employment and the Rise of Crowd-Based Capitalism*: 'Although the broader socio-economic effects of the gig economy are as yet unclear, it is obvious we must rethink the provision of our safety net, decoupling it from salaried jobs and making it more readily available to independent workers.'[218]

For those that do remain formally employed, the millennial generation is shaking up workplace rules.[219] Typically, they are not motivated by the same factors as previous generations, such as job security; instead, they value a good work–life balance and a sense of purpose beyond financial success. In response, organisations seek to create a relaxed office environment, where staff feel as comfortable there as they do at home. As co-founder of Airbnb Nathan Blecharczyk, says, 'We're constantly trying to remind our employees of what business we are in, in creating an environment where they can be totally comfortable and where they actually want to hang out after work.' They are also providing more opportunities for workers to take sabbaticals.[220] Leadership coach Barbara Pagano explains: 'Time is the new currency [of work] ... people don't want to work for 40 years – and then retire ... They don't want to wait that long to pursue their goals...'[221] Adjacent to this, and as the world becomes smaller and a generation of global itinerant networked workers comes of age, more executives are consciously seeking to blend business and leisure – 'bleisure'[222] [223] – choosing to work away, to take longer breaks or even job share and job switch.

With the collaborative economy growing quickly and with more 'workers' becoming producer-participants for the likes of Uber, Airbnb, Etsy, Lending Club and Zopa, there is a blurring between the very definition of worker, producer and consumer – and even the notion of an organisation's workplace. Shared, collaborative and co-working space (for example, WeWork, The Hub) have emerged as very real alternatives to the organisation specific spaces that dominated the 20th century.

Creative Economy

> *The creative economy helps to build inclusive and sustainable cultures. What's more, it generates wealth. To build scale it requires a workforce comfortable with collaboration, critical thinking and the ability to take a risk.*

Creativity is a core part of the knowledge economy, so much so that it is worth thinking about what the next decade has in store for this particular sector. Publishing, film, television, music production, broadcasting, architecture, advertising, visual and performing arts are all part of this (Figure 39). While many others are suffering a downturn, creative individuals are blending culture and technology to generate jobs. Often they are capable of revitalising depressed areas and building cultural heritage – and the sector is also increasingly profitable. A 2013 UNESCO (UN Educational, Scientific and Cultural Organization) report highlighted that the creative economy employed nearly 30 million people worldwide and generated $2.25trn in revenue – or 3 per cent of the world's GDP.[224] This is substantially more than global telecommunications ($1.57trn) and greater than the GDP of India, Russia or Canada. Television is the largest sector with $477bn in revenue, followed by visual arts, and newspapers and magazines. Together, these three sectors account for more than $1.2trn in global revenue, and roughly half of the total for the creative economy worldwide. In the UK the creative economy generates £8.8m an hour[225] while attracting tourists, enhancing the overall cultural life of citizens and acting as a focus for social cohesion, irrespective of age, geography and religious belief.

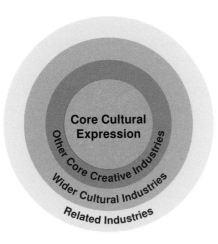

Core Cultural Expression
Literature
Music
Performing arts
Visual arts

Other Core Creative Industries
Film
Museums, galleries, libraries
Photography

Related Industries
Advertising
Architecture
Design
Fashion

Wider Cultural Industries
Heritage services
Publishing and print media
Television and radio
Sound recording
Video and computer games

Figure 39: The cultural and creative industries.
(Source: UNESCO)

Although harder to quantify, investing in culture and the creative sector as a driver of social development can contribute to the overall well-being of communities, individual self-esteem and quality of life. It also makes the most of an abundance of renewable resources, using knowledge, experience and imagination to generate value, and produce goods and services that can often be developed, bought and sold, and even delivered, online. In tough times for ageing economies, many politicians and business leaders look to the creative industries as a means of generating fast growth with a relatively low initial investment in soft infrastructure.

Creative types are often inspired by others so they generally fare much better in cities where they can easily meet and collaborate with like-minded individuals: Hollywood, Mumbai and Lagos for the film industry, Seoul for electronics and digital media, New York and London for the performing arts. Sydney, Los Angeles, Berlin, Tokyo and Barcelona are also global creative centres. However, artists of all kinds are often poorly paid, so, despite their importance to economic growth and the vitality of neighbourhoods, rising rents and high living costs often means those in the industry do not have the funds to live in the very cities they enhance. Affordability is crucial – hence the ongoing need for continued government or philanthropic support.

Artistic centres often act as magnets to attract other professionals who are keen to share the creative vibe. Although there have been failures along the way, on occasion city planners have been able to harness this to their advantage – the Museo Soumaya, now the most visited museum in Mexico, acted as a catalyst for the transformation of Plaza Carso from a rundown industrial wasteland into one of the most sought-after areas of Mexico City. Sometimes the effects can last for generations; Paris's Left Bank still attracts thousands of visitors, there to catch a lingering whiff of the bohemian counterculture that belonged to Colette, Henri Matisse and Jean-Paul Sartre. Some cities try to establish creative hubs; subsidised rents in Dublin's Temple Bar have been used to attract musicians, filmmakers and the like. Singapore has classified an area of the city-state as a creative zone, while Dubai has a Creative Clusters Authority.

What is certain is that from one side of the globe to the other, a growing number of cities are attracting high flying professionals thanks, in part, to burgeoning arts and culture sectors which make them attractive places to live and work. From London to Lagos, Berlin to Buenos Aires, cities have used their cultural credentials to attract people who want to enjoy the arts. These cities are driving new business, spurring innovation, attracting talent and investment, accelerating urban development and, in the process, improving the overall quality of life for all their residents.

The creative economy can also help to build social inclusion and can often be found addressing some of most intractable social issues of today, such as poverty eradication, women's empowerment, environmental protection and mental illness. For example, the Earthen Symphony, a decorative arts and design studio in Bangalore, India, trains women to be designers, artisans and craftsman, as well as promoting a healthy work culture in the local community. Or the Avatar Therapy Project, led by King's College London, which is a computer-based system aiming to treat schizophrenics who suffer from hallucinations despite drug treatment.

In some instances, the creative economy offers developing countries a feasible option to leapfrog into emerging high-growth areas. Some are embracing this challenge. China, for example, leveraging low-cost connectivity and a large domestic market, has invested significantly in the video games industry, aiming to compete with the USA and South Korea. Many East Asian cities are also now becoming creative hubs. Latin American countries, most notably Brazil and Mexico, already have significant local music industries, and with the emergence of fresh music genres such as Cumbia, many are reaching new global marketplaces.

Given the possibilities set out above, it seems curious to many who attended our events that more schools are not better preparing students to be creative. Professor Sugata Mitra, author of our initial perspective on the future of education, pointed out, 'The education systems in almost all countries are obsolete', and this view was echoed in workshops from London to Dubai, India to Singapore. As also proposed by Ken Robinson in his TED talks, many children are obliged to be part of an old-fashioned, over-structured, bureaucratic system which does not allow them time or provide them with the skills to work in the collaborative and increasingly creative world we now live in. Although there are some indications of change ahead, such as the rise of liberal arts degrees in universities such as Ashoka and Flame in India, Habib in Pakistan, Warwick and University College London in the UK, the pressure to produce similarly qualified, systems-driven students is hard for many to resist. This is particularly challenging in developing countries where often the difficulty is to provide any sort of education – let alone one that with a focus on free expression.

Adjusting the way we teach to ensure that the next generation is better able to adapt quickly to different environments, think nimbly and more discerningly, and collaborate more effectively, might be the best way to future-proof our creative industries.

Deeper Collaboration

Partnerships are shifting to become more dynamic, long-term, democratised, multi-party collaborations. Competitor alliances and wider public participation drive regulators to create new legal frameworks for open, empathetic collaboration.

Given the pace of global change, the uncertainty of markets, and the social and economic challenges we face, teaching our children to be more agile and adaptive is vital if we want to create more stability and security in our ever-shifting world. To be successful this will, clearly, require much effort and multiple levels of cooperation between organisations, pressure groups, governments (both local and national) and tech companies. Some businesses have already recognised the need to drop old habits and explore new ways of working, and are beginning to incorporate processes to become more dynamic and agile; over the next decade expect others to take similar action.

Addressing some of the big, meaty future challenges will rely on deeper and wider collaboration that will no longer be driven solely by intellectual property and value considerations; instead, more dynamic, agile, long-term, democratised and multi-party cooperation is on the horizon.

Let's look again at rising air pollution. Tackling this will demand partnerships across transportation operators, energy providers, city planners, public health organisations, governments, regulators, financiers and citizen groups. Addressing the obesity challenge is not just about food and drink companies changing direction, but also involves health-care professionals, behavioural psychologists, regulators, transport and city planners, educational institutions and the media. The type of cooperation needed to innovate and address these (and similar) challenges will require the collaborating organisations to rethink the fundamental nature of how such partnerships are designed, operated and rewarded. Bilateral agreements, while easier to establish and execute than global ones, are implicitly limiting.

The residual approach to intellectual property creation, ownership and trading is more of a barrier to collaboration than an enabler. While concepts such as patent pools have worked within industries, be that sewing machines and cars a century ago or Bluetooth, MPEG and DVD standards in the past 20 years, some think that they too are not the right model for the deeper and wider levels of collaboration envisaged for the future. The answer could be emerging in the way we increasingly collaborate around content production online via layered authorship – copyright is shared as more of us collaborate and swap ideas as thoughts are built upon again and again. As a result, multiple authors are recognised and shared information is not owned by any individual. Clearly, remuneration models for collaborative programmes need to evolve.

Although often criticised in some areas in the West, across Asia and South America the need for and benefit of closer collaboration between governments and companies is evident. In Ecuador and elsewhere, the successful transformation of Medellín in Colombia was highlighted as an outcome of closer public-private partnerships in city management and facility operation.[226] In India, our discussions on improving health care, education, transport and food supply all highlighted what can be achieved when government ambitions can be executed more efficiently through collaboration with faster-moving and more flexible private companies. As part of a shift towards more participatory government in some regions, citizens will increasingly be more involved in both decision-making and execution. The state may take a step back and, instead of leading, will become the facilitator of building new relationships with people and industry that can co-create and co-provide solutions to problems.

The need for greater collaboration in the future will drive many companies to reorganise themselves based more on social networks than traditional functional or business unit silos, so changing the structure of collaboration as well as the platforms upon which it operates. This could bring about a divide between meaningful networks based on shared values and emotions, and those more superficial connections built purely on data. Within collaboration, time may well become a social currency, and time spent on working on collaborative projects addressing real societal issues could become the metric that drives reputation and social status. Rather than putting in cash, either from a philanthropic standpoint or as a more active investor, we may soon see a shift to individuals proactively seeking to give up their free time to help solve emerging problems, ensuring that the scale of action and impact can be far greater than that achieved when a couple of organisations decide to form a partnership on a traditional joint venture.

Already, collaboration in innovation is increasingly becoming more public and shifting from bilateral partnerships to grand challenges focusing on problems currently seen to be unsolvable, or that have no clear path toward a solution. One timely example of this is the award-winning SunShot initiative run by the US Department of Energy.[227] This initiative focuses on accelerating the point at which solar energy becomes cost-competitive with other forms of electricity by the end of the decade, essentially bringing the cost-per-watt of solar energy down from $3.80 to $1. Rather than starting within energy companies, the approach has been to engage the wider public first to generate new concepts that could help achieve the ambition. By funding the best ideas through cooperative research, development and deployment projects undertaken by a combination of private companies, universities, state and local governments, non-profit organisations and national laboratories, the SunShot approach choreographed the ideal collaboration network for each concept. Halfway into the decade-long initiative, it has been able to use its resources more intelligently and fund 250 projects that have collectively already achieved 70 per cent of the target cost reduction.

Going forward, big problems are seen to require completely different ways of thinking and cooperating, and for many, deeper, wider, more meaningful collaboration is an important part of the puzzle. As such, the nature of work and the role of the organisation blurs. Organisations will change radically in this environment, and flatter, project-based, collaborative, virtual, informal organisations will become the new normal.

The Real Sharing Economy

> *Increasing collaboration drives organisations to reconfigure, based on social networks and social impact. Real sharing enterprises, not driven by profits, seek to share resources, knowledge and decision-making responsibilities.*

When talking about the sharing economy, it is worth exploring the principles behind collaborative consumption. This has grown since Napster's disruption of the music industry in 2001, to become a vast online-exchange market economy now attracting more than $12 billion of investment a year. Will the next stage be a real sharing enterprise, not driven by profits for shareholders, but instead seeking to share resources, knowledge and decision-making responsibilities?

Based on online marketplaces creating transparency of demand and matching it to supply, at a competitive price, the sharing economy already encompasses a wide range of models, including the likes of Airbnb, Uber and TaskRabbit, most founded on a for-profit approach. Many of them have been established around the more open and transparent sharing of information that enables more peer-to-peer business models to be developed. While many of the current successes are considered as being part of the sharing economy, a good number are using Internet platforms to run disruptive and profitable new businesses. Many see hope, going forward, that a more meaningful approach to sharing may emerge and so we will see a real sharing economy – one where people genuinely share skills, information and knowledge with each other in a way that creates additional value for everyone, and not just for some.

Whether considering platforms such as eBay, the original online marketplace; Lyft, the car sharing competitor to Uber; or TaskRabbit, connecting odd jobs to people in your neighbourhood, the majority work on the basis that the platform takes a cut of every transaction. Whether that is 5 per cent (or, as with Uber, 30 per cent), the attraction for investors is that the companies both control and acquire the majority of the value. The new models mean that the marketplaces don't need to support any of the assets but simply match supply to demand as and when needed. So-called sharing platforms are distorting communities as they have become less about sharing and more about access. What began as a peer-to-peer, idealistic and egalitarian movement has, to some, become a commodifier of other people's resources. The platforms are extracting most of the value created by their users and seeking to create, often unregulated, monopolies with little – if any – competitors of scale. Regulators in some cities are starting to raise concerns about how some of the recent start-ups are going against the public interest.

Some, such as the New Economics Foundation, are seeking a real sharing economy where information, power and profits are more genuinely shared.[228] Localised sharing platforms such as freecycle allow people to recycle products without payment; apps such as Leftoverswap are enabling excess food to be made freely available to the homeless; Couchsurfing freely matches people to spare sofas, without the Airbnb intermediary overhead; and tool library networks are enabling pools of farmers to share access to specialised machinery and equipment that are too expensive for individuals to acquire. These are popular and growing movements, but are currently tiny compared to the for-profit platforms.

As resources become more constrained and waste is seen as a resource, more cooperative platforms that give access to goods to those who can't afford them will accelerate more sustainable consumption (especially in cities), reduce our impact on the environment and maybe even help build stronger communities. As the smart grid evolves to allow consumers of energy to be producers, this infrastructural shift could drive a change in the systemic view of sharing – one that may, in the end, lead to improving our quality of life through greater social interactions, fairer wealth distribution and stronger community relationships. Local time-banking projects, such as those run via Echo in the UK, are seen to be a more equable and effective approach than that of TaskRabbit; OuiShare has expanded from France across Europe to the Middle East and Latin America as it creates a global network of collaborators. Instead of creating enterprises that let well-off people pay less well-off people to do their chores – without providing the benefits and security of traditional employment – many are looking at more cooperative, collaborative platforms as a means to both improve efficiency, and collectively create a good or service, and then share the results equitably.

How far will we get to this more egalitarian view of sharing by 2025? The momentum behind the likes of Uber, Airbnb and their peers is evidently significant – the challenge is whether the not-for-profit alternatives can draw in wider support and hence scale.

Last-Mile Delivery

Seamless, integrated and shared last-mile delivery replaces inefficient competition and duplication of goods distribution. Greater efficiency in moving things is as important as moving people and so a major focus for innovation.

One area where more efficient collaboration could be transformational, whether for passengers or goods, is to save money on what is the most expensive portion of the delivery chain – what's known as 'last-mile delivery'. If it can be organised in simple ways, then the opportunities for businesses are obvious.

In the complex world of logistics, vast improvements have already been made in the efficiency of moving goods around the world. The speed at which packages are sorted, loaded and transported has increased substantially over recent years. The main efficiency challenge is in the last mile – from distribution centre to final destination, be that a home, an office, a car or an individual. This, typically accounting for up to 50 per cent of distribution costs, is the most difficult and expensive leg of a package's journey and integral to many areas of development focus (Figure 40). Proposed solutions lie mostly in drones or autonomous delivery vehicles.

A core aim, no matter what system is deployed, is to deliver goods on the same day they're purchased. Amazon Prime Air videos are already showing how a 30-minute drone delivery system might work, and the company has filed patents for several advanced vehicle systems. But other, equally nimble, players are also making bets on future options, for instance, Uber. With its rapidly extending infrastructure and heavy investment in algorithms to help route deliveries, Uber is the only newcomer who can match up to the size and scale of incumbents such as United Parcel Service (UPS), FedEx and their counterparts. UPS delivers 35 million parcels a day and is investing heavily in new technologies to make these deliveries cleaner and more efficient.[229] Meanwhile, shared capacity models have been tried out as other organisations have collaborated in Uber-esque networked business models that also seek to bring down driver and vehicle costs per delivery. Amazon's Flex programme in the USA is one of the more recent of these, allowing independent drivers to make between $18 and $25 an hour delivering packages.

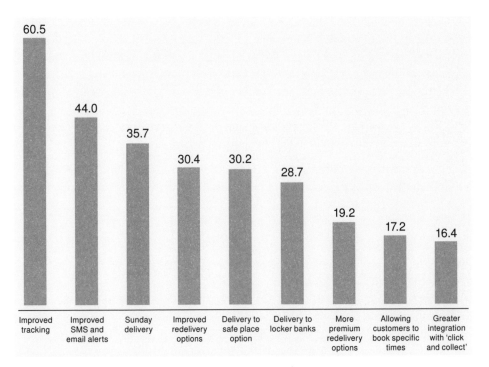

Figure 40: Focus areas of future development for UK logistics firms, 2015.
(Source: Barclays)

Fulfilment costs currently account for 15 per cent of sales for Amazon and so reducing these while improving service is a fine balance. But it is not only Amazon looking to make an impact; Alibaba and Google are also in the mix. Google's 'Project Wing' is aiming to have a commercial drone business up and running by 2017. Although gaining approval from the Federal Aviation Administration (FAA), Civil Aviation Authority (CAA) and other regulators is currently in negotiation, many see these and similar activities starting to have a significant impact by 2020.

Back on the ground, there is also interest in the adoption of autonomous vehicles. Warehouses and fulfilment centres have been using autonomous vehicles for years, moving products and packages around as directed. While in the past they have largely followed pre-determined routes (so requiring a fixed infrastructure), the next generation of vehicles uses 3D vision guidance systems. These vehicles not only transport goods, and can load and unload packages quickly and safely, they also automatically join together to transport large products – and whenever an obstacle is encountered automatically replan routes.

What many find interesting is how this technology can migrate from inside buildings to the outside, and start to change how goods are moved around cities. If multiple white vans can be replaced by a swarm of autonomous electric delivery vehicles, then the efficiency improvements could be significant. Although they will be slow moving for safety reasons, supporters argue that they can navigate through urban districts, choose routes that avoid causing congestion and deliver goods when and where required.

This will work not just for deliveries to end consumers but also in the B2B (business-to-business) environment. Offices, restaurants, retailers and even manufacturers, it is argued, could gain from the network efficiencies that will be realised. Self-evidently, eliminating the need for drivers has social and economic implications, but within the logistics arena would lead to significant cost savings. Although there are a number of regulatory hurdles to be overcome, supporters, including many in the logistics sector, see that the technology is fast-becoming scalable; the business case is compelling and the environmental benefits attractive.

At one extreme these vehicles can be so small that, effectively, they are only slightly larger than the parcels themselves, and we may end up with a fully automated system of self-driving parcels. One such example, from the founders of Skype, is the Starship project: a self-driving robot, holding up to 10kg of goods, travels along pavements at a sedate 4 miles per hour so as not to disrupt pedestrians.[230]

Another level up in complexity, but one even more attractive in terms of overall system efficiency, is to coordinate the simultaneous movement of people and goods. If someone is using a taxi to take them home, then the same vehicle can deliver a package to a neighbour. Coordinating putting the right package into the right vehicle in this scenario is no easy task, but Volvo, for one, already has developed its On Call app to give access to shared vehicles. By overlaying package distribution with known customer journey plans and routes, Volvo plans for delivery companies to pay for access to cargo space, put the packages in the car, and allow the customer to use a digital key to open the car and collect their parcel when it has arrived at its destination. Audi has already taken a different but related approach; trials in Munich have allowed owners to use their car as a shipping address for online orders. Using the Audi in-car communications system, delivery drivers track the location of the vehicle and use a one-off digital access code to unlock the boot and deliver a package. The trials to date have been in partnership with Amazon and DHL but the principle can clearly be extended.

All of these innovations are evidently competing in the same space and there seems to be plenty of opportunity to go around. For many years the last mile has been highlighted as one of the untapped inefficiencies to be addressed. Whether by drones, driverless trucks, autonomous robots, the wider adoption of simple vehicle-sharing schemes or a combination thereof, it looks like greater transparency of what needs to go where is going to have significant impact over the next decade.

Sometime Nomads

> *Elective migration, cheap travel, international knowledge sharing and increasingly transient working models create connected nomads who mix the traditions of home with the values and customs of their host location.*

The movement of goods is clearly an ongoing challenge that organisations have to deal with. Alongside this, people are more mobile than they have ever been before and companies are going to have to work hard to retain talent. Continuing globalisation, connectivity and the availability of information at one's fingertips has made the world a smaller place. This, combined with cheap travel, international knowledge sharing and increasingly transient working models, has begun to make a real impact on the culture of work, in particular creating opportunities for the adventurous. The next decade will see a growth in the number of the so-called 'connected nomads', the global workers who mix the traditions of home with the values and customs of their host location.

People move around for all sorts of different reasons, good and bad. The World Bank estimates that about 250 million people live outside the country of their birth and, adding in those who have moved internally, about one in every seven of us could be defined as a migrant. Increasing numbers of people are fleeing violence but many others move for work, love and adventure. This mass movement of humanity, combined with cheap and easy travel options and free-flowing communication technology, is creating a world where cultures are dissolving, and the traditional understanding of what it means to belong is being challenged.

The privileged few, fortified by sought-after skills and protected by the passports of their choice, dominate the top echelons of the corporate world. Their lifestyles, irrespective of location, remain broadly unchanged; tapping into local culture is an option but not an obligation. Their peers also hail from diverse corners of the globe and many will find more in common with those in similar circumstances than friends and family back home. Corporate executives, working on a global scale, are able to use the power and influence of the organisations that employ them to drive material change in ways that national governments can only dream of. Unilever, for example, has set a target for 2020 that aims to help more than a billion people improve their health and hygiene and help to reduce obesity. The Tata Group spends around 3 per cent of its net profits (US$17m in 2014) on programmes related to education, health and the environment.

Many people who migrate for professional reasons use their education as a ticket to riches, making their homes in centres such as Silicon Valley. The USA is the number one destination of choice for many, and the previous record high in 1890 of 14.8 per cent of the population being foreign-born will be surpassed by 2025, with the figure rising to nearly 19 per cent by 2060. These days most arrivals are qualified in some way – in 2013, 41 per cent of newly arrived immigrants to the USA had at least a bachelor's degree (in 1970, that share was just 20 per cent).[231] Indian Americans are now the richest ethnic group with a median household income of about $88,000,[232] compared with an economic output of less than $1,600 a head in India. As the focus of world trade shifts, and the opportunities for corporate development expand, expect this tiny but influential group to look towards new locations in the emerging economies in South America or Asia.

China has been encouraging students to study abroad in order to improve their education since the late 1970s. Chinese youths currently make up over a fifth of all international students in higher education in the OECD, with more than a quarter of them in the USA – making it likely that that there are more US-based Chinese PhD students than Americans. Meanwhile, the number of returnees has grown even faster: more than 350,000 Chinese returned from overseas study in 2013, up from just 20,000 10 years earlier.[233]

The Western population's absorption of other cultures is not always reciprocal, however. In 2013/14, the USA hosted 886,000 of the world's 4.5 million mobile higher education population – more than twice the UK, the next entrant on the list, yet less than ten per cent of US college students travel abroad in their undergraduate years.[234] If this imbalance continues, it could begin to create questions around the readiness of the US workforce to participate in a more globalised world.

From cleaners in Hong Kong to lawyers in London, migrants also send cash to their families, which has a huge impact in developing economies. The World Bank estimates that Nigerians abroad sent back some $21bn in 2013, about a quarter of their country's earnings from oil exports. Many send money either through Facebook or via their mobile phones. Such has been the impact of technology on economic migration that global remittances are now worth more than twice as much as foreign aid, comprising 10 per cent of the Philippines' GDP and 42 per cent of Tajikistan's.[235] Last year India received $70bn, more than any other country.

For the majority of migrant workers the 'hubs' of choice remain New York, London and Singapore, and it is there that the influence of that cultural blending is most obvious. Wealthy Indians consider London, Singapore and Dubai to be the three largest 'Indian' cities outside India. Few in London would think it curious for an Argentinian woman to eat at a Japanese restaurant before enjoying an evening of Russian ballet, but even for London, the extent of internationalism has been a transformation of the comparatively recent past. Many individuals are making the most of a global citizenship to forge more nomadic lifestyles and careers. For some, making the most of the opportunities that a globalised world offers is providing a richer existence, one less focused on the rat race but also more legitimised than simply 'opting out'. For others, the global community is just a better, more connected way to do what they always done – have conversations, share knowledge and work collaboratively.

Other, somewhat darker, factors are also at play as global uncertainty makes life planning difficult. Not every migrant is privileged. Increasingly the less fortunate find themselves in unfamiliar places where there is little opportunity or hope for a better life. Obliged to leave all their possessions behind to start again, these displaced people may only have tradition and belief to give them a sense of self. Low-cost connectivity links the poor and the displaced to their past, enabling them to retain a sense of identity and belonging even as they live in the most taxing environments. What seems certain is that the next decade will see an increase in the number of people who feel, at least for some of the time, that they do not fully belong to a specific nation or country.

Internal migration has become a significant issue. Some cities in the West are disproportionate in size and scale to the rest of the country, and this is not just confined to London. China is concerned that some of its major conglomerates are becoming too large and, as such, tries to restrict movement between provinces through regulation. The government has long used the *hukou* system to control migration flows, especially of labourers from villages looking for work in cities. Because cheap health care and education in cities are only provided to people with local *hukou*, the system acts as a brake on migration. Young workers eager for relatively well-paid city jobs are undeterred, but they usually leave children and older relatives behind. No one yet knows of the long-term impact that this will have.

Returning home with money and experience are not the only benefits that migrants can offer their homeland. With their knowledge of the ropes on both sides, many also help companies in their host country operate in their home country – and vice versa – as understanding of language and culture becomes less of an issue. Such is their value to their home nation, both politically, economically and as cultural ambassadors, that some governments work hard to ensure they do not lose touch, even appointing a minister for diasporas in order to embrace as many people as possible: Ireland counts everybody of Irish descent as Irish, similarly Israel claims all Jews. Some diasporas, however, are particularly influential in specific areas. For example, many Lebanese are highly educated and have well-paid jobs all over the world but they have a particular influence in the Middle East, which has a poor track record in tertiary education. Looking ahead, as education across the Gulf improves and local residents become more qualified to take on skilled work, it is possible opportunities will diminish, leaving many with the challenge of where to go next. With Lebanon home to more than 2.5 million refugees and the knock-on implications this has for work, it is unlikely that they will either wish or be able to return home.

As the world becomes smaller through migration and mobility, both virtual and real, it may be that people and groups will express themselves more insistently through multiple-identity lenses. Blended cultures may become the new norm.

Conclusion: Business and Society

Should business be optimistic or pessimistic about the future? Perhaps it's fair to say the jury is currently out. Certainly, to achieve lasting, inclusive growth, many now believe that business and society should align around a wider agenda, adopting a broader definition of success in order to achieve a better balance between short- and long-term gain. There are uncertainties around this, such as who will lead and how, but there is also a general consensus that commercial organisations have the potential to take the lead in establishing a future that benefits wider society. To achieve this, tough decisions need to be made, a number of which may well lead to significant change in the systems within which many currently operate. However, despite being increasingly integrated and interconnected, the world is more becoming more fragmented and imbalanced. This diffusion of power makes it increasingly difficult to act collectively and in turn has created an apparent paradox – the tendency for the world to grow further apart, even as it draws closer together.

At the same time the boundaries between governments, business and civil society have begun to blur, with a growing consensus that there is a strong need to collaborate on key issues, such as resource constraints and societal stress. This is hampered by a lack of trust in both the traditional institutions of leadership and corporates, which, if not managed successfully, will potentially reduce the possibility of positive change. Many, especially the young, are disillusioned with today's political and business leaders, and are looking for new networks to trust, those who will set a more positive direction for the future.

Different approaches to more appropriate corporate governance and more aligned behaviours are being suggested, debated and even piloted around the world. Notable among these are the clarification of the legal obligation for companies to maximise shareholder value, and adopting the principles of B-Corp, to aid a return to a focus on stakeholders rather than pure profit. Beyond this, the notion of large-scale collaboration with shared mutual interests at the fore is providing the opportunity for a radical step-change to occur. Some see the need for companies, governments and wider society to pool their resources, better leverage available capital and focus more on common forms of intellectual property that accelerate rather than constrain knowledge sharing, in order to drive positive change. Some organisations will make these changes but whether business as a whole will respond is another question; after all, a good number are happy with the status quo, and still benefit from it.

Reflections on Common Views of the Future

The insights gained from our multiple discussions have helped us to form a response to some of the concerns and occasional misconceptions that have been raised about the future.

- Reflections on concerns
- Building on opportunities

Returning to the 12 common views shared at the start of this book, what have we learned that may help give us a more informed angle?

After exploring the varied insights from our multiple discussions, we have certainly gained different perspectives from countries across the world which have helped us form a response to some, if not all of those views. Some are clear for the next decade, others are uncertain.

Reflections on concerns

1. Too Many People

Even with slowing rates of growth, the global population is plainly set to rise to between 9 and 11 billion people this century. Exactly how many we will be by 2100 is open to debate. If we assume mass migration taking place to rebalance the natural distribution of where the babies will be born, then we are evidently going to see both increasing urbanisation and a general move north.

As we saw with food waste, where we are currently losing between 30 and 40 per cent of production every day, there is a huge opportunity to improve the efficiency of the system, and potentially therefore have enough food for everyone without the need for more land. Add in technology developments and improved farming practices, and many believe that there will be no need for us to double our food production. Perhaps most significant, though, is that we need to get used to a change in our diets – particularly away from beef. With around one billion cattle today – and a third of them in India – averaging out at two acres per cow, the amount of land taken up rearing the global herd is around eight million square km. That is just under the total land area of the USA. Coping with more people seems doable, but more cows are going to be a challenge for many countries.

Urbanisation is evidently *the* major shift within nations, and with 70 per cent of us living in cities by the middle of the century, it will be down to the master-planners to design and build more flexible spaces to house everyone in an effective manner. We know the models and, as long as we make sure the infrastructure is up to the demands that will be placed on it, the extra two to four billion that will be added globally this century looks feasible. Locally there will undoubtedly be challenges in some countries, but that is why migration is the key balancing lever. We need to recognise that living standards are going to have to change for some to accommodate more people, and that people living in closer proximity to others are going to have to adapt to and accept different cultures.

2. Running out of Resources

If we are able to make intelligent decisions around food and land use, then hopefully we can also follow the right path on other resources. Energy is always front of mind and with it the need to change the supply away from fossil fuels and as quickly as possible. Here the end game is widely seen as the majority of power coming from solar, but other sources, such as nuclear, wind and, for the next 50-odd years, gas, are all in the mix. During the next decade or so several countries will face an energy squeeze. Reducing our dependency on oil and coal while ramping up the alternatives is therefore a big concern for many. Achieving this as a smooth transition is no easy task.

Ensuring a fresh water supply for more people is largely a technical challenge as the net volume of water is constant. So, expect to see advances in desalination, grey water reuse and irrigation. Other major resources under threat of fast depletion (such as antimony and iridium) seem to be the main immediate challenges here within the decade; alternative options for batteries and solar PV cells are top of many a to-do list. Longer term, at current rates of consumption, we have 17 years of silver and zinc, around 30 years' worth of copper and 45 years of titanium. Then we are back with food as the problem, as we hit peak phosphorous use in around 2030. After that, we are going to need alternatives, yet to be invented.

3. Pollution is Out of Control

Now that the naysayers to global warming in most, but not all, regions appear to be in the minority, hope for the much-needed changes in our use of fossil fuels is rising. Carbon-capture technologies are being trialled to help, and so managing the energy-mix transition is a considerable area of focus. However, given the damage already done, and the particular issue of air pollution, it is clear that major action is required at a far faster rate than many expect. Air quality is perhaps the most visible problem and, as it kills more people every day, it is, in many eyes, already out of control. As we have highlighted, fixing this problem is a complex collaboration but certainly possible if the key actors align around a common purpose.

Pollution in the oceans is the more hidden issue, and with more plastic than fish in the seas by 2050 it is apparent that what we really need is a fundamental behaviour change before the damage is irreparable. With the UN, for one, leading action, many hope that something can be done, especially by, but not only, China. And then, after air and water, we have land pollution. Contamination of soil by pesticides and herbicides grew significantly throughout the 20th century. Soil contaminants can have significant deleterious consequences for ecosystems; in several nations, this is a fast-building concern. So in the next decade, we can probably take the necessary moves to start to get pollution under better control, but not eradicated. The unknown factor here is what will 2°C, 3°C or even 4°C temperature increases do? The forecasts are very scary.

4. Migration is Bad

As mentioned above, migration is and will continue to be a necessary element in rebalancing the natural distribution of the world's population. Further internal migration to cities seems to be inevitable and with it come multiple trials. It is, however, cross-border migration that will be the biggest problem. Current anti-migration sentiment looks to be building, not just in Europe and the USA but probably also in Russia, which had more than 11 million international migrants in 2015.[236] There is a clear economic argument that migration is good for many countries with low fertility ratios. But in several countries extremist politics and right-wing media are increasingly drowning this out, and popular sentiment is evidently moving against further migration. The irony is that the countries making the most noise about immigration are also some of the key sources of emigrants to the likes of Singapore, the UAE, Qatar and Kuwait – but they are generally white and called ex-pats. The big question is whether more countries will indeed follow the shining example of Canada with its open and transparent approach.[237] [238] Canada has one of the highest net immigration rates in the world; this is likely to remain a fixture of Canadian policy and demography for the foreseeable future. So too is an emphasis on human capital, as immigration becomes ever more tightly woven into economic policy. Elsewhere, in more crowded nations, the ideal models are hard to find. Germany has been a good example for some in the past, but current challenges are raising whopping questions about the future.

5. There will not be Enough Jobs

It is also obvious to many that automation will be having an impact. Coupled with the rise of AI is its growing potential to have the capability to take over certain jobs, notably shown with Google DeepMind beating the world champion at the Chinese board game Go. While the high-value, information-rich, largely repetitive jobs (pharmacists, accounts, lawyers, etc.) seem to be the most attractive for replacement, dangerous roles (in mining, underwater, extreme temperatures, etc.) will also be in focus. Although some fear that more 'mundane' low wage jobs in warehouses and supermarkets may also be vulnerable, it seems that many are not viable for automation as yet. The return on investment (ROI) is not yet attractive, at least not while humans seem to be good at those. A big issue seems to be that with the ageing keeping their jobs for longer, there will be fewer jobs being released for the young to take up. What we have seen in Spain and Greece as a consequence of the 2007/08 crisis may become commonplace elsewhere. Youth unemployment heading towards 50 per cent in more countries may cause systemic problems. Add in an increase in lower-wage jobs, especially for migrants, and achieving sustained employment will be a challenge for many a government.

We have, however, had similar fears in the past. As manufacturing jobs in some nations declined, the service sector role grew to bridge the gap. With new roles emerging from the creative economy, a burgeoning demand for health care globally and the continued growth of the digital economy, several experts feel that net impact on the number of jobs may well be neutral. The underlying concern, however, is that as competition and technology have an impact, we will see lower wages for many.

Building on opportunities

6. Female Education can Address Many Issues

Many believe – with a passion – that providing better and wider access to education to girls in particular will have positive knock-on effect across many areas. With the UN pushing strongly via its Girls Education Initiative and female education core to the 5th SGD (achieve gender equality and empower all women and girls), the top down impetus is there. Add in all the CSR activity focused on the same target, and momentum looks highly likely to continue to build.

The World Bank sees girls' education as a strategic development investment – it brings a wide range of benefits not only to the girls themselves but also for their children and their communities, as well as society at large in terms of economic growth. 'More educated women tend to be healthier, participate more in the formal labour market, earn more income, have fewer children, and provide better health care and education to their children, all of which eventually improve the well-being of all individuals and can lift households out of poverty. These benefits also transmit across generations, as well as to communities at large.' The links are clear and compelling and, in most countries, but unfortunately not yet all, are now a persuasive priority.

7. Technology will Solve the Big Problems

While many of the challenges we face rely on policy, behaviour and planning changes, technology has a big role to play. Increasing digitisation is, in some industries, truly leading to transformation. And in health care, energy, transport and food production, to highlight just a few, there are major developments on the horizon that well help provide solutions to some of the key problems we face: gene editing, new lithium-ion batteries, self-driving cars, drought tolerant crops, etc. will all play a role.

However, there seem to be questions around what technology can do in the face of some of the fundamental issues that we face. For such challenges as climate change and obesity, as yet there is no silver bullet or magic pill on the horizon, and unlikely to be one any time soon. While some are delaying action on these major concerns in the hope that a new technology will come to the rescue, more are recognising that other avenues have to be pursued. As agreement on global warming has become more widespread and agreements such as Paris COP21 come into force, it will be changes in government policy that really make the difference. At some point we will also have similar recognition on biodiversity and hence more behaviour focused change. Some would also argue that the same applies to obesity – sugar tax, personal health-care budgets and withdrawal of insurance for the severely overweight are all on the cards.

8. Solar is the Answer

As stated above, solar power is not only the goal for many in the energy sector but it is also probably the primary global answer. With many thousand times our envisaged future power requirements available every day from the sun, it is little surprise that investment in solar energy is top of many a government's to-do list. However, the economics are opaque. While some have resisted or downgraded subsidies, and others with vested interests are pushing other agendas, as we talked to politicians, technologists and leaders in the energy sector, the majority said they believed that solar is indeed a big part of the answer. Although some expect faster returns than are credible, the journey and the speed of the transition is a matter of both improvements in cost per watt and scale.

Some regions, obviously, get more sunlight than others, and so can benefit more from solar energy. However, with breakthroughs in energy storage and long-distance electricity transmission now emerging from a number of research labs, the role that solar can play in the energy mix by the end of the century is building. With China's eco-civilisation initiative gaining momentum and significant investment in solar research taking place there, improving PV efficiency is the immediate priority.

And now let's turn to the potentially less extreme, more underlying issues:

9. We Need to Rethink Retirement

As life expectancy increases, many countries are facing an ever-growing ageing society. Several, worryingly, already have dependency ratios of more than 50 per cent. The central challenge in those with a state-supported pension system is one of balance between work and retirement: 40 years in work cannot support 30 years of retirement, especially with most pension systems designed to support an average of ten years post-retirement. We are ageing faster than we can pay into the pension kitty and, unless we are going to put an even greater tax burden on the next generation, it is time for action. With 70 now being openly discussed as a retirement age in Europe, when we talked to actuaries, many saw 75 as credible by mid-century.

Attitudes are changing about the transition from full-time to part-time work and then to retirement. Professor Laura Carstensen, Ken Smith and Dominika Jaworski of the Stanford Center on Longevity, shared the following: 'For those who have inadequate retirement savings, the most obvious solution is to work longer ... One major potential barrier, however, is that employers remain ambivalent about older workers. Currently, most employers view older workers as expensive and sometimes less productive than younger workers. Research findings increasingly suggest that the latter reflects stereotypes more than evidence. The productivity of workers tends to increase with age. This is especially true for knowledge workers ... Offering bridge jobs or flexible work arrangements such as flex hours and part-time work will allow employers to retain the expertise of older workers while reducing costs.'

10. Health-care Spending will Only Go Up

Led by the benchmark of the USA, it is obvious to many that health-care spending is indeed going up. As the health-care spend in the USA approaches 20 per cent of GDP over the next decade, and in many other Western countries rises above 10 per cent, putting the brakes on is a much-debated challenge. Equally, in other countries across Asia and Africa currently focused on improving basic health, the scale of spending is also going up – although not yet likely to reach the same 10 per cent figure. Chronic disease, public health and an ageing society are all having an impact.

In the West there is only one country that is now reducing its health-care spend on a real-basis. That is the UK, where the NHS system is both equally praised and under pressure for delivering more with less. Although budgets for the next five years have been increased by £8bn, population growth and inflation mean that keeping things equal would require an extra £30bn by 2020. As such, the UK is the only country currently planning to cut its health-care spend – in its case by £22bn. How successful this will be remains to be seen. Many doubt if the target efficiencies can be achieved without lowering standards of care.

However, elsewhere innovative approaches are being developed that may well hold global solutions. Most notably, as mentioned previously, in India the likes of Aravind (cataract operations) and Narayana (cardiac surgery) are re-engineering the whole system. They are providing high-quality support as good, if not better, than that available at the best hospitals in the West, and are doing so at as little as two per cent of the cost of facilities such as those of the celebrated Cleveland Clinic. More of this, as well as the so-called 'frugal' innovation applied to health care, could well be the answer for surgical intervention. It is highly likely that answers will come from outside the EU/USA. Add in greater preventive health care, pandemic early warning and gene-based prediction emanating from the West, and many are trying to halt the steady rise of health-care spending per head. The reality is that, at some point soon, health-care spending has to be levelled off; the question is whether it can be, and when.

11. This is the Asian Century

China's economic success in recent years is without question; its ability to maintain recent levels of growth is, however, now being challenged. Are the wheels coming off the Chinese engine, or is it just slowing down a bit (albeit to around twice the growth rates seen in the West)? This is being asked on the front pages of the *Financial Times*, *Wall Street Journal* and elsewhere on a regular basis. With India now experiencing around seven per cent GDP growth per annum, more are becoming aware of the momentum that is being gathered for the other significant Asian economy. It is unquestionable that the centre of global economic power is heading East. However, when we think of an Asian century, we are not just talking about economics.

We must also think of military influence, cultural reach and the all-important reserve currency status presently dominated by the US dollar. Few see the end of American military supremacy any time soon, but a potential US withdrawal from the global stage was a frequently raised issue in our discussions. With no remaining dependency on Middle East oil and low export exposure when compared to other countries, the idea that the USA could choose to focus on its Atlantic and Pacific buffers, and leave the rest to others, is being voiced around the world. This will be a US decision rather than one imposed on it from elsewhere, but it will create a potential military vacuum that many see China, far more than India, seeking to fill. Culturally India, via Bollywood, food and its diaspora is already a major global influence; China may not be that far behind. Again, however, the ability of either to usurp the 20th-century dominance of Western, and particularly US, culture is questioned. Lastly, even with the concerted action now taking place with the IMF, the renminbi taking over from the dollar as the world's reserve currency seems a 30 to 40 year possibility rather than a high probability for the next decade or two. Perhaps the 22nd century will be Asian? This leaves the 21st century as potentially a period of bumpy transition.

12. GDP Growth is the Best Way to Measure Progress

Perhaps more significant to underlying change than many other issues, is how we measure and judge success. GDP growth is the default for countries, but may not be the best option, even for economists. In his review of Diane Coyle's 2014 book, *GDP: A Brief but Affectionate History*, Sir Samuel Brittan of the *Financial Times* highlighted that, 'Other things being equal, a higher real GDP per head is better than a lower one ... GDP is simply gross national income without deducting depreciation, which came to be regarded as too difficult to measure on a national scale. It would probably aid understanding if discussion switched back to the national income concept.'[239] While many agree, others are intrigued by such views as that of the Fourth King of Bhutan, Jigme Singye Wangchuck, who, in 1970, first proposed that Gross Domestic Happiness would be a better option and 'sustainable development should take a holistic approach towards notions of progress and give equal importance to non-economic aspects of well-being'.[240] Subsequent analysis such as the World Happiness Rankings[241] has sought to add detail; in 2016 it ranked the top five countries as Denmark, Switzerland, Iceland, Norway and Finland: notably these are the same countries that feature well in the UNDP HDI.[242] They are also all to be found in the top twenty-five countries when ranked by GDP PPP (purchasing power parity) per head: Switzerland and Norway are in the top ten but none is in the top five. Maybe a non-GDP view would be better primary measure of a country's progress – if only we could all agree.

Turning to companies, a recent *Economist* view came out in favour of shareholder value being the primary measure for any organisation: 'A firm's worth is based on its long-term operating performance, not financial engineering. It cannot boost its value much by manipulating its capital structure.'[243] Although recognising that social and financial impact are being discussed alongside one another by the likes of Siemens and Unilever, the *Economist* sees problems in identifying a goal that could replace the pursuit of shareholder value. 'If firms had to promote employment, they would be less productive and riskier borrowers, as China is discovering. The objective of maximising wealth is deeply embedded in the global savings system, with asset managers obliged to protect clients' money.' Others clearly disagree, and with momentum building for a more informed view of how society judges success, some see a shift gradually occurring. The question is how quickly things will change and whether the incumbent mindset, largely supported by the banks, will dominate ... at least for now. Down the line, many hope that a multi-capital view[244] could prevail.

Chapter 9

Cross Topic Insights

- Trust
- Privacy
- Inequality
- Transparency
- Identity

When we ran the first Future Agenda programme in 2010, we gained around 50 major insights into the decade to 2020 that we grouped into six clusters. These were: health, wealth, happiness, mobility, security and locality. Cutting across all of these there were two issues that seemed, at the time, to be underlying many of the major prospective changes, and so potentially significant to how quickly or slowly change would take place. We called them the moderators of the future: trust and privacy.

Five years ago, our understanding of trust was:

> 'It is a reflection of our belief in the fairness and honesty of others. It influences not only the way people and organisations co-operate but it is also an essential part of the contract between government, organisations and society. Understanding how and who to trust is important because when it is broken, or not established, there are often negative consequences. Sometimes this can be catastrophic, providing fertile ground for the growth of radical or extreme ideologies. Some argue that the 2008 economic downturn, fears about climate change, geopolitical uncertainty and widespread corruption in established institutions from church, state and corporations, have shaken trust in the capitalist system itself. Over the previous decade, belief in previously held convictions has been questioned and many people are now looking for a new frame of reference and new organisations in which to trust. This makes the world a very uncertain place.'

Our view on privacy was:

> 'The growing prevalence of data and the sophistication of its analysis for almost all aspects of public life has led to many social benefits from smarter cities to better health-care delivery. However, in some eyes, this has been at a cost to personal privacy. As the public become more aware of the value of the data they generate, individuals will better understand its vulnerabilities and their need to balance their right to a private life with the advantages of sharing personal information for public good. The desire to control who and what has access to personal information will become increasingly important, and the way we manage our privacy will change. Cultural attitudes will play a significant role in this, so expect approaches to vary between nations. As society adjusts to this new normal, sentiments will change. However, future generations who have grown up in an online world are likely to find negotiations between their public and private lives much easier.'

As we have seen across the core chapters of this book, both of these issues are having a significant impact across multiple areas and as a result, in some ways, have changed our views over the past few years.

Trust

Since 2010 there has been an evident shift – not just in the level of trust but also in its nature. The Edelman Trust Barometer is one of the standard references for global trust: in 2015 it saw 'an evaporation of trust across all institutions, as if no one has the answers to the unpredictable and unimaginable events'[245] such as the spread of Ebola in Western Africa, the disappearance of Malaysia Airlines 370, the arrest of top Chinese government officials on corruption charges, the rigging of foreign exchange rates by six of the world's largest banks, and the rising number of data breaches. In 2016 it highlighted that 'a yawning trust gap is emerging between elite and mass populations'.[246] Trust is seen to be 'rising in the elite or "informed public" group – those with at least a college education, who are very engaged in media, and have an income in the top 25 per cent. However, in the "mass population", trust levels have barely budged since the Great Recession.' Whether from the rise of fundamentalism in several faiths, a fear of the impact of AI or the rising tide of evidence of corporate and personal tax evasion, it seems as though the decline in trust is set to continue for some time.

Privacy

At the same time, there has been a huge increase in the number of companies with chief privacy officers. Professional organisations such as the Internal Association of Privacy Professionals, with whom we partnered on five events in 2015, now have thousands of members. The revelations by Edward Snowden about the extent of the activities of the US National Security Agency (NSA) have changed many laypeople's views of government interception and surveillance. We have also seen major data breaches from the hacking of, among others, Sony, Home Depot, eBay and JP Morgan, all of which have shown that many of our assumptions about data security need to be challenged. Most significantly, perhaps, is the 2016 Apple–FBI confrontation focused on Apple's unwillingness to write the code to break into its phones. The subsequent adoption of end-to-end encryption by WhatsApp, part of Facebook, has shown a potential future standard emerging for all. Privacy is certainly no longer niche.

Reviewing the new insights gained from the 2015 Future Agenda discussions, it is apparent that again there are cross-cutting issues that there are common 'red threads' that ran through the numerous views we heard. They interweave within, and underpin, a number of important potential shifts. They may not be issues that will undergo specific changes between today and 2025 and beyond, but are rather matters that may moderate some of the other probable changes taking place around the world. This time we have identified three such issues: inequality, transparency and identity.

Inequality

Given the way the world is, and where it is heading, it is little surprise that inequality is such a big issue. With economists, politicians and the media all highlighting the growing rich–poor gaps around the world, it is a common topic in many discussions about today, as well as the future. Concerns are raised not just about rising income and wealth inequality and their impacts on society and the economy, but also on other types of inequality beyond the purely financial. Reviewing the six core chapters in this book, it is clear that numerous facets of inequality will feature on the future agenda.

In *Future People*, there is evident inequality between many areas: how different populations are growing, and the stresses they are putting on their regions; the number of children per family; life expectancy; the availability of jobs for the middle classes and the youth; varied age profiles between countries, dependency ratios and the opportunities and care made available to the elderly; retirement ages in different nations; access to and quality of health care; and between women and men.

In *Future Power*, we can see inequality not just between rich and poor countries but also between those within and outside trade agreements; those complying with global vs local standards; ownership and access to resources; the connected and the unconnected; those who understand privacy and its implications and those who do not; and those with access to clean, reliable energy and those that have to rely on dirty, infrequent supply.

In *Future Place*, there is inequality driving migration and the rights that different migrants have in different nations; within cities, between those that live in the planned vs unplanned areas; around access to public and private transport; in the diverse impacts of air quality, flooding and sanitation; in those likely to be more or less affected by climate change; and also between urban and rural populations.

In *Future Belief*, we can also see inequality across an equally broad spectrum between those with a vote and those without; between those with a vote that counts and those where it is anathema; between those that are most affected by environmental changes, and those that are least; between public and private good; between the trusted and the trusting; between humans and machines; and still, in some nations, between different faiths and religions.

In *Future Behaviour*, there is inequality between those with and without secure access to key resources (food, water, land, precious metals, etc.); perhaps those with GMO crops and those without; those who waste food and the hungry; the obese and the underweight; those who own data and those who do not – as well as those who make money from others' data and those who get nothing. In addition we have the banked and the unbanked; tax payers and tax dodgers; the educated and the illiterate; those with good degrees and those with no qualifications; as well as the savvy and engaged, and those left behind.

And, lastly, in *Future Business*, there is also inequality between companies that focus on short-term gains vs long-term contribution; the spiralling value of the 'unicorns' that employ a few, and the more traditional firms that provide jobs for many; again those who benefit from owning data and those that supply it; the companies that have access to clever algorithms to maximise yields and their competition who do not; and the organisations that are part of the real sharing economy vs the marketplaces that take advantage of the low paid via alleged 'sharing economy' platforms. Inequality is rife.

Something has to be done. Oxfam, for one, highlights the target proposed by Joseph Stiglitz, former chief economist to the World Bank and Nobel Prize winner, to reduce income inequality so that the income of the top ten per cent is no more than that of the bottom 40 per cent. Since the world is already on track to end $1 a day poverty, Oxfam advocates that we should set the bar higher and eradicate $2 a day poverty.[247]

However, it is clearly not just about the money. If we are going to accommodate more people on an increasingly crowded and resource-constrained planet, we must address inequality in its broadest sense. Yes, rising Gini coefficients and the 50 per cent of the world's wealth owned by the top one per cent are hard facts that regularly appear in headlines of some media channels, but these are probably as much the consequence of inequality beyond just monthly income.

As mentioned earlier, in the 30 years or so after the Second World War, many countries, especially in the West were able to reduce inequality. Three key factors are seen to have been a fear that lack of reform would cause social and political turmoil, the practical impacts of two world wars, and a decline in the belief in individual responsibility for one's destiny.[248] 'These trends created a political and intellectual basis for policies that redistributed wealth and reduced economic inequality across the advanced industrial democracies throughout the middle decades of the 20th century, even without any theoretical consensus about justice or equality.' However, since the 1980s all these objective factors have disappeared, and with them, the support for egalitarian public policy. There are no longer strong exogenous factors driving developed countries toward policies that keep inequality in check.

Economists rightly analyse all the varied data on household income per head, disposable personal income, mean and median wages, wealth per capita and their like. They show the effects of varied government policies, social structures and behaviours, but they don't always highlight the causes. If we are going to make an impact on the drivers of change for inequality, then perhaps our focus should be less about taxation rates for individuals and companies around the world, and more about investment in infrastructure, education, health and connectivity.

One of the most well-known philanthropy organisations, the Bill and Melinda Gates Foundation, takes a broader view.[249] A big supporter of focused aid coupled with innovation, it identified that when poorer countries have spent development funds on education, agriculture and health care there has been dramatic change. For example, in 1969 in Southeast Asia the likes of Bangladesh, Indonesia and South Korea all relied on aid for more than 5 per cent of their GDP. By 2009, the figures for Bangladesh were below 1 per cent, for Indonesia below 0.5 per cent and South Korea had become a major donor country. The Gates Foundation argues that public–private partnerships, focused on specific issues and not general ones, is the way forward.

Inequality in its varied forms is here, and growing in many areas, but not all: we are making progress on race and gender. Nevertheless, overcoming inequality is one of the big challenges facing us for the years ahead. How well we achieve this, where, and by tackling which specific causes is very much part of the current debate. What is clear, not just to the economists but also to the sociologists, the scientists, the police and even the politicians is that a more unequal society will increasingly become less stable. As social geographer Professor Danny Dorling points out,[250] 'Since the economic crash of 2008 inequalities have risen almost everywhere, but so has the opposition to rising inequality. We have been here before, in the 1840s rising inequalities were opposed and great social progress began to be made (in Europe); this happened again (80 years later) in the 1920s.' We can do it again – hopefully this time globally.

Transparency

One way to ensure trust, and hopefully improve equality, is to be transparent about our actions – and this applies as much to governments and corporations as it does to individuals. Indeed, transparency has now become a bit of a buzzword in the corporate lexicon: the more transparent a business, the argument goes, the better it is for consumers, the more profitable it will be and the more likely it is to perform in a socially responsible fashion. But although campaigners make much noise about holding multinationals to account, transparency could have a bigger impact on the governments they deal with. Publication of what the taxman receives will, in many countries, increase pressure on government departments to show how money is spent. They could be held even more accountable if organisations were forced to disclose which of their payments go to central governments, which to regional ones and which to local administrations.

It is certainly true that the global financial crisis increased the public appetite for transparency. Investigative journalists and NGOs, often backed by impassioned social media campaigns, are seeing to that. This has the potential to have a positive impact – provided there is agreement about what should be transparent. At the time of writing, the US Foreign Account Tax Compliance Act (FATCA) has caused great frustration: it obliges financial institutions abroad to report details of their American clients' accounts, or face withholding taxes on American-sourced payments. Aside from the fact that implementing this is expensive, in jurisdictions such as Singapore or Hong Kong, the Internal Revenue Service (IRS) rules appear to contravene local privacy laws. At the same time, the OECD is also leading efforts to force multinationals to reveal more about where and how profits are made, and the deals they cut with individual governments in order to curb aggressive tax-planning. So far 96 countries, including Switzerland, have signed up and will soon start swapping information; however, the effectiveness of this deal is limited, unfortunately, because, as it has signed a host of bilateral data-sharing deals, the USA sees no need to join the process that it itself initiated.

Experience has shown that gaining agreement around what should be made public will never be easy. Take, for example, the Extractive Industries Transparency Initiative (EITI), with its 'multi-stakeholder' model, giving equal board representation to its three constituencies: governments, companies and civil society. This continues to have a combative record, but at the same time – thanks in the main to its efforts – governments in Africa and other corruption-plagued places now disclose a lot more about their dealings in oil, gas and mining. Its members have delivered more together than they could have done apart.

Sometimes, of course, there can be too much of a good thing. Demands for more information could tempt some to be disingenuous, making information available but difficult to understand and analyse. For instance, companies can aggregate their profits so it is difficult to judge what assets and revenues they have in any one country. The EU is passing into law a new directive requiring country-by-country, and in some cases project-by-project, reporting in some areas, particularly the extractive industry. The USA, on the other hand, is dragging its feet. Agreement around global standards would really help.

Transparency does have natural limits, particularly if not everyone plays by the rules. Opponents point to the fact that EITI can be unfair on those forced to disclose, because it hands a competitive advantage to non-Western rivals that are not held to the same standards. In addition, abiding by an EU requirement to be open, for instance, could mean breaking the law in a country of operation that forbids disclosure. Finally, it is not clear yet whether country-by-country reporting can really capture what is going on in a group that, for example, produces in Australia and Canada, markets through Singapore and sells in China. Even some transparency campaigners acknowledge a risk of drowning in data or of comparing apples with oranges.

Increased global transparency, however, helps us to better understand issues from a systemic viewpoint, as well as dive further into the detailed causes and effects of change. Consider health care, where knowing more about disease progression and management has the potential to mitigate the growing threat of global pandemics. Some countries are more willing to embrace this idea than others, who fear that full disclosure could cause local panic, deter foreign tourists and lose valuable exports. Organisations such as the Global Pandemic Initiative, a collaboration between the WHO and the CDC together with IBM and a number of other organisations, are working to change this. Others, including Google and Sun Microsystems, are also collaborating to create an open source, non-governmental, public access network that will help the world move quickly whenever necessary. 'The threat of a pandemic is a definitively global phenomenon,' argues Samuel Palmisano, IBM's chairman. 'Our response must be similarly global, and must rely ... on open, collaborative innovation.' In the next ten years expect more countries to work towards addressing this challenge.

In many areas, smartphones have provided the key to grass-roots transparency. Their ability to share information instantaneously with a global audience has had a profound effect on low-level corruption, giving individuals power. No one likes to be named and shamed; policemen are no longer so keen to ask for bribes if they know they might find a video of their request for *baksheesh* on YouTube, victims are more inclined to report crimes if they can do so via the Internet, without fear of reprisal. Not only that, but smartphones spread dissenting information, helping protest movements to form and challenge. Looking ahead, it seems likely that as increasing numbers of people come online, the power to challenge authoritarianism at any level will flourish in the hands of individuals.

At the bottom of the food chain, increased transparency and traceability has been very effective in addressing information inequality simply by making it more widely available. A study by Deloitte states that, by tracking weather conditions and crop prices through mobile phones, farmers in India increased their profits by eight per cent, resulting in a four per cent drop in prices for consumers.[251] Having market and pricing information enables small-scale farmers direct access to markets instead of being obliged to act through intermediaries. As increased connectivity rolls out, this will be transformative across the developing world, where about 40 per cent of the labour force still works in agriculture. Deloitte estimates that up to 360 million individuals will benefit from lower and more stable prices.

Lastly, for business, full transparency is only really needed if trust is absent. It certainly does not mean a requirement to share mountains of information as a means to ensure ethical behaviour. Many argue that full disclosure potentially means sacrificing competitive advantage, which is in no one's interest, but it might also mean disengaging with customers, most of whom would be comfortable with minimal information – provided they trusted the organisation behind the brand.

Notably, increased access to information will continue to shift public opinion, and regulators are struggling to keep up. Recent scandals around payment of taxes have reduced public trust in some organisations (Google, Facebook and Starbucks to name but a few). But what is perhaps interesting here is not the fact that companies have played hard and fast with the concept of tax efficiency, but more that public outcry has supported the idea of appropriate behaviour that goes beyond that outlined by the legal system. Google's public affairs chief might be right when he says, 'Governments make tax law, the tax authorities independently enforce the law, and Google complies with the law', but he does not get much public sympathy for his comment.

Reviewing the multiple insights gained from the Future Agenda workshops, we can see the thread of transparency touching almost all the areas we discuss. The provision and availability of data has, of course, made it much easier for us to track the activities of governments, corporates and individuals, and is the basis of many of the arguments that we put forward around unequal access, our habitat and the changing business environment.

Identity

Identity is the collection of attributes that defines how we see ourselves. It is the answer to the question: who am I? The answer is never straightforward, in part because we change and evolve as we mature. But more recently it seems that, for many, our sense of self has become defined less by a sense of nationalism or place, and more by a compilation of beliefs around faith, social mobility, language, gender and age, among others. It is this which shapes our action within, and reaction to, society.

Many agree that the main reason that the pegs on which we hang our identity have shifted is, in part, because of the ease with which information and ideas can now be shared. New technologies connecting us to others has allowed us to develop relationships which until recently were impossible to create. As we spend more and more time online, these connections become more intimate and solid, making it possible to share ideas and reach out to others who have the same interests, albeit from seemingly different cultures and backgrounds. As a result, *who* we are is no longer defined by *where* we are.

Curiously, alongside creating a sense of intimacy, technology also engenders a sense of detachment, thus making it possible for individuals to create a range of identities, some of which conflict, that can be adopted or discarded as the occasion demands. This could be as simple as having different email addresses for work and home life, for example, but as our world becomes smaller through migration and mobility, both virtual and real, it may be that people and groups will express themselves more insistently through multiple- rather than single-identity lenses. This is the 'cocktail identity' – the combination of personas and their consequences – that many believe will profoundly influence the future. As the world becomes more urban, expect communities to become ever more diverse, and a significant issue will continue to be the uncertainty relating to how well we will manage to coexist.

It is clear that people will continue to be mobile and migrate in huge numbers as a result of economics, politics, climate change and so forth. Some will be able to adapt to their new environment quickly, but others will not, holding fast to traditions of their lost homeland. Many believe that the ways in which society adjusts to this mass movement of people will define future generations; some suggest that the best way to ensure peaceful coexistence is to develop a cohesive set of values with due regard for diversity and individual rights. This means finding ways of celebrating difference while also building, identifying and embedding a shared identity among community members. Others reflect that the more marginalised and excluded groups have been increasingly troubled by the rapid erosion of national borders and identities, and are uncomfortable with the growing diversity they see around them. They also fear that cultural differences are too significant to be easily brushed aside. This view cannot be ignored, as there really is a cultural gulf between rich, liberal, secular Europe and some of the countries from which recent migrants come. For example, the 2013 Pew poll of Muslims suggests that 90 per cent of Tunisians and Moroccans believe that a wife should always obey her husband, and that only 14 per cent of Iraqi Muslims and 22 per cent of Jordanians think a woman should be allowed to initiate a divorce.

Looking ahead, some of the key challenges we face can only be addressed if there is collaboration and action. Finding ways of bringing people from different groups together and encouraging collaboration between these people helps create more comfort with difference. Recent work suggests that *contact* is successful in bringing about more positive attitudes towards others, reducing prejudice and also building long-lasting friendships. The approach is based on the premise that everyone, individually and as a nation, benefits from knowing, experiencing and working with other cultures, as the focus of these projects are the commonalities that bind groups together, rather than their differences. Intercultural dialogue is one of the ways in which people can be brought together for such collaboration.

Just as trust and privacy have risen in significance and helped to shape the world since 2010, we can expect inequality, transparency and identity to also play a greater role going forward. While not the panacea for all of the challenges facing us, and certainly not specific to individual contexts, it looks as though these are the three big cross-cutting topics that may well define how far we progress – or not – in the next decade.

Conclusion

The Future Agenda project was created to provide an open foresight platform that could stimulate innovation. We believe that to address the challenges we face, we need to be better informed. Our ambition was to create a space in which some of the best minds from around the globe could identify and discuss the greatest challenges of the next decade and, in doing so, map out the major issues, agree potential solutions, suggest ways forward and, as a consequence, create a platform for collective innovation.

To uncover what the world could look like in 2025 we have combined different perspectives and cut across different sectors. This has allowed us to have a clearer view of the probable versus the possible, and make connections between different events that may occur in order to help us to make better informed decisions based on what we hope is a richer, deeper picture of the future.

The insights that we have shared are designed to act as stepping stones towards additional activity. We want to encourage people to think about the 'so what?' in order to help companies, governments and individuals build strategies to prepare for the future. This is why we decided to make the information we collated as widely available as possible, in order that everyone could have immediate access and use it to stimulate their thinking.

We all seem to agree that 'business as usual' is no longer an option and therefore something has to change. Most people also acknowledge that it is likely that the choices we make in the next few years will have an impact well beyond the next decade, in all likelihood affecting the lives of our children and grandchildren. The responsibility to make the best choice we can is in our hands. This is why we believe that, when thinking about the future, it is important to be as open to different approaches as possible and, for example, consider the opportunities presented by different industries and seemingly unrelated initiatives. After all, real innovation often occurs at the intersection of disciplines and the crossover between sectors as technologies and business models jump from one area to another.

It is also worth considering the possibility that change could emerge from unlikely places, stimulated by unexpected events rather than being driven from a top-down global initiative. Policy-makers, businesses and key influencers can often take advantage of this and have a significant role to play in amplifying and accelerating the pace and scope of change by investing in supporting infrastructure, encouraging the 'right' habits and choices through education, information and incentives, developing reinforcement policies and bringing to market new products and services.

Throughout all our 120 discussions, there was general agreement that, if we are to deal with some of the major challenges that evidently face us over the next decade, we need to innovate across all sectors. We need new policies and regulations to both accommodate and moderate some of the events that we can now see on the horizon, and we also need to create new products, services and business models that will generate value, both social and economic, as well as change the rules of the game so that, as an increasingly global society, we can make tangible, sustainable and positive progress.

Questions

Having explored the certain and probable changes for the next decade, including the drivers and moderators of these changes, it is worth spending some time considering the questions that have arisen as a result.

Some of the salient issues that deserve further consideration could include the impact of public debt in the West; the rise of the Asian consumer; concerns over security of supply of key materials and their associated prices; the need to shift to a low-carbon economy; the possible split of the developed world into a two-speed grouping; increasing security; societal shifts around privacy; the interconnectedness of global systems; fragmented organisational structures and new alliances; the impact of new technologies; advances in medicine; the role of the elderly in society; the shift from ownership to access; or the impact of growing unemployment in mega-cities.

While governments, organisations and individuals will have a different understanding of the specific impacts and implications of many of the issues discussed, it is clear there are some common questions to answer. To help start additional conversations and stimulate further thoughts, in the following pages we have outlined ten questions for each of these levels that we hope will be useful.

Ten Questions for Governments

1. *Are we really focusing on the right big issues for the next decade?*

   We know about climate change and the energy challenge, but are health, food and water as near the top of our agenda as they should be? Are we making inaccurate assumptions about who our citizens are, and their willingness to share data?

2. *Do we share our understanding about the big challenges we all face in an effective way with the right people and organisations?*

   How many of us are being straight with the public on the likely impact of a 4°C rise in temperature, the increasing cost of health care for the ageing and those with chronic disease, and how to pay for it all?

3. *To what extent can we really use taxation and policy to change behaviour?*

   Can we nudge people to adapt to a new world, eat less meat and use less energy, or will we have to ban certain products and, if that does not work, how effective will the tax lever be? Are there any other tools available to us?

4. *Which new areas of the economy should we be investing in for the future?*

   Will our current local strengths be long-term global successes?
   Should we stop supporting legacy industry and shift to a new
   world and, if so, where can we have the greatest effect?

5. *What new skills will we need to build or have access to in order to support
   higher growth?*

   Does our population have the capabilities best suited to the challenges
   ahead? How quickly can we re-equip our workforces with the right skills?
   Should we review our migration policies to attract new and able workers?

6. *With which regions of the world will we need to cooperate more effectively?*

   Will our current trading partners be the best ones in 2025? As
   the centre of power continues to shifts East, should we forge new
   bilateral agreements or is collaboration a better approach? Should
   we align according to geography, ideology or economics?

7. *Which currency should we be saving and trading in?*

   Do we have the right balance of foreign reserves? Are we too
   dependent on the US dollar? How prepared are we to trade in
   alternative and digital currencies and change our reserve mix?

8. *Should we readdress the balance between economic growth and societal needs?*

   Should we focus on taxation to redistribute wealth or provide
   greater support for the key catalysts of change?

9. *How well are we prepared to deal with inevitable surprises?*

   Do we have the right bio-surveillance in place to protect our nation's
   health? Are we over-dependent on the wrong sorts of food? How good
   is our data security and can we be self-sufficient in energy by 2025?

10. *Will we tackle the big challenges in isolation or will we collaborate?*

   How well aligned are we with other countries on the pivotal issues?
   Will we all agree on the right path and work in unison or are
   there areas where we will go our own way and, if so, where?

Ten Questions for Organisations

1. *How well do we recognise the big issues on the horizon?*

   Are we really challenging ourselves to look beyond the status
   quo, to understand how changes outside our control will
   impinge on our sector and to plan for a different future?

2. *How well do we understand the full implications of resource constraints?*
   Will we face problems from water shortages? How will we cope
   with less energy? How will we secure access to the materials that
   are running out and what options do we have for change?

3. *Where can we use our existing capabilities to create new sources of value?*
   As the world changes, what new activities will come to the fore
   where our skills and experience can be more effectively deployed
   and how can we best take advantage of the opportunities?

4. *To what extent do we expect to have influence over our human resources?*
   If the world is getting smaller and flatter and the best talent is mobile,
   how can we attract the key people we need for the future to work with
   us? How can we stimulate them and how will they be rewarded?

5. *How will we operate in an increasingly transparent world?*
   How will increasing access to information impact on our reporting processes?
   What about the multi-capital view? Will intangibles be more important
   than fixed assets and what levels of risk will be acceptable to the market?

6. *Are we paying enough attention to what we do not know?*
   Is our understanding of future areas of opportunity any better than that of our
   peers? Do we understand the future any better than others? How vulnerable are
   we to change from outside, and how and where can we best understand this?

7. *How well equipped are we to respond to adjacent sector changes?*
   If new technology developments or changes in customer relationships occur
   in other areas, how can we best take early advantage of these in our own
   space and do we know how they could threaten our current activities?

8. *How well are we tracking the possible future risks and challenges?*
   As well as looking at the upside for growth opportunities, are we
   paying enough attention to monitoring threats to both our core
   and potential new areas of activity? Can we create competitive
   advantage by spotting new opportunities earlier than others?

9. *Are we ready to participate in deeper collaboration with others?*
   Will we be able to remain competitive if knowledge and intellectual
   property (IP) is freely shared? How will we manage value across diverse
   private public collaborations? Are we prepared to change the way we act?

10. *Are we sufficiently influential in new regulatory change?*
    Where will the new international standards emerge from and how can we be
    involved? Are we able to match our global and local operations to changing
    legal frameworks?

Ten Questions for Individuals

1. *How can I play a part in changing the status quo?*
   How and where can I, as one person, make the greatest impact? What issue is most relevant to me? Who will I trust to give me accurate information?

2. *How can I better live within the means of the planet?*
   Will technology allow me to do everything I want to do or will I have to use fewer resources? What sacrifices might I need to make? Should I judge wealth in the same way as my parents did?

3. *Which of my daily choices will have greatest influence over the future?*
   Should I walk to work or buy a bike? Should I learn to drive or not? Should I become a part-time vegetarian? Is living in the city the best option for me and should I have a smaller home?

4. *Am I prepared to pay the full cost for things in the future?*
   Will I pay $5 a gallon for fuel, €2 a litre for milk or £5 for a loaf of bread? Will I pay my carbon tax and fat tax on each purchase or against my monthly personal allowance? What am I willing to do without?

5. *To what extent should I openly share information about myself?*
   How will I make and maintain friendships in the future? Will my virtual networks be as important as the people I meet in the 'real' world? Will I only share my personal information with my closest friends but be prepared to give all my health data to the government?

6. *Where in the world will I find the greatest opportunities?*
   If I stay here, will there be enough for me to do or will I need to move? Do national boundaries matter? Should I consider moving to another country or continent or just be willing to travel further to work?

7. *What professions will exist in 2025?*
   What should I learn? How will I manage and plan for a changing career portfolio? Should I become a bio-informationist, a privacy broker, a freelance wechatter or an urban farmer? Or am I actually better off as a teacher, a doctor or a lawyer?

8. *How can I best plan for retirement?*
   Can I afford to live to be 100? Shall I expect to work beyond 75? How will I keep myself healthy and active? What foods should I eat and where should I live?

9. *How should I raise my children to prepare them for their future?*
   What is the best way to educate them? Who should set the standards? How do I ensure they have the right expectations and values?

10. *What will I believe in?*

How will I know what I should believe in? What and who will I trust? Should I listen to the crowd?

Moving Forward

Our list of questions is not exhaustive and, of course, you may have different issues that resonate with your own future agenda. However, these, or a similar collection of questions, could provide the fuel for further debate. We offer the results presented in this book – and available via our website www.futureagenda.org – to organisations around the world so that they can build on the research we have carried out to date and identify potential areas of innovation and change. We will continue to keep the insights refreshed and, as we do this, we hope that they prove useful to you in provoking new thoughts and actions.

The world is facing some major challenges in the next decade and beyond. Imbalanced population growth and key resource constraints are just two of the ones we are certain about. Add in health-care costs, urbanisation, more travel and clean energy, and the list is getting pretty full. We hope, however, that the insights we have presented around global connectivity, the rebalancing of the economic centre of gravity, medical innovations, changing business models, new technologies and our increasing ability to manage resources in a more sustainable way give you food for thought. We also hope they gives the confidence that we have the tools at our disposal to create a host of new innovations that will enable us all, in our different ways, to make significant and tangible improvements to the world we live in.

Endnotes

Chapter 2: CHALLENGE 1: FUTURE PEOPLE

Imbalanced Population Growth

1 http://esa.un.org/unpd/wpp/

2 http://www.who.int/gho/mortality_burden_disease/life_tables/situation_trends_text/en/

3 http://www.bbc.co.uk/news/world-asia-19630110

4 http://data.worldbank.org/indicator/SP.POP.DPND

5 https://www.cia.gov/library/publications/the-world-factbook/fields/2261.html

6 http://www.metoffice.gov.uk/climate-guide/climate-change/impacts/four-degree-rise/map

7 http://www.pewsocialtrends.org/2015/12/09/the-american-middle-class-is-losing-ground/

Shrinking Middle

8 http://www.pewglobal.org/2015/07/08/a-global-middle-class-is-more-promise-than-reality/

9 http://www.theatlantic.com/magazine/archive/2015/05/the-disintegration-of-the-world/389534/

10 http://www.s4.brown.edu/us2010/Data/Report/report10162013.pdf

11 http://www.brookings.edu/blogs/the-avenue/posts/2015/06/09-city-middle-class-berube-friedhoff

12 http://www.economist.com/news/leaders/21637393-rise-demand-economy-poses-difficult-questions-workers-companies-and?fsrc=scn/tw_ec/workers_on_tap

13 http://www.truelancer.com/blog/india-and-usa-comparing-freelance-economies-2/

14 http://www.economist.com/news/business/21625801-forecasting-internets-impact-business-proving-hard-pointers-future

Agelessness

15 http://apps.who.int/iris/bitstream/10665/186463/1/9789240694811_eng.pdf?ua=1

16 https://www.gov.uk/government/collections/future-of-ageing

17 https://t.co/MM1YvTyrdW

Working Longer

18 http://www.mckinsey.com/mgi/overview/in-the-news/the-productivity-challenge-of-an-aging-global-workforce

19 http://www.dw.com/en/german-pension-plans-prompt-eu-reply/a-17588981

20 http://www.economist.com/news/essays/21596796-democracy-was-most-successful-political-idea-20th-century-why-has-it-run-trouble-and-what-can-be-do

Rising Youth Unemployment

21 http://www.ilo.org/wcmsp5/groups/public/---ed_emp/---ed_emp_msu/documents/publication/wcms_181907.pdf

22 ILO, World Employment and Social Outlook – Trends 2015.

23 http://www.weforum.org/community/global-agenda-councils/youth-unemployment-visualization-2013

Affordable Health Care

24 http://www.who.int/gho/publications/en/

25 http://www.economist.com/blogs/democracyinamerica/2015/06/pharmaceutical-pricing?zid=318&ah
    =ac379c09c1c3fb67e0e8fd1964d5247f

26 http://www.stgeorgeshouse.org/wp-content/uploads/2016/02/Redefining_the_UKs_Health_Services_
    Report.pdf

27 http://www.bbc.com/future/story/20150805-will-machines-eventually-take-on-every-job?ocid=twfut

Care in the Community

28 http://www.caregiving.org/caregiving2015/

29 http://apps.who.int/iris/bitstream/10665/186463/1/9789240694811_eng.pdf?ua=1

30 http://www.caregiving.org/wp-content/uploads/2015/05/2015_CaregivingintheUS_Final-Report-
    June-4_WEB.pdf

31 http://www.oecd.org/newsroom/healthspendingineuropefallsforthefirsttimeindecades.htm

32 https://www.metlife.com/mmi/research/caregiving-cost-working-caregivers.html#key findings

Female Choice Dilemma

33 http://europa.eu/rapid/press-release_STAT-15-4555_en.htmhttp://www.mckinsey.com/insights/
    growth/how_advancing_womens_equality_can_add_12_trillion_to_global_growth

34 http://www.prowess.org.uk/facts

35 http://reports.weforum.org/global-gender-gap-report-2015/report-highlights/

36 http://www.prowess.org.uk/facts

37 http://www.prowess.org.uk/facts

38 http://www.icrw.org/what-we-do/emerging-issues/innovation-transform-womens-lives

Conclusion: Nordic Answers

39 http://www.iea.org.uk/in-the-media/press-release/scandinavian-success-is-not-due-to-high-taxes-
    and-welfare-spending

40 https://www.jacobinmag.com/2015/08/national-review-williamson-bernie-sanders-sweden/

41 http://hdr.undp.org/sites/default/files/2015_human_development_report_1.pdf

Chapter 3: CHALLENGE 2: FUTURE PLACE

42 http://www.unfpa.org/urbanization

43 https://urbanage.lsecities.net

Accelerated Displacement

44 http://www.bbc.co.uk/news/world-europe-34131911

45 https://issuu.com/unpublications/docs/wmr2015_en

46 http://unhcr.org/556725e69.html

Infrastructure Deficit

47 http://www.weforum.org/communities/global-agenda-council-on-infrastructure

48 http://www.thenational.ae/business/economy/uaes-infrastructure-investment-not-affected-by-oil-
    slump

49 http://web.worldbank.org/WBSITE/EXTERNAL/TOPICS/
    EXTINFRA/0,,contentMDK:23154473~pagePK:64168445~piPK:64168309~theSitePK:8430730,00.
    html

50 http://ec.europa.eu/economy_finance/publications/occasional_paper/2014/pdf/ocp203_en.pdf

51 http://reports.weforum.org/strategic-infrastructure-2014/introduction-the-operations-and-
    maintenance-om-imperative/the-global-infrastructure-gap/

52 http://www.mckinsey.com/industries/infrastructure/our_insights/infrastructure-productivity

53 http://reports.weforum.org/strategic-infrastructure-2014/introduction-the-operations-and-maintenance-om-imperative/the-global-infrastructure-gap/

54 http://reports.weforum.org/strategic-infrastructure-2014/executive-summary/

55 http://www.pwc.com/gx/en/industries/capital-projects-infrastructure/future-of-infrastructure.html

56 http://online.wsj.com/ad/cityoftheyear

Built-in Flexibility

57 http://www.gci.uq.edu.au/building

58 http://www.energyplan.eu/smartenergysystems/

59 http://www.prnewswire.com/news-releases/global-water-metering-market-66-billion-per-year-by-2025-300058768.html

Access to Transport

60 http://www.artba.org/about/transportation-faqs/#9

61 https://www.cia.gov/library/publications/the-world-factbook/fields/2085.html

62 http://reports.weforum.org/global-competitiveness-report-2014-2015/rankings/

63 http://www.transport.govt.nz/ourwork/keystrategiesandplans/strategic-policy-programme/future-demand/

64 http://peakcar.org/category/car-use/

65 http://www.archdaily.com/462616/qianhai-integrated-transportation-hub-gmp-architekten/

66 http://www.futurecommunities.net/case-studies/hammarby-sjostad-stockholm-sweden-1995-2015

67 http://www.teriin.org/div/pro-poor-mobility_policy-guidelines-case-studies.pdf https://lsecities.net/media/objects/articles/mobility-and-the-urban-poor/en-gb/

68 http://www.teriin.org/div/pro-poor-mobility_policy-guidelines-case-studies.pdf

69 http://www.sustrans.org.uk/lockedout

70 http://www.slocat.net/sites/default/files/pro-poor_mobility_guidelinesbest_practices.pdf

Autonomous Vehicles

71 http://www.economist.com/news/business/21644149-established-carmakers-not-tech-firms-will-win-race-build-vehicles

72 https://www.eutruckplatooning.com/home/default.aspx

Air Quality

73 http://www.who.int/phe/health_topics/outdoorair/databases/cities/en/

74 http://www.theguardian.com/world/2015/aug/14/air-pollution-in-china-is-killing-4000-people-every-day-a-new-study-finds

75 http://www.economist.com/news/middle-east-and-africa/21657805-does-united-arab-emirates-really-have-dirtiest-air-world-dust-up

76 http://www.oecd.org/env/the-cost-of-air-pollution-9789264210448-en.htm

77 https://www.london.gov.uk/what-we-do/environment/pollution-and-air-quality

78 http://www.cdc.gov/air/

79 http://www.bbc.co.uk/news/world-asia-india-32193742

80 http://www.economist.com/news/asia/21642224-air-indians-breathe-dangerously-toxic-breathe-uneasy

81 http://www.oecd.org/env/the-cost-of-air-pollution-9789264210448-en.htm

Flooded Cities

82 http://www.metoffice.gov.uk/climate-guide/climate-change/impacts/four-degree-rise/map

83 https://www.weforum.org/agenda/2016/02/how-can-cities-improve-their-climate-resilience-f6fb69b3-2680-473f-9239-4f6b98b0ed78

84 https://www.weforum.org/agenda/2015/11/major-cities-under-water

Basic Sanitation

85 http://www.economist.com/news/asia/21607837-fixing-dreadful-sanitation-india-requires-not-just-building-lavatories-also-changing

86 WHO/UNICEF Joint Monitoring Programme for Water Supply and Sanitation, Water Supply and Sanitation Sector Monitoring Report 1990: Baseline year, JMP, Geneva, 1992

Eco-Civilisation

87 http://epi.yale.edu/epi/country-rankings

88 http://www.theclimategroup.org/_assets/files/china-ecocivilisation.pdf

Intra-city Collaboration

89 http://www.mckinsey.com/global-themes/urbanization/urban-world-mapping-the-economic-power-of-cities

90 http://inhabitat.com/how-the-cheonggyecheon-river-urban-design-restored-the-green-heart-of-seoul/

91 http://www.unicefchina.org/en/index.php?m=content&c=index&a=lists&catid=130

92 http://www.c40.org

Off-Grid

93 http://newsroom.fb.com/news/2015/02/the-state-of-global-connectivity

94 http://solar.m-kopa.com/about/

Conclusion: Smart Cities vs Smarter Citizens

95 https://urbanage.lsecities.net

96 http://www.seguridadjusticiaypaz.org.mx/sala-de-prensa/1356-caracas-venezuela-la-ciudad-mas-violenta-del-mundo-del-2015#.VqZQNwJ4GSI.twitter

Chapter 4: CHALLENGE 3: FUTURE POWER
Shifting Power and Influence

97 http://www.lse.ac.uk/IDEAS/pdf/COX-Waltz.pdf

98 http://www.mckinsey.com/insights/urbanization/urban_world_cities_and_the_rise_of_the_consuming_class

99 https://qzprod.files.wordpress.com/2013/01/global-middle-class-consumption-2.png?w=640

Rise of the Cult of China

100 http://www.mckinsey.com/business-functions/strategy-and-corporate-finance/our-insights/why-chinas-consumers-will-continue-to-surprise-the-world

101 https://www.weforum.org/agenda/2015/09/china-king-of-commodity-consumption/

Africa Growth

102 http://www.mckinsey.com/global-locations/africa/south-africa/en/rise-of-the-african-consumer

103 http://www.mckinsey.com/global-themes/middle-east-and-africa/whats-driving-africas-growth

104 https://www.bcgperspectives.com/content/articles/globalization-growth-dueling-with-lions-playing-new-game-business-success-africa/

105 http://www.mckinsey.com/global-themes/employment-and-growth/the-growth-opportunity-in-africa

Declining Government Influence

106 https://www.eiu.com/public/topical_report.aspx?campaignid=Democracy0115

107 http://www.economist.com/news/essays/21596796-democracy-was-most-successful-political-idea-20th-century-why-has-it-run-trouble-and-what-can-be-do

108 http://index.okfn.org/place/

109 http://www.top500ngos.net/the-new-top-500-ngos/

Everything Connected

110 http://www.ericsson.com/news/1925907

111 http://www.bloomberg.com/news/articles/2013-08-05/trillions-of-smart-sensors-will-change-life-as-apps-have

112 http://networks.nokia.com/innovation/technology-vision

113 http://www.ericsson.com/news/1925907

114 http://www.statista.com/statistics/333861/connected-devices-per-person-in-selected-countries/

115 http://www.ibm.com/smarterplanet/us/en/

116 http://www.theguardian.com/cities/2014/jun/25/predicting-crime-lapd-los-angeles-police-data-analysis-algorithm-minority-report

Privacy Regulation

117 http://www.theguardian.com/cities/2014/jun/25/predicting-crime-lapd-los-angeles-police-data-analysis-algorithm-minority-report

118 http://www.theguardian.com/cities/2014/jun/25/predicting-crime-lapd-los-angeles-police-data-analysis-algorithm-minority-report

119 http://www.hoganlovells.com/files/Publication/cee0104e-9625-4a3c-9d57-dc7c810da2fe/Presentation/PublicationAttachment/7f46bf34-5f15-4aeb-9ec6-e79f28981d95/100273_CM3_Data%20Privacy_BRO_E_link.pdf

120 http://www.nytimes.com/2016/02/07/opinion/congress-starts-to-get-serious-about-online-privacy.html?ref=topics&_r=1

121 https://www.whitehouse.gov/sites/default/files/docs/big_data_privacy_report_may_1_2014.pdf

Standards Driving Trade

122 http://docplayer.net/3305636-Global-trade-2020-achieving-the-vision-of-interconnected-customs.html

123 https://ustr.gov/tpp/

124 http://www.fmprc.gov.cn/mfa_eng/wjdt_665385/zyjh_665391/t1170143.shtml

125 http://ec.europa.eu/trade/policy/in-focus/ttip/index_en.htm

Open Supply Webs

126 https://www.wto.org/english/res_e/booksp_e/world_trade_report13_e.pdf

127 http://www2.deloitte.com/us/en/pages/about-deloitte/articles/press-releases/global-supply-chain.html

128 Camarinha-Matos, L., *Adaptation and Value Creating Collaborative Networks*, 2011, São Paulo, Virtual Enterprises

129 http://venturebeat.com/2015/10/19/dyson-acquires-sakti3-for-90m-to-help-commercialize-breakthrough-solid-state-battery-tech/

Energy Storage

130 http://www.greenbiz.com/blog/2014/04/21/how-10-innovative-companies-are-giving-energy-storage-jolt

131 http://www.greenbiz.com/article/energy-storage-could-change-power-paradigm

132 https://www.teslamotors.com/en_GB/gigafactory

133 http://storage.pv-tech.org/news/tesla-hints-at-further-gigafactory-ramp-up-consulting-with-utilities-on-sto

Chapter 5: CHALLENGE 4: FUTURE BELIEF
Capitalism Challenged

134 http://www.theguardian.com/commentisfree/2014/apr/12/capitalism-isnt-working-thomas-piketty

135 https://hbr.org/2015/12/a-better-scorecard-for-your-companys-sustainability-efforts

136 https://www.equalitytrust.org.uk/among-equals-spring-2015-0

Nature's Capital

137 http://quaternary.stratigraphy.org/workinggroups/anthropocene/

138 http://www.theguardian.com/environment/2015/jun/19/humans-creating-sixth-great-extinction-of-animal-species-say-scientists

139 http://www.nature.com/news/biodiversity-life-a-status-report-1.16523

140 http://www.sciencedirect.com/science/article/pii/S2212041614001648;http://www.fs.fed.us/pnw/about/programs/gsv/pdfs/health_and_wellness.pdf;http://www.pnas.org/content/112/28/8567.abstract

141 http://naturalcapitalforum.com/about/video-wall/

142 http://www.teebweb.org/

143 http://www.sciencedirect.com/science/article/pii/S0959378014000685

144 https://www.gov.uk/government/uploads/system/uploads/attachment_data/file/462472/ncc-natural-capital-gov-response-2015.pdf

145 https://brightfuture.unilever.co.uk

Full Cost

146 http://www.trucost.com/published-research/99/natural-capital-at-risk-the-top-100-externalities-of-business

147 http://integratedreporting.org/the-iirc-2/

148 http://www.naturalcapitalcoalition.org

Human Touch

149 https://www.google.co.uk/landing/now/

150 http://www.forbes.com/sites/micahsolomon/2015/01/03/dont-forget-the-experience-part-of-the-customer-service-experience/#554ca976ffac

151 http://eu.wiley.com/WileyCDA/WileyTitle/productCd-0470598824.html

152 http://www.forbes.com/sites/jaymcgregor/2015/07/06/siri-cortana-google-now-are-the-future-of-mobile

153 http://money.cnn.com/2015/07/01/technology/siri-easter-eggs/

154 http://uk.businessinsider.com/robotic-cat-is-the-perfect-pet-for-seniors-2015-11

155 http://www.singularity.com/

156 http://www.kurzweilai.net/the-law-of-accelerating-returns

Changing Nature of Privacy

157 http://www.theguardian.com/technology/2014/sep/28/tim-berners-lee-internet-bill-of-rights-greater-privacy

Ethical Machines

158 https://deepmind.com/publications.html

159 https://www.technologyreview.com/s/527336/do-we-need-asimovs-laws/

Keeping the Faith

160 Stonawski, M., Skirbekk, V., Potancokva, M., Connor, P. and Grim, B.J., 'Global Population Projection by Religion', 2015. *Yearbook of Religious Demography 2015*, pp99–116.

161 http://www.brill.com/products/book/yearbook-international-religious-demography-2014

162 http://www.state.gov/j/drl/rls/hrrpt/

Chapter 6: CHALLENGE 5: FUTURE BEHAVIOUR
Key Resource Constraints

163 http://resourcesfutures.org/#!/introduction

164 http://www.bbc.com/future/story/20120618-global-resources-stock-check?selectorSection=science-environment

165 http://www.theguardian.com/environment/blog/2011/oct/31/six-natural-resources-population

166 http://www.globalagriculture.org/report-topics/water.htm

167 http://www3.weforum.org/docs/WEF_FutureAvailabilityNaturalResources_Report_2014.pdf

Food Waste

168 https://next.ft.com/content/09d28fda-98e4-11e5-9228-87e603d47bdc

169 http://www.fao.org/save-food/resources/keyfindings/en/

170 https://www.youtube.com/watch?v=s_JLmxhnpNY

Urban Obesity

171 http://www.mckinsey.com/mgi/overview/in-the-news/the-global-obesity-threat

172 http://www.medpagetoday.com/upload/2012/5/7/AMEPRE_33853-stamped2.pdf

173 http://www.worldobesity.org

174 http://www.cdc.gov/obesity/data/index.html

Plastic Oceans

175 http://www.plasticpollutioncoalition.org

176 http://www.plasticseurope.org/information-centre/publications.aspx

177 http://education.nationalgeographic.org/encyclopedia/great-pacific-garbage-patch/

Data Ownership

178 Lanier, J., *Who Owns the Future?*, 2014, London, Penguin.

179 http://www.economist.com/blogs/economist-explains/2013/07/economist-explains-12

180 Topol, E., *Patient Will See You Now*, 2015, New York, Basic Books.

Digital Money

181 The Ascent of Money, Niall Ferguson

182 http://betterthancash.org/why-e-payments/cost-savings

183 http://www.pymnts.com/news/2015/global-card-fraud-damages-reach-16b/

184 US Federal Reserve http://www.federalreserve.gov/paymentsystems/coin_data.htm

Education Revolution

185 https://www.ted.com/talks/sugata_mitra_build_a_school_in_the_cloud?language=en

186 http://www.ungei.org/

187 http://www.unicef.org/esaro/7310_Gender_and_WASH.html

188 https://www.edx.org/school/mitx

Mass Engagement

189 https://www.change.org/

190 https://home.38degrees.org.uk/

191 https://hbr.org/2012/01/mass-medias-new-engagement-mea

192 Phillips, R., *Trust Me, PR is Dead*, 2015, London, Unbound.

193 http://www.huffingtonpost.com/margaret-heffernan-/is-pr-really-dead_b_6660032.html

194 Farrar-Myers, A. and Vaughn, J.S., *Controlling the Message*, 2015, New York, NYU Press.

195 Wang, R., *Disrupting Digital Business: Create an Authentic Experience in the Peer-to-Peer Economy*, 2015, Cambridge, Mass., Harvard Business Review Press.

196 http://www.acceleratedimprovement.co.uk/culture-change-engagement

197 Ronson, J., *So You've Been Publicly Shamed*, 2015, New York, Riverhead Books.

Caring for Those Left Behind

198 http://www.womenofchina.cn/womenofchina/html1/news/china/1602/655-1.htm

199 http://mirror.unhabitat.org/stats/Default.aspx

200 https://oxfamblogs.org/fp2p/why-ending-poverty-in-india-means-tackling-rural-poverty-and-power/

201 http://www.irap.org/en/

202 http://www.who.int/mental_health/en/

Chapter 7: CHALLENGE 6: FUTURE BUSINESS

Companies with Purpose

203 http://www.theguardian.com/commentisfree/2015/apr/27/divestment-fossil-fuels-apartheid-barclays

204 http://www.oecd.org/tax/aggressive/

Speed-to-Scale

205 https://www.cbinsights.com/research-unicorn-companies

206 http://www.forbes.com/sites/liyanchen/2015/08/11/the-most-valuable-employees-snapchat-doubles-facebook/#257ecebcf754

207 http://www.thehindubusinessline.com/info-tech/reliance-jio-sets-a-target-of-100-million-users-in-first-year/article8037571.ece

208 http://articles.economictimes.indiatimes.com/2015-09-20/news/66731180_1_cyrus-mistry-tata-sons-tata-group

The Value of Data

209 Harbour Research, 'Where Will Value Be Created In The Internet Of Things & People?', available at: http://harborresearch.com/where-will-value-be -created-in-the-internet-of-things-people/ (09/12/2014)

210 Little, M., 'Personal Data and the Big Trust Opportunity', available at: http://www.ovum.com/big-trust-is-big-datas-missing-dna/ (accessed 10/11/2014)

Dynamic Pricing

211 http://www.forbes.com/sites/prishe/2012/01/06/dynamic-pricing-the-future-of-ticket-pricing-in-sports/#2c11616355ac

212 https://www.washingtonpost.com/news/wonk/wp/2015/04/17/how-uber-surge-pricing-really-works/

Organisation 3.0

213 Abrams, R.S., 'Uncovering the Network-Centric Organization.' Ph.D. dissertation, University of California, Irvine, 2009.

214 http://www.zapposinsights.com/blog/item/a-memo-from-tony-hsieh

215 http://www.fastcompany.com/3046371/the-new-rules-of-work/what-kind-of-leadership-is-needed-in-flat-hierarchies

216 http://www.theguardian.com/commentisfree/2015/jul/26/will-we-get-by-gig-economy

217 http://www.fastcompany.com/3046387/the-new-rules-of-work/4-things-freelancers-wish-you-understood

218 https://mitpress.mit.edu/books/sharing-economy

219 http://www.bbc.co.uk/news/business-35460401

220 www.fastcompany.com/3046532/the-new-rules-of-work/how-you-can-realistically-make-a-sabbatical-happen

221 http://yoursabbatical.com/about/team/

222 http://skift.com/wp-content/uploads/2014/10/BGH-Bleisure-Report-2014.pdf

223 http://www.economist.com/blogs/gulliver/2015/03/mixing-business-and-leisure

Creative Economy

224 http://www.unesco.org/new/en/culture/themes/creativity/creative-economy-report-2013-special-edition/

225 https://www.gov.uk/government/statistics/creative-industries-2015-focus-on

Deeper Collaboration

226 http://www.forbes.com/sites/ashoka/2014/01/27/the-transformation-of-medellin-and-the-surprising-company-behind-it/#642e62df4752

227 http://energy.gov/eere/sunshot/sunshot-initiative

The Real Sharing Economy

228 http://www.neweconomics.org/blog/entry/the-sharing-economy-the-good-the-bad-and-the-real

229 https://pressroom.ups.com/pressroom/ContentDetailsViewer.page?ConceptType=PressReleases&id=1445948452077-607

Last-Mile Delivery

230 http://uk.businessinsider.com/skype-cofounders-launch-starship-delivery-robot-2015-11

Sometime Nomads

231 http://www.pewhispanic.org/2015/09/28/modern-immigration-wave-brings-59-million-to-u-s-driving-population-growth-and-change-through-2065/

232 http://factfinder.census.gov/faces/tableservices/jsf/pages/productview.xhtml?pid=ACS_10_SF4_B19013&prodType=table

233 http://www.economist.com/news/china/21644222-yearning-american-higher-education-has-driven-surge-overseas-study-georgia-their

234 http://www.iie.org/Who-We-Are/News-and-Events/Press-Center/Press-Releases/2014/2014-11-17-Open-Doors-Data

235 http://www.economist.com/news/finance-and-economics/21663264-how-torrent-money-workers-abroad-reshapes-economy-manna

Chapter 8: Reflections on Common Views of the Future

236 http://www.migrationpolicy.org/programs/data-hub/charts/top-25-destination-countries-global-migrants-over-time

237 http://www.migrationpolicy.org/article/canadas-immigration-policy-focus-human-capital

238 http://www.cic.gc.ca/english/

239 https://next.ft.com/content/cf550f34-a396-11e3-aa85-00144feab7de

240 http://www.grossnationalhappiness.com/articles/

241 http://worldhappiness.report

242 http://hdr.undp.org/en/2015-report

243 http://www.economist.com/news/business/21695940-enduring-power-biggest-idea-business-analyse?fsrc=scn/fb/te/pe/ed/biggestideainbusiness

244 http://www.multicapitalscorecard.com

Chapter 9: Cross Topic Insights

245 http://www.edelman.com/insights/intellectual-property/2015-edelman-trust-barometer/trust-and-innovation-edelman-trust-barometer/executive-summary/

246 http://www.edelman.com/insights/intellectual-property/2016-edelman-trust-barometer/executive-summary/

247 http://www.huffingtonpost.com/winnie-byanyima/overcoming-inequality-and_b_5498804.html

248 https://www.foreignaffairs.com/articles/2015-12-14/how-create-society-equals

249 http://www.gatesfoundation.org/What-We-Do/Global-Policy/G20-Report

250 http://www.dannydorling.org/?p=5206

251 http://www2.deloitte.com/content/dam/Deloitte/ie/Documents/TechnologyMediaCommunications/2014_uk_tmt_value_of_connectivity_deloitte_ireland.pdf

Index